THE THINGS
OUR
FATHERS SAW

VOLUME II:
THE UNTOLD STORIES OF THE
WORLD WAR II GENERATION
FROM HOMETOWN, USA

WAR IN THE AIR:
FROM THE DEPRESSION TO COMBAT

MATTHEW A. ROZELL

WOODCHUCK HOLLOW PRESS

Hartford · New York

Information at matthewrozellbooks.com.

Photographic portrait of Earl M. Morrow used courtesy of Robert H. Miller.

Front Cover: B-17 Flying Fortresses from the 398th Bombardment Group fly a bombing run to Neumunster, Germany, on April 13, 1945. Credit: Public Domain, U.S. Air Force photograph.

Additional photographs and descriptions sourced at Wikimedia Commons within terms of use, unless otherwise noted.

Publisher's Cataloging-in-Publication Data

Names: Rozell, Matthew A., 1961-
Title: The things our fathers saw : war in the air, from the Great Depression to combat : the untold stories of the World War II generation from hometown, USA / Matthew A. Rozell.
Description: Hartford, NY : Woodchuck Hollow Press, 2017. | Series: The things our fathers saw, vol. 2.
Identifiers: LCCN 2017912885 | ISBN 978-1-948155-45-8 large print pbk. | ISBN 978-0-9964800-5-5 (pbk.) | ISBN 978-1-948155-06-9 (hbk.) | ISBN 978-0-9964800-4-8 (ebook)
Subjects: LCSH: United States. Army Air Forces. Air Force, 8th--History--World War, 1939-1945. | United States. Army Air Forces--Airmen--Biography. | World War, 1939-1945--Personal narratives, American. | Bombing, Aerial--History--20th century. | Military history, Modern--20th century. | BISAC: HISTORY / Military / Veterans. | HISTORY / Military / World War II. | HISTORY / Military / Aviation.
Classification: LCC D810.V42 R691 2017 (print) | LCC D810.V42 (ebook) | DDC 940.54/8173--dc23.

matthewrozellbooks.com

Printed in the United States of America

THE THINGS OUR FATHERS SAW
II
WAR IN THE AIR:
FROM THE GREAT DEPRESSION
TO COMBAT

*For the mothers who saw their children off to
war,
And for those who keep the memory alive.*

MY BEST 4 FRIENDS
of our Crew all Killed in
action But me

I get a little emotional. I'm almost 93; I hope to see them all again in heaven.
— JOHN SWARTS, B-17 TAIL GUNNER

Dying for freedom isn't the worst that could happen.
Being forgotten is.
— SUSIE STEPHENS-HARVEY, REFLECTING ON HER BROTHER,
STEPHEN J. GEIST
MIA 9-26-1967

I think we shall never see the likes of it again.
— ANDY DOTY, B-29 TAIL GUNNER

THE THINGS OUR FATHERS SAW

II

THE STORYTELLERS

(IN ORDER OF APPEARANCE):

ANDY DOTY

DICK VARNEY

RICHARD ALAGNA

KEN CARLSON

EARL MORROW

MARTIN BEZON

SEYMOUR SEGAN

JOHN SWARTS

THE THINGS OUR FATHERS SAW

II

TABLE OF CONTENTS

THE BOMBARDIER 415

RESURRECTION 451

ABOUT THIS BOOK 487

ACKNOWLEDGEMENTS 487

NOTES 491

Twenty-year-old waist gunner Clarence McGuire,
(tallest in back row, center)
and the crew of the 'Pugnacious Ball'
England, springtime 1944

Author's Note

Twenty-year-old Clarence McGuire was always lurking around the periphery of my childhood. My knowledge of my father's older cousin begins with the memory of a familiar far-off sound. From several blocks away, my brothers and sisters and I could pick out the bass drums punching faintly into the air. Our eyes traveled the length of Main Street, lined with cars parked on either side for as far as we could see. A police officer stood in the intersection, arms folded, with little traffic to direct, and turned towards the thickening beat. Kids began scampering for the best car rooftop positions, though our neighborhood gang had the best seats all around. Our family address was 2 Main Street, Hudson Falls, and for one day of the year, we were the kings.

In our small town near the falls, the traffic began thinning out in the morning hours. Our front porch steps were prime real estate for the parade, and my parents' friends in town would come over with lawn chairs for the best views in the village.

The front door of the house led directly from the porch into the foyer and thence the kitchen, where my mother had her crockpot cooking up hours in advance with hotdogs; rolls and condiments and sides were piled high on the table nearby. Our American flag on the white front porch column fluttered softly in anticipation in the late May morning breeze; the maples that lined our street gently sent their seedlings helicoptering to the pavement below.

An All-American Memorial Day morning was underway. Soon enough, a crawling police car with its flashing emergency lights appeared in the distance as the marching band grew louder and the first flags swayed forth in a rhythmic cadence in step with the beat. The firemen in their snappy uniforms with brass buttons and white gloves waved out of their gleaming red trucks, following the rescue squad and their ambulances, the Little League teams, the pickup trucks pulling the flatbed floats, adults flinging penny candy from baskets into the street at the children's feet. My father's friends in the fire company and ambulance corps tipped their caps in our direction. The parade climaxed as the grand marshal for the year was chauffeured past in a gleaming convertible, waving to the crowd. We knew he was important, but had little idea who he was from year to year: just an important old man, decked out in his finest, a military-style cap peaked on his head.

All this meant that summer was finally here. The holiday known originally as "Decoration Day" originated at the end of the Civil War when a general order was issued designating May 30, 1868, *'for the purpose of strewing with flowers or otherwise decorating the graves of comrades who died in defense of their country during the late rebellion.'* When Congress passed a law formally recognizing the last Monday in May as the day of national celebration, we effectively got our three-day weekend and our 'de facto' beginning of summer.

As American schoolchildren of the 1970s, we had a vague *'something is important here'* feeling, but like a snake that slowly winds away and retreats out of sight, that feeling dissipated with the rearguard of flashing police cars, the highway truckers, and the 'stuck behind the damned parade' summer travelers anxious to get to wherever they were in a hurry to go. The cars lining Main Street started up almost on cue, pulling away from the curbs as our family and friends made their way to the kitchen to gorge on my mother's picnic fares. But Cousin Clarence never came to our Memorial Day get-togethers. He was dead. I never even knew him; I was born twenty years after the war that killed him began.

*

I don't quite remember the year that it dawned on me. I forsook the family picnic and folded in with the tail end of the parade after it passed the house, walking a few blocks on slate slab sidewalks to the black wrought iron entrance to Union Cemetery. Here I was notified by a volley of shots that I was too late for the words of wisdom from the town fathers, but that was okay. Amidst the parade flotsam on the side of Main Street, I saw a small American flag lying in the sand. I stopped to pick it up, and continued on further to the smaller cemetery behind Union where I knew a special grave marker was located, the one my father would bring me to on our occasional walks in my boyhood:

SGT. CLARENCE B. McGUIRE

A COURAGEOUS AND GALLANT GUN-
NER
WHO GAVE ALL FOR GOD AND COUN-
TRY
JULY 29, 1944
MAY HIS SOUL, AND ALL THE SOULS
OF THE GALLANT MEN WHO DIED, REST
IN PEACE

Clarence B. McGuire. Dad remembered Clarence coming to visit and teasing him in a playful
manner when Dad was only in grade school. We
had a crew photo of him, which I saw from time to
time growing up, and which I rediscovered while
cleaning out Dad's desk after he passed. It was the
only photo I had ever seen of Clarence: tall, centered in the rear row, just beaming and smiling.
'Clarry' was one of the waist gunners in this B-17
crew; you get the impression that they all got
along, that maybe they were pals, teammates,
probably friends for life. But somebody—maybe
his mother?—anointed this picture with a cross
over his head. He didn't come back, you see. The
entire crew in this picture was killed on a bombing

mission when the plane exploded on July 29, 1944, somewhere over Germany.

Friends for life. Blown out of the sky, just parts of twisted metal and burning chunks tumbling to the German soil. Even as an adult, the photo always haunted me a bit. All died in an instant, probably only months after this was taken. Flowers scythed down in the springtime of life. All gone.

Or so I thought. I planted the tiny flag at his memorial, and walked away. A seed was also being planted. I would be back.

***

I've given a good deal of thought on how to approach telling the story of the Air War in Europe in World War II. In my first book, I unfolded the War in the Pacific through the words of the veterans, specifically using the wartime prisoner diary of Joe Minder as a chronological guide. My original goal was to do something similar here, but it was proving more difficult. I had different airplanes my subjects were on, different theatres and Army Air Forces, different times and objectives during the European war. Some readers may be disappointed by a lack of technical detail or a political history, but my focus wound up being drawn to an entirely different path.

As it turned out, most of the veterans interviewed for this book served in the U.S. Army Eighth Air Force based in England. But rather than serve up to the reader another rehashing of the Mighty Eighth's story (there are already many detailed books out there—and I'd probably recommend Donald L. Miller's *Masters of the Air* over most of the others), I decided it would be fairer to our storytellers if they could share their own experiences individually. As I racked my brain for a narrative thread, I walked away and sat down to do some proofing. Then I noticed something. As it turned out, each of the men I was drawn to held a different crew position on the heavy bombers of the B-24 Liberator or the B-17 Flying Fortress. I had a new angle; I went with that.

*

In this and the upcoming books in *The Things Our Fathers Saw* series, we visit with more of the people who were forged and tempered in the tough times of the Great Depression and went on to 'do their bit' when even rougher times came calling. Most hailed from or later settled near or otherwise have a connection to the 'Hometown, USA' community where I grew up and taught in for over 30 years. (So that readers of all the books in this series can start in any place, the background chapter on the origins of the 'Hometown, USA' sobriquet from the first book is condensed and re-presented in the introduction.)

I don't know how to explain the feeling of sitting down and going back to re-listen to and edit these conversations, which in many cases took place years ago. As the writer/historian you spend days, if not weeks, with each individual, researching their stories, getting under their skin. You really have the feeling that you are doing a kind of cosmic CPR, taking their original words and breathing new life into them in a readable format that places readers at the kitchen table with that person who had something important to say. The reader shares the intimate moments with them as he/she gets absorbed in a real story being told. As an interviewer it happened many times to me directly with our World War II veterans, in living rooms, kitchens, and dining rooms all over 'Hometown, USA,' in the classroom, and at reunion 'hospitality rooms' and hotel breakfast tables across America. As a history teacher I also turned loose a generation of young people to bond with their grandparents' generation in the same way. We gave all of our first-person interviews to research institutions so that they might not be lost. The New York State Military Museum was the primary beneficiary, with over a hundred interviews deposited for future generations to learn from. As one of the most active contributors to the program, I also leaned on them for video recordings of some of the interviews I edited for this book. My friends Wayne Clarke and Mike Russert, the workhorses of the NYS Veterans Oral History Program, traversed the state for several years gathering these stories under the leadership of Michael Aikey; they know the feeling of bonding with these extraordinary men and women well. In bringing these stories back to life, I hope I did a service to them as well as to the general public.

But memories are short. A World War II memoirist once wrote, 'Ignorance and Apathy are the greatest dangers to Freedom.' I agree, but as a lifelong history teacher, I contend that it begins with people simply not being exposed to the history to begin with. For how could one not be drawn into these stories, the human drama, the interaction and the emotion that goes into putting an ideal first? After sitting at their table, how could you not give weight to what they have seen, and where they think we are going, as a people, as a nation? I saw this spark kindled time and again in my classroom, when we got to hear from real people who had a front row seat, who acted in the greatest drama in the history of the world.

Perhaps now I ramble. Now it is better to have them tell you themselves, about the world they grew up in, the challenges and obstacles placed on life's course, and how a generation of Americans not only rose to the challenge but also built the country and the freedoms that we enjoy today. They truly saved the world. Be inspired. Share their stories; give them voice. Lest we forget.

Matthew Rozell
August 2017

General Electric's Fort Edward plant is the only completely government-financed factory in the Glens Falls area. A half of its workers live in Glens Falls. Above, Jean Fitzgerald, Eleanor Penders, Phoebe Francato and Ruth Lopen test synchronous motors for automatic gun turrets on our largest bombers.

'General Electric's Fort Edward plant is the only completely government-financed factory in the Glens Falls area. A half of its workers live in Glens Falls. Above, Jean Fitzgerald, Eleanor Penders, Phoebe Francato and Ruth Lopen test synchronous motors for automatic gun turrets on our largest bombers.'
LOOK Magazine, 1944.[1]

---

[1] Fort Edward High School's sports teams are still known as the "Flying Forts," after the Boeing B-17 Flying Fortress heavy bomber and the motors for the gun turrets built here.

Hometown, USA

During the greatest conflict humanity has ever known, a cluster of small towns in upstate New York sent its sons and daughters off to war. In 1945, after six years of savage fighting, the devastation was unprecedented and incalculable. Between sixty and eighty-five million people—the exact figure will never be known—would be dead. Overseas, the victors would be forced to deal with rubble-choked cities and tens of millions of people on the move, their every step dogged with desperation, famine, and moral confusion. American servicemen, battle-hardened but weary, would be forced to deal with the collapse of civilization and brutally confronted with the evidence of industrial-scale genocide.

John Norton, American sailor at Hiroshima, after the atomic bombing: We walked around. The people, the civilians, were looking at us wondering what we were going to do to them. And, oh my God, the scars on their faces and burns. Oh God, it was sickening. Women and children—it was just sickening.

World War II would become the gatepost on which the rest of the twentieth century would swing.

Just what did our fathers see?

*

In the study of World War II, we are tempted to teach and learn the history as if the way things turned out was somehow preordained, as if it was a foregone conclusion that Americans and their allies were destined to win the war from the outset. As historian (and Pacific Marine veteran) William Manchester noted, because we know how events turned out, we tend to read the history with a sense of inevitability. Nothing could be further from the truth. It is easy to forget that during World War II the United States would be essentially engaging in two full-blown wars at the same time, taxing America's resources and families to the hilt. The story of World War II has been told many times, but only recently have we allowed those who actually lived it to speak for themselves. The narratives in this book are reflective of many of the places in the United States 75 years ago, but most have never been heard before. Most of them are drawn from those who share a connection to the communities surrounding the 'Falls' in the Hudson River, some 200 miles north of where the river joins the sea at New York City. Over a span of six months in 1943 and 1944, *LOOK Magazine* dispatched a team of photographers to Glens Falls, New York, and its environs for a patriotic six-article series on life in what was then dubbed 'Hometown, USA' to a national audience.[2]

---

[2] Assistant Secretary of War Robert P. Patterson had a hand in influencing the selection of the Glens Falls region by the magazine's editors. Born in Glens Falls in 1891, Patterson allegedly helped to steer the magazine towards the North Country in promising the availability of color film, which at the time was scarce and prioritized for military use. Over 5000 photographs were taken by magazine photographers presenting Glens Falls as a model of the home front during World War II.

'Near Falls-Finch, Pruyn & Co., Inc. on Left'
Glens Falls-Hometown USA—LOOK Magazine, 1943-44.
Credit: Crandall Public Library, Folklife Center, Glens Falls N.Y.

Esthetically and demographically, it seemed an apt decision. The counties on either side of the waterfalls on the Hudson River, Washington and Warren, give rise to the Adirondack Mountains and the pristine waters of Lake George to the north. To the east lay Lake Champlain and the Green Mountains of Vermont; just to the south, Saratoga with its historic racetrack, a summertime destination for over 100 years. Beyond Saratoga lay the industrial city of Troy and the state capital of Albany, less than an hour away by rail or automobile. In the early days these counties played pivotal roles in the formation of the United States, given their geographic strategic importance on the Great Warpath, the almost unbroken stretch of water linking New York City with Canada. It was around the vicinity of the 'Falls' that watercraft had to be taken out and portaged. Two major fortifications were constructed here by the British during the French and Indian War, and this was the setting for James Fenimore Cooper's classic *The Last of the Mohicans*. Half a generation later, a British army sweeping through here would be repulsed by county sons at the Battle of Saratoga.

Following the American Revolution, the early settlers engaged in agricultural pursuits such as dairy farming and, later, sheep raising. Mill-based operations on the river were centered around the upper falls at Glens Falls and the lower falls just downstream at Hudson Falls and evolved into significant lumber and papermaking operations. With the opening of the Erie and Champlain Canals two generations after the Revolution, new worlds opened up, but the 'North Country' counties remained relatively small in population.

Living here required hard work in all four seasons, but it was a quiet, close-knit place to raise a family, like many rural areas across America.

Then the war came.

*

Like most every other community in America, from the outside this region seemed untouched by the war. As documented by LOOK, life went on to its rhythmic beat—children went off to school, the mills hummed, department stores filled their storefront windows, and farmers sowed and reaped according to the seasons. The beat quickened as young men and women stirred to volunteer, notices arrived in the post box, and many left town for the first time in their lives. Life went on but was now accentuated by rationing, victory gardens, blackouts, and paper and scrap drives. Soon, the arrival of telegrams announcing sons missing or captured, teary phone calls from military hospitals, or worse, the static rings of the front porch doorbell would drive this war home into the heart of 'Hometown, USA' with the fury of hammer blows. Things would never be the same again. Like the 'hard times' of the Great Depression in the preceding decade, this war affected every family. Few American communities would remain unscathed by the emotional detritus of World War II.

Glens Falls-Hometown USA—LOOK Magazine, 1943-44.
Credit: Crandall Public Library, Folklife Center, Glens Falls N.Y.

John Norton: There was a family that lost two sons in World War II. The family got a telegram on a Monday that one of the boys was killed, and that Thursday they got another telegram saying that his brother had been killed. There were about 35 young men from [this town] who were killed in World War II, and I knew every one of them.

Thus the war came and went. Of the sixteen million Americans who donned uniforms, nearly three-quarters of them went overseas. Most returned home to a nation on the cusp of a change not imaginable to their younger selves who had struggled through the Great Depression. The GI Bill of Rights brought new opportunities everywhere, and the economy began to boom. It was best to forget the war and to get on with normal life.

Art LaPorte, U.S. Marine at Iwo Jima: I've had a nightmare down through the years. When I worked at the paper mill sometimes I would be working on something, with all the noise and whatnot, and I would go back in the battles and I could almost smell the gunpowder. I would see all the action for a few seconds. If you had waved your hand in front of me, I would not have known you were there. I was right back there.

'Normal' life. Except maybe it was not going to be that easy.

*

Twilight

Nearly seventy-five years after the beginning of those dark days, the twilight of living memory is now at hand. Day after day we open the newspaper to see that more American veterans have passed on, and we are suddenly on the other side of the 'bell curve' of deaths per day—the downhill slope. By September 30, 2018, the U.S. Department of Veterans Affairs estimates that fewer than 450,000 will remain with us; in just 20 years, the World War II generation will have all gone the way of the veterans of World War I and the Civil War.

I don't know exactly when I was struck by the notion that this day would come, though on some cosmic level I have been planning for it for years. I was born sixteen years after the killing stopped, and I grew up in the company of men and women who fought in World War II. Probably like most kids my age, I had no idea what they did, and like most kids, I did not think to ask. I was raised in this sleepy hamlet on the 'Falls' in many ways not unlike their generation: an innocent in an intact home surrounded by brothers and sisters and community-minded parents. I seemed to draw strength from the study of history at a young age, spending my summer mornings wandering in the woods down near the waterfalls that gave the town its name, searching for evidence of colonial skirmishes and settlements of the French and Indian War and the American Revolution. As I got older I became interested in the conflicts of the twentieth century but remained blissfully unaware of the veterans who were all around me. Some of my teachers in school were veterans of World War II, but I don't remember anyone ever specifically launching into a story about their time in the conflict. It's also possible that they did, but I was not paying attention.

In the late spring of 1984, all of that would change. On television I watched as the 40th anniversary of the Normandy landings was being commemorated over in France. Thousands of American veterans joined their Allied and German counterparts for a solemn tribute and reunion tours of the battlefields where they had fought decades earlier. Many of these men would have now been just hitting their stride in retirement. It was also the first time in nearly 40 years that many would be back together to ruminate on their rea-wakening past. And here it was that I woke up and was moved.

I returned to my high school alma mater in 1987 as a teacher of history. I found myself spending a good chunk of time each spring lecturing enthusi-astically about World War II, and it was conta-gious. There was a palpable buzz in the classroom. All the students would raise a hand when I would call out for examples of grandparents or other rel-atives who had served in the war—frequently two hands would go up in the air. Every kid had a per-sonal connection to the most cataclysmic event in the history of mankind—and in the late eighties, many of the soldiers, airmen, Marines, and sailors who came home from the war were still with us.

A few years later my students and I watched as the nation observed the 50th anniversary of the Pearl Harbor attack. After that we had the 50th an-niversary of the Normandy landings, which again attracted much interest. The films *Schindler's List* and *Saving Private Ryan* were released to much fan-fare and critical acclaim. The United States Holo-caust Memorial Museum, a work in progress for over a decade, opened its doors on a cold April day in 1993. These events signaled to those who had lived through World War II that it was okay to begin to talk about these things, that maybe people were finally ready to listen.

Building on that blossoming interest, I created a simple survey for students to interview family members. I had hit upon something that every teacher searches for—a tool to motivate and encourage students to want to learn more, for the sake of just learning it.

I was haunted, though, by one survey that was returned. When asked to respond to a simple question, a shaky hand wrote back in all capitals:

I DON'T KNOW HOW YOU COULD MAKE YOUNG PEOPLE TODAY UNDERSTAND WHAT IT WAS LIKE TO GO THROUGH A NIGHTMARE LIKE WORLD WAR II.

He was right—nobody can interpret history like those who were there. Maybe I took that as an unconscious push to bring the engagement into the students' lives even more personally. Every spring we produced themed seminars and veterans' forums, and at every step of the way students were actively involved. We began to conduct videotaped interviews, inviting veterans into the classroom, and I also conducted dozens of interviews on my own outside of school. It seemed that for every facet of the war, if we dug deep enough, we could find someone who had lived it and would be willing to share his or her story. Young people who despised school stopped me in the hall to voice appreciation after listening to the veterans. I learned a lot about World War II, but I also learned a lot about teaching.

Shortly after the 50th anniversary of the end of the war we initiated a dedicated project, and to date, young people have fanned out into the community and collected nearly 200 stories, forging bonds and bridging generational divides, bringing happiness and companionship to their elders. They became 'collectors of memory' and brought back much of what you will read here, improving their 'people skills,' honing their capacity for sustained concentration and analytics, and sharpening their writing chops for college in the process. Just as importantly, students of history had a hand in creating new history, adding an important tack on the scholarship of World War II that would have probably otherwise been lost. In that regard, the books in this series are unlike other World War II titles on the bookshelves today.

The Ripples

Still, as we recount these stories, the overarching question for some may be *'So what? Who cares?'*, and I suppose in our busy world that is to be expected. But somehow I believe that there is a higher purpose to this endeavor. There are always the lessons of sacrifice and service, of duty and honor, and that is enough to warrant a work like this. But in the end it comes down to simply listening, and pausing to consider all we have gone through together in a broader scope as a nation. It helps us to understand the essence of the eternal truths of the human condition, and ultimately, ourselves. World War II brought out the worst in humanity, but it also brought out the best. In studying World War II and the Holocaust, the ripples created generations ago remind us that history is not static, that these events will continue to flow and reverberate down through the ages.

Most of the subjects for this book have now passed on. Thirty years after it all began, sometimes I will lie awake at night and wonder about it all; it appears that the past beckoned, and we channeled a portal. Here are the stories that a special generation of Americans told us for the future when we took the time to be still, and to listen. In these narratives I hope you can draw your own lessons.

8th AF B-17 Flying Fortresses, 396th Bomb Group, 1943.
Credit: USAF. Library of Congress, public domain.

CHAPTER ONE

Air Power

The transition of the young men in this book from the Great Depression to aerial combat, from boyhood to manhood, paralleled the American development of air power and the emergence of new tactics and philosophies of coordinating and waging 'air war' on a scale that had never been done before in history. The concept of waging war from the sky on a large scale after World War I was not a novel idea, but it was met with resistance by the established branches of the U.S. services. During the 1930s, proponents like Billy Mitchell, Jimmy Doolittle, and Charles Lindbergh made gains at home, as did the Royal Air Force in Britain. The German Air Force, or Luftwaffe, under Air

Marshal Herman Goering, increased in size and range with the growth of Nazi militarism; these terrible weapons were tested during the Spanish Civil War and then the invasion of Poland to great effect. During the lull in the fighting between the fall of Poland in September 1939 and the German attacks in the west the following spring, Germany and Great Britain geared up for the battles that loomed on the horizon. The British had established the Royal Air Force, or RAF, as an independent wing of their armed forces. Led by independent thinkers who believed that air power and strategic bombing would be the key to winning the next conflict following its emergence in the First World War, RAF Bomber Command began their first missions with daylight attacks on German warships in the North Sea. In the course of a December 1939 daylight raid, half the bombers sent out as a force of 24 were shot down by the faster German fighter planes. The RAF quickly switched to experimenting with flying at night; survival rates for the planes dropping propaganda leaflets and the occasional bombloads thereafter improved dramatically, although bombing results were far less satisfactory.

After the German invasion of the Low Countries in the spring of 1940, British Prime Minister Winston Churchill issued a cautionary warning to the Luftwaffe that any attack on civilian populations would lead to an 'appropriate' response.[1] On May 14, the Germans bombed Rotterdam in the Netherlands, killing 800 civilians. Although part of the rationale for the Allied use of air power was precisely to avoid the constant slaughter that ground on and on along the stalemated Western Front for four long years in the First World War, no one could predict how much air power, once unleashed, would be difficult to contain. The first strategic targets were aircraft factories, synthetic oil plants, and marshalling yards for rail transport.[2] Wildly inaccurate, bombing by night led to much collateral damage.

After the fall of France in the summer of 1940, Britain stood alone. Hitler's plan, in simple terms, was to have the German Luftwaffe wreak havoc and terror from the skies, and have the U-boat fleet blockade the island country. Once Operation

Sea Lion's first phase was completed, an invasion by navy barges and infantry troops could occur.

It never got that far. While London was initially avoided by German bombers, on August 24, 1940, two German pilots veering off course jettisoned their bombloads before heading home, hitting areas of the city. This gave Churchill the opportunity to order up an 81-plane retaliatory nighttime mission on the German capital. Though it did little damage, it was a public relations success, and was also sure to bring German retaliation, which would in turn garner American public opinion towards helping Britain in some way.[3] Outnumbered four to one, the pilots of the RAF, the use of newly invented radar, and effective anti-aircraft flak kept the German bombing campaign at bay.[4] In the ensuing Blitz of London, where German bombers appeared over the city in a daily parade of terror bombing, the RAF claimed 56 bombers over the city on a single day in September.[3] Even the

---

[3] *the RAF claimed 56 bombers*-The number of RAF kills on September 15, 1940, is frequently cited as 185, but both sides were obviously prone to exaggeration; nevertheless, the punishment dealt the Luftwaffe that day stunned the German High Command. See Dodds, Laurence, 'The Battle of Britain, as it happened on September 15, 1940' *The Telegraph*, September 15, 2015.

royal family's quarters were not spared, but Londoners did not fold. Hitler called off the invasion indefinitely two days later, though the onslaught would go on at night for the next two months. Forty thousand had been killed in the Battle of Britain, and the notion that 'civilian populations be spared' rendered almost quaint. The strategic air offensive against Germany would last for five years, 'the most continuous and grueling operation of war ever carried out.'[5] Hitler turned his attention to the East, convinced that the conquest of the Soviet Union, with its teeming agricultural lands and resources, was paramount to Germany's ultimate victory in the war.[6] He could return to finish Britain off later. And now, on December 6, 1941, with Hitler's legions literally at the gates of Moscow, came Marshal Zhukov's massive Red Army counterpunch. A world away, Japanese fliers were conducting last minute preparations for launching their strikes against a place most Britishers, or Americans for that matter, had never heard about—Pearl Harbor. Germany declared war on the United States on December 12, and the sleeping, lumbering giant stirred. The Americans would finally be on their way.

*

In January 1943, Franklin Roosevelt and Winston Churchill met in Casablanca, French Morocco, to hammer out a rough blueprint for the Allied invasion of Europe. One of the first priorities was to destroy the German Luftwaffe, and as such, a 'Combined Bombing Offensive' was to be undertaken, with the Americans bombing German targets during the day and the British following at night in an unrelenting bid to soften German resistance. The goals were clear—in order to bring the war to an end, the effects had to be total and overwhelming. That meant bombing not only industrial targets but also densely populated urban centers where the working people lived; a skilled worker was more difficult to replace than a machine, and many machines escaped destruction in the bombing raids. Euphemistically termed 'de-housing,' British strategists in Bomber Command never denied that those efforts constituted an attempt to terrorize the population.[7] In Operation Gomorrah, the repeated attacks by the Royal Air

Force and the Eighth Army Air Force targeting Hamburg during the last week of July 1943, more than 45,000 people were killed and 400,000 left homeless in conflagrations that resulted in manmade 'firestorms'—howling tornado-like updrafts which conducted superheated air skywards, drawing oxygen out of subterranean bomb shelters and incinerating human beings by literally sucking them into the flames.[8] In this one raid alone, more civilians died than in all of Germany's air attacks against English cities, though neither Bomber Command nor Churchill felt any moral qualms; many pointed out that the Germans had begun it with their raids over London during the summer nights of 1940. Given the brutal nature of initial German attacks and the necessity of defeating Hitler, this is hardly surprising.

'Typical bomb damage in the Eilbek district of Hamburg, 1944 or 1945.'
Royal Air Force Bomber Command, 1942-1945. 'These were among the 16,000 multistoried apartment buildings destroyed by the firestorm which developed during the raid by Bomber Command on the night of 27/28 July 1943.' Source: RAF, Imperial War Museum, public domain.

More direct efforts to hit specific industrial targets fell primarily to the American air command. By the end of 1943 there were more than a million Yanks in Great Britain laying the groundwork for the destruction of Nazi Germany, with the American air bases dotting the eastern English countryside. From here, the Eighth Air Force mounted raids with her heavy bombers, the formidable B-17 Flying Fortress and the B-24 Liberator.

Boeing B-17G Flying Fortress "Shoo Shoo Baby" at the National Museum of the United States Air Force. Credit: USAF. Public domain.

The first mass-produced model, the B-17E, was heavily armed with nine .50 caliber machine guns mounted in Plexiglas 'blisters' and could carry a 4000 pound bomb load.[9] Subsequent models made various improvements, and from the beginning, the B-17 'Flying Fortress' was a workhorse of the American air campaign over the skies of Germany, with nearly 13,000 manufactured for the U.S. Army Air Corps. Improvements would gain the crews of the B-17 the capacity to carry three tons of bombs to the target, up to 2000 miles. The aircraft was also armed with thirteen .50 caliber guns.[10]

The B-24 Liberator was the most heavily produced bomber in history, with 19,000 manufactured; at one point, a mile-long assembly line at Ford Motor Company's Detroit plant cranked out a B-24 every 63 minutes.[11] It sported a twin tail and four engines, with a top speed of 303 miles per hour, ten .50 caliber machine guns, and the ability to carry 8,800 pounds of bombs. It was also used in a variety of capacities throughout the war. Complex tight bombing formations kept these bombers together to increase their accuracy and firepower against German fighters rising up to attack them, and several missions involved more than a thousand bombers carrying 10,000 or more airmen into enemy territory.

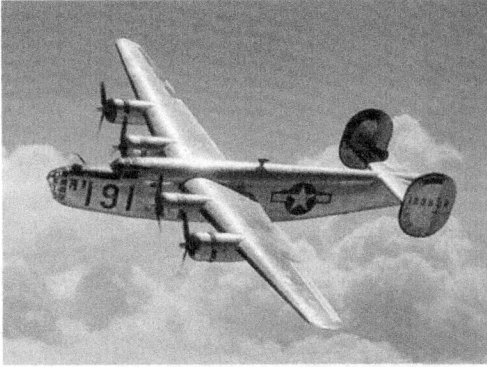

Consolidated B-24 Liberator from Maxwell Field, Alabama, 1940s. Credit: USAF, public domain.

By the time the European bombing campaign ended in mid-April 1945, nearly 10,000 of these bombers would be lost, along with another 8,500 fighters and almost 80,000 American airmen.[4] Manning these planes and others, it would be up to the boys of the United States Army Air Forces to get the job done. They would come from the depths of the Great Depression, and they would become men.

---

[4] *nearly 10,000 of these bombers would be lost*-British losses were even higher, having been in the war longer. Miller, Donald L., *The Story of World War II*. New York: Simon & Schuster, 2001. 481.

Hudson Falls, on the Hudson River, in 1946.
Source: Hudson Falls High School Yearbook, 1946.

CHAPTER TWO

Hard Times

Andy Doty was born in 1925. A 1943 graduate of Hudson Falls High School, he compiled the memories of his World War II experience at the fiftieth anniversary of the war, remembering growing up during the Depression and the inevitability of entering the service. Andy became a B-29 tail gunner, completing 21 combat missions in the skies over the Japanese home islands (detailed in my first book on the Pacific War) and even surviving an emergency crash landing in the vast Pacific—all before his 22nd birthday. He recounts the tempering experience of being raised in small-town America during the Great Depression, an experience that played out all over the United States:

'I present to the reader my memories of that era—the impact of 'hard times' and a world war on a quiet

village, the experiences of one of the last truly innocent generations of Americans, and the transition of a young man who hated fist fights into a seasoned tail gunner. Throughout my wartime training, I was aware of what was being done to prepare me to kill or to be killed.'

Andy Doty

Our town stretched for nearly two miles along the high east bank of the Hudson River, fifty miles north of the state capital at Albany. Main Street runs parallel to the river; along its length during the 1930s were the public library, the village fire and police stations, five churches, three department stores, a bank, three drug stores, one hotel, the tiny Strand theater, the high school, the post office, and a mysterious 'cigar store' where you could buy cherry bomb fireworks and where men 'played the horses' in a dark, smoky poolroom in the back.

Extending east at right angles to the main thoroughfare were the usual small town streets—Maple, Elm, Willow, Chestnut. By pedaling a single-speed bike half a mile out Maple Street you could see far across the broad valley to the Green

Mountains of Vermont thirty miles away. Looking down from Main Street, you saw the wide river tumbling along the long terrace of rocks that gave the village its name.

Hudson Falls, formally known as Sandy Hill, was a peaceful place where there were no serious crimes, scandals, or disasters to mar the slow pace of life. Snow sifted down onto the homes in the winter, lilacs bloomed beside long porches in the spring, katydids chirped on soft summer nights, and the scent of burning leaves filled the air in the fall. The best part of the village was the tree-shaded streets at the center of town, at right angles to Main Street. The poorer sections were at the north and south ends of town, and 'under the hill,' an area near the falls and the Union Bag and Paper Company mill.

My fraternal twin Chuck and I were born on October 12, 1925. Our family lived at the south end, seven of us, in a large, two-story rented house. A porch ran along the front and one side. Inside were a parlor and front room, the kitchen, dining room, and several bedrooms. The furnace stood in the center of the cellar like a huge oak, its big pipes spreading upward to the hot air registers in the rooms above. A dark coal bin stood nearby; there was a small garden in the back of the house.

My father was a lean, angular, quiet man, proud of the fact that he had become a night shift 'back tender' on one of the paper company's big machines. He made sure that wide swaths of paper rolled smoothly through without tears or wrinkles, and he wrestled huge rolls that were half his height in diameter. He earned eighteen dollars a week and was happy to have it.

Mom was a pretty, pink-faced, somewhat disorganized woman who engaged in long, dull monologues that we learned to let slip by. She was not a gifted cook; she would become so engrossed in reading the *Ladies' Home Journal* that countless smoking dishes had to be hurriedly retrieved from the oven. Mom would scrape away the burned portion, telling her children that carbon was good for them. She raised a large family while taking in sewing from the local shirt factory to augment Dad's income.

Three older children and a set of twins lived in the house—Bill, a taut, wiry replica of his father;

Agnes, who continually drank coffee and smoked cigarettes; and Ann, as pretty as her mother. The twins—Chuck and I—came along years later, no doubt to the great dismay of their parents. Two older sisters, Betty and Ruth, had left home earlier after dropping out of school to go to work.

Chuck and I turned out to be quite different. I did all the 'right' things—finished my chores, studied hard in school, and earned Boy Scout merit badges. In high school, I played on four sports teams, had leading roles in dramatic productions, and was named president of our senior class. I was the fair-haired son, and knew it—something I still feel guilty about. Chuck marched to his own drummer. He was taller and stronger than me but he cared little about sports. He was self-taught in many ways; I was amazed by the store of information he acquired about nature, animals, electricity, and many other subjects. He quietly handled the lighting and other electrical details of our high school drama productions.

It was not at all unusual that my older brother and sisters had dropped out of school early. The vast majority of Depression-era children did not proceed beyond eighth grade, for they had to work or marry to ease the economic burden on their families. Agnes proudly showed us the razor-sharp, crescent-shaped blade attached to a ring that she wore on her finger while working on a production line at the paper company. Her job was to bundle paper bags as rapidly as she could. She tied up the batches, and then cut the cord with a sweep of her razor, losing little time in the process. Ann, Chuck, and I were the lucky ones in the family; we were able to continue into high school, thanks to our older brother and sisters.

Our family was poor, but lucky to have jobs. Forty million Americans had no work or regular income in the mid-1930s, and unemployment ran as high as 80% in some cities. Fortunately, the paper products of the mills were in demand. Dad worked six days a week, and Mom sewed when she was not cleaning, washing, or scorching dinner. We had no car, no telephone, no family vacations, and no bicycles for many years (the Montgomery Ward model cost a staggering $29). I have a clear memory of dinners consisting of a slice of bread in a soup plate, covered with milk and sprinkled with sugar. At one time we ate dandelion greens that Dad dug up from a field. We complained about the bitterness but were told that the greens, like charred cake, would make us strong. We needed only to add some butter and salt.

Doctors were too expensive for casual use. One winter night I was sliding down a hill at the same time a girl was pulling her Flexible Flyer sled up the slope. The sled was behind her, trailing at the end of a long rope. Without her realizing it, the sled strayed out into my path. I was flat on my stomach, hands extended out to the steering handles as I sped down the hill. There was no time or room to turn. I smashed into her sled, the bridge of my nose catching the steel frame at the front. I rolled off my sled as blood spilled onto the snow. My companions placed me on the sled and pulled me home, where my mother applied her favorite remedy, a 'cold poultice'—a bandage soaked in cold water. No doctor was called, nor did we ever visit one. I still bear the scar and skewed nose.

Chuck and I asked Dad for a dime apiece one Saturday to attend the afternoon matinee at the Strand Theater. 'I just don't have it, boys,' he said, and turned his pockets inside out to show us. Although disappointed, I felt an even deeper sadness for him. Waitresses were averaging $520 a year in income, construction workers $900, textile workers $435, and secretaries $1,000. Wages were routinely reduced at the same time work weeks were extended, and no one dared complain. In fact, Dad had been 'let go' from an earlier paper mill job in another town when he dared talk about the need for a workers union.

Christmas brought few gifts. Chuck and I could expect a new penknife each year from Betty, knitted mittens (with our initials on the cuffs) from maiden Aunt Gertrude, and an article of clothing or two and a homemade toy from Mom and Dad.

The announcer during the 'Fibber Magee and Molly' radio show would tantalize us with his descriptions of Mars candy bars. He spoke in slow, mellow tones of the 'rich, creamy caramel,' the crunchy almonds,' and the 'smooth chocolate' that made up the candy we could not afford. As we walked the sidewalks of Hudson Falls our eyes scanned the pavement ahead, searching for lost coins. A penny was great, a nickel was a real find, and a quarter would send the finder into ecstasy. I dreamed of finding that much money.

The Delaware and Hudson railroad tracks were not far from our house. My father called the D & H the 'Delay and Halt,' but it did succeed in carrying some of that era's one million homeless—men called 'hoboes'—into northern New York. They stole rides in railroad boxcars, cooked food in tin cans over wood fires, and slept in 'jungles' in the woods. They chalked secret codes onto village curbs and sidewalks to direct others to hospitable homes—or to warn them away from unfriendly ones. Some made their way to our house, where my mother gave them a slice of bread and butter when it was available. They were courteous, grateful, and subdued as they sat on our back steps. Chuck and I stole glances at their bearded faces, grimy clothes, and worn shoes.

'Where are you from?' we asked one.

'From all over. You name it, I bin there.'

'Where you going?'

'Wherever I can catch onta something.'

When we were able to go to the theater, we watched the Fox Movietone News coverage of bloody strikes in automobile and steel factories. There were other scenes of men in black overcoats standing stoically in block-long bread lines, and of former executives selling apples, pencils, and shoe-strings from tiny sidewalk stands. There were dirty, seamed 'Okies' fleeing the dust storms that had overwhelmed their farms. We saw an army of World War I veterans march on Washington to demand early payment of bonuses due them in 1945.[5] Those were 'hard times' indeed.

A new president came into office, his cigarette holder cocked at a jaunty angle, and announced a 'New Deal' of relief, recovery, and reform to lift the nation out of the Depression. Among Franklin Roosevelt's programs was the WPA (Works Progress Administration). It created jobs for the unemployed all over America. An empty corner lot near our house that lacked sidewalks and curbs was

---

[5] *We saw an army of World War I veterans march on Washington-* the so-called 'Bonus Army' of 17,000 veterans who arrived in DC at the height of the Depression to demand early payment of WWI certificates. On July 28, 1932, President Hoover ordered his Army Chief of Staff General Douglas MacArthur to clear the gathering; supporting roles in clearing the marchers were played by then Majors George S. Patton and Dwight D. Eisenhower. At least two people were killed and over a thousand injured; the 'Bonus Army' was dispersed with their demands rejected, and it became a public relations nightmare for Hoover, one more notch that would lead to his re-election bid disaster the following November.

targeted for improvement. One day a truck and a dozen men arrived, hammered a WPA sign into the ground, and began shoveling. They worked leisurely that summer, stretching out the job as long as possible. 'Do you know why the WPA needs a crew of eight and a portable outhouse to hoe a field that two men can handle?' my father would ask with a slight smile. 'Because there are always two coming, two going, two peeing, and two hoeing.'

Our village was the perfect place for boyhood. The river, vacant lots, and nearby ponds and wooded areas were our playgrounds. Riding two on a bike and carrying a scruffy football, we challenged other gangs to Saturday morning battles. We tangled in the dust and mud without benefit of Pop Warner League helmets, padding, or cleated shoes. There were no obnoxious 'high-fives' or show-off victory dances after a touchdown. Neither a coach nor a parent was in sight. Our school classes were small, and our summer vacations were delicious. Sprung free in June like colts turned out to pasture, our gang of boys hiked across a bridge to roam the wooded Fenimore banks, named after James Fenimore Cooper, whose *Last of the Mohicans* was set in our area. We tried to run silently along paths through the trees and walk with our toes pointed straight ahead, as we were told the Indians once did. We swam naked in the river at a remote shale beach. An old row boat washed up onto the shore after a storm; we lugged it home, where we replaced broken bottom boards, pounded rope into the cracks, and sealed it all with chunks of tar melted in a tin can over a small fire. We paddled about happily on sunny afternoons in our resurrected craft; we fished for slippery, long-whiskered bullheads. My father told us his favorite recipe for preparing river carp; 'You put the carp on a board, bake it in the oven for an hour, pull it out, throw the carp away, and eat the board.'

The seasons dictated our activities—football in the fall, ice hockey and basketball in the winter, baseball and track in the spring. We entertained ourselves in many ways—by building, defending, and storming snow forts in the winter, by racing match sticks down a street gutter in the spring runoff, or by nudging a small wheel along the street with a T-shaped device we had hammered together. A kite could be built from strips of wood, string, newspaper, some paste, and a tail of torn rags. It was serviceable and was no great loss when it tangled inevitably in a tree or telephone lines.

We believed our gang to be unique. 'McGoosey' Walsh was a freckled imp who could drop two-handed set shots into a hoop almost at will. Bob Burns was a skinny Irishman. He was a choir boy in the Catholic Church, but was far from angelic. Bob could swear with the best of us, but he could go to confession on Saturday to be absolved of his guilt. As a Methodist, I envied the protection he gained by dipping his fingers into the water to cross himself before we went swimming or before he took a foul shot in basketball. Later in life I wondered if a controlled experiment would show that Catholics who crossed themselves drowned less often or made more foul shots than Methodists who did not.

Bill DeCamillo could not look more Italian than he did. So we called him 'Irish Bill.' Later on, in high school, he affected a 'zoot suit.' He wore a bright yellow, absurdly long jacket. His lavender pegged pants, supported by bright suspenders, reached up to his rib cage. A key chain drooped nearly to the ankles. His wide-brimmed fedora hat would have done justice to a Chicago gangster. His were the first male fingernails I ever saw that were an inch long.

'Bud' Reed was devilishly inventive. One dark night, as we were liberating apples from someone's backyard trees, the owner heard us, turned on a light, and looked out the door. As we ran away, Bud called back: 'Get down out of that tree, Mark LaRue, son of Reverend LaRue.' Mark was a popular boy who of course was not with us. The next day, his kindly father received a phone call from the angry owner.

Although we grew up in a small village and came from humble stock, we were surprisingly literate. We prided ourselves on the nicknames we devised for village characters—'Shufflefoot' Gleason, 'Choo Choo' Trayne, 'Carstairs' Lethbridge (after his favorite whiskey), and 'Commodore' Logan. The Commodore was tall, handsome, and distinguished in his castoff clothing. He had no job, and, as far as we could tell, no home. He was allowed to sleep at night in a barbershop chair or in the back of Harry Baker's Square Deal Drugstore.

Our days were enlivened by the arrival on our street of the ice man, the rag man, and the vegetable man. Their coming was announced by loud calls, bells, or whistles. The ice man's truck was piled high with large, clear blocks covered by bits of sawdust and wet canvas. He snagged the blocks down with his tongs, chipped them to the right size, hoisted them onto a leather patch on his shoulder, and bore them to the ice boxes in our homes. While he was away, we sucked on the ice shards on hot summer days.

The rag man was a shrewd old fellow who offered a few coins for all the cloth and scrap metal we could collect. 'Rags, rags, rags,' he called, and we dragged to his truck a burlap bag half filled with rusted nuts and bolts we had dug up from the Sandy Hill Iron and Brass Company yard. He was engaged in recycling long before the word was invented.

A ringing bell told us when the vegetable man was in our neighborhood. His wares were displayed on slanted racks in the back of his truck, shaded by an awning. A scooped scale dangled from a chain. Our mothers came out, wiping their hands on their aprons, to select from the fruits and vegetables when they could afford them.

As soon as we could, we found jobs. Three of us weeded Mr. Bushbaum's yard and garden at fifteen cents each for the full Saturday morning. Ten cents got us into the afternoon movie, leaving five cents for candy. 'Vaht robbers!' he roared one day when we gathered the courage to ask him for twenty cents a morning. We did not pursue it further; his was a buyer's market.

At age fifteen, Bob Burns, McGoosey, Chuck, and I obtained our working papers and began caddying at the Glens Falls Country Club. After two years we worked our way up to the highest 'Double A' status. That qualified us to advise golfers on which clubs to use, and to carry a heavy golf bag on each shoulder for thirty-six to forty-five holes on a good day. If we were polite, quickly handed out the proper clubs, and complimented our clients for their solid shots, we could expect a modest tip. As we trudged up and down the hills on those summer days the voices of the Andrews Sisters carried across a lake from a pavilion loudspeaker. They sang 'I'll Be With You in Apple Blossom Time' and 'Bei Mir Bist Du Schon,' and my heart sang with them. We were young, healthy, outdoors, and earning money.

Between rounds, we sometimes walked through the pine woods to the tenth hole, where we hid in the low-hanging branches, over a hill from the tee. As the golfers' drives came bounding over we dashed out, picked up the balls, and threw them far down the fairway. Back in the trees, we laughed as the resplendent bankers, doctors, dentists, and lawyers marveled at how far they had driven their balls. What wonderful clubhouse stories must have followed!

My friends and I were caught up in building model airplanes and in identifying aircraft of all kinds. We knew the name of virtually every plane in the world, ranging from tiny American Gee Bee racers to giant Italian Caproni bombers. Balsawood kits could be purchased for fifteen to twenty-five cents. The models were built from scratch—ribs cut out with a razor blade; stringers glued into notches with airplane cement to form the fuselage; wings and tails assembled, covered with tissue paper, and attached. A World War I Spad, a Sopwith Camel, and a tri-winged Fokker took shape on my table, as did a Piper Cub, a Seversky P-35, and a Gloster Gauntlet biplane. The Gauntlet cost a dollar, my most expensive purchase. Tears came to my eyes the night an entire wing burst into flame when I held it too close to the stove to make the doped skin tight enough to impress my friends. It took hours to reconstruct from surplus balsa.

Our schoolteachers were dedicated women, mostly unmarried, who demanded that we diagram the structure of sentences properly, recite the multiplication tables without a slip, and remember the outcome of the Peloponnesian Wars. Their right to grab an unruly boy by the ear and hustle him out the door and into the principal's office was unquestioned.

I was filled with the ambivalence of youth—quite confident at times, but insecure and uncertain at others; sometimes terribly shy, but pleased by attention; gregarious, yet often preferring to be alone; able to lead, but quite willing to follow.

I dreaded the fist fights that broke out after school or during our sandlot games. Honor required a boy to fight when challenged, so I often found myself taking a longer route home from school to avoid one thug in particular whose major reason for attending class seemed to be to pick fights afterward. There was a chip on his shoulder at all times. It actually came to that. He would place a bit of wood there and dare another boy to knock it off. Of course the other had to; great loss of face would result if he did not. Then the scuffle would begin, starting with wildly swung fists and invariably ending up with the two grappling in the dirt or snow—one, if not both, hoping all the while that they would be broken apart by their friends or a teacher or a mother who happened on the scene.

Although our gang engaged in pranks, stole apples from trees, and later found ways to sneak into the Strand Theater without paying, we were among the last truly innocent generations in America. We did not drink or smoke, or gamble. Drugs were unheard of, except for the rumor that certain big band drummers used something called marijuana. We did not swear in front of girls or insult them in any way. When an opponent took his foul shots in a basketball game, fans and players alike remained silent and unmoving so as not to disturb him. We fought fair. Two boys never picked on one, nor one boy on a smaller opponent. Kicking was not tolerated. Anyone caught carrying a knife was subject to permanent banishment. Firearms were totally out of the question.

*

Over the years our attention shifted from bicycles and ice skates to how we combed our hair, to our clothing, to shaving—and to girls. We watched the movie actors shave—men lathering, screwing up their faces, tugging at a cheek with one hand as the other drew a broad razor through the thick, white cream. We timidly roller-skated with girls to organ music at Brennan's Roller Rink on the Lake George highway, hands sweating and minds groping for a few words of conversation. There were later games of 'Spin the Bottle' and 'Post Office,' with chaste kisses at stake. We knew next to nothing about sex, even though some of our high school classmates told us they were experts on the subject. Our parents avoided the topic and our

THE THINGS OUR FATHERS SAW (VOL. II)| 63

schools taught us little. The movies were discreet, songs were discreet, and magazines were discreet. The most salacious material available to us was the silk stocking ads in the Montgomery Ward catalog. Hand-holding and kissing were allowed after several dates with a girl, but a boy did not try to go 'too far' if he really cared for her. Parental wrath, peer disapproval among the girls, and the fear of pregnancy hung over our era.

Sports brought many rewards. I was not big, but could run fast and far. During my high school years I ran the mile in track, played guard on the basketball team and second base on the baseball team. The eleven starters on our football squad played the full game, on offense and defense. We received only rudimentary football training, had a slender playbook, and did not confuse our opponents with a sophisticated offense. The team photo shows uniforms that did not match perfectly and helmets without face masks. Nevertheless, we were a good, solid team, and went undefeated in my senior year. We beat the fearsome Golden Horde of Granville in a War Bond benefit playoff game before a monster crowd of 2,100 at Derby Field—with most of the fans standing along the sidelines. 'Tex' Bailey, the owner of a village saloon, bet an astronomical fifty dollars on the game, an unheard of amount in those days. He happily pummeled us all the way back to our tiny, cement block locker room.

The summer before that final season, Bob Burns and I went to work at the Imperial Paint and Paper Company in Glens Falls. We were assigned to the yard gang, where we unloaded by hand railroad box cars filled with knee-high stacks of cement bags that weighed one hundred pounds apiece. We stood on a high platform in the oppressive heat and fumes, shoveling heavy, tinsel-like shreds of lead into wide vats of acid as the metal dropped relentlessly from a conveyor belt onto a steel plate. We pushed carts of crushed ice up to the paint mixers—men whose hats, overalls, shoes, faces, and hands were red, green, blue, or yellow. They must have sweated primary colors. It was at the Imperial factory that the name of Eleanor Baker, daughter of our town pharmacist, first came to my attention. A fellow worker from Glens Falls said he had noticed her and thought she was 'cute.' Had I ever thought of dating her? I had not. Her family was high on the Hudson Falls social ladder, while ours was out of sight on the rungs below. But the seed was planted. Eleanor sat in front of me in history class that fall and I finally worked up the courage to ask her to go on a hayride. She accepted and other dates followed. She was pretty, poised, intelligent, and totally unpretentious. Freshly washed, light brown hair fell to her shoulders. She wore soft, baggy sweaters, a pearl necklace, pleated plaid skirts, bobby socks, and saddle shoes. I was hooked. The day after our first date, I dramatically announced to my teammates that I had found the girl I would marry someday.

Life was good that fall of 1943, except for one thing—the guns of war had been rumbling over the horizon during most of my boyhood, and the sound was coming closer.

CHAPTER THREE

'Ye Shall Hear of Wars'

The war had come to our small town. Like all of those who would soon find themselves in the thick of it, Andy Doty was forming his youthful impressions of a world careening out of control, and finding his place in the swirling storm.

Andy Doty

Hardly a week passed during the 1930s when our school *Weekly Reader*, the local newspaper, the *Glens Falls Post-Star*, or *LIFE Magazine* failed to carry news of some far-off conflict. Aggressors were on the march and little stood in their way.

Japan invaded Manchuria and China, Italy subdued Ethiopia, and the Spanish Civil War ran its cruel course. We were shocked by a *LIFE* photograph of a naked Chinese baby crying in bombed ruins, by the Japanese rape of Nanking, and by photos of Nipponese soldiers bayoneting and beheading bound Chinese prisoners. An Italian pilot—the son of Dictator Benito Mussolini—casually observed that when his bombs exploded among Ethiopian natives, a 'beautiful' pattern resulted that reminded him of the petals of a flower slowly unfolding.

Hitler came to power in Germany and began building one of the most formidable military machines in history. He annexed Austria in 1938 then demanded that Czechoslovakia's Sudetenland be turned over to Germany—even a thirteen-year-old boy could see war coming to Europe. The major nations made no secret of the fact they had tested their weapons in Spain's Civil War, and Hitler's appetite seemed insatiable.

'Ye shall hear of wars, and rumors of war,' my father told us fatalistically, quoting from the Bible. Although Matthew went on to say, 'see that ye not be troubled—for all these things must come to pass, but the end is not yet,' I understood Dad to mean that war was an inevitable fact of life. I could see no reason to disagree.

Later in 1938, Prime Minister Neville Chamberlain of England returned from a meeting with Hitler in Munich, smiling as he waved a signed agreement he declared had won 'peace in our time.' Chamberlain had given Hitler the land he wanted, over the protests of the Czechs. Half a year later, the German dictator scrapped the agreement and occupied the rest of the country.

World War II broke out on September 1, 1939, after Germany invaded Poland. England and France, finally realizing that appeasement had failed, declared war. Poland fell in a matter of days, the victim of swift panzer tank divisions and Stuka dive bombers.

A long lull—the so-called 'Phony War'—followed, during which little fighting occurred. America debated whether or not to take sides. My youthful sympathies clearly lay with England and France, but the memory of World War I was still fresh in the minds of older, wiser men and women. 'What did we get from the first world war but death, debt, and George M. Cohan?' the isolationists asked; their cries of 'Never Again' and 'America First' held strong appeal. Congress passed yet another Neutrality Act as public opinion polls in December of 1939 showed more than two-thirds of the people opposed involvement in Europe's problems.

An amazing reversal took place during the next six months. German troops occupied Denmark and Norway in April of 1940, paused, and then swept across the Netherlands, Belgium, Luxembourg, and northern France in a devastating 'blitzkrieg' attack. After only ten days of battle, Hitler stood on the shores of the English Channel. Newsreels showed long lines of British troops at Dunkirk, farther to the west, waiting to be evacuated by a flotilla of every English naval or pleasure craft that could cross over to France. England was standing alone, and a surge of pro-British feelings resulted. A survey that May revealed a dramatic shift in public opinion—more than two-thirds of Americans favored active aid to England.

Shortly afterward, Congress passed the Selective Service Act of 1940, and the nation began arming itself. In the next two years, the Army grew from a force of 190,000 men to 1.5 million. Isolationism had been a persuasive force, but it gave way to America's instinctive support of freedom and democracy. The feeling slowly grew that England had to be saved and Hitler defeated.

Photos began to appear of raw recruits at the Plattsburgh Army Base practicing with wooden cannon, or with trucks bearing signs that read 'Tank.' Real equipment was not yet available in any great number. In Glens Falls, a hotel was taken over to house fledgling aviation cadets. We saw the uniformed young men marching to their pre-flight classes on the way to becoming pilots, navigators, and bombardiers.

The 'Battle of Britain' swirled over England that summer. To pave the way for an invasion of the island, Hitler sent out his bombers to hit military targets and destroy the Royal Air Force. After suffering heavy losses—and not knowing that his

Luftwaffe had worn the RAF down to its last reserve squadrons—he changed tactics and ordered
the blanket nighttime bombing of London and
other cities. That shift saved the RAF. London
could absorb the terrible punishment, but the RAF
could not have fought much longer.

'This... is London!' was Edward R. Murrow's
dramatic introduction of his nightly radio broad-
casts. We listened as Londoners huddled in deep
underground shelters, bombs erupted, and smoke
shrouded St. Paul's Cathedral. But Hitler had
missed his chance to invade England after Dunkirk, and failed to subdue England through bombing. He called off the invasion, and turned his
armies and air force south and east in 1941 to attack North Africa, Yugoslavia, Greece, Crete, and
the Soviet Union. Britain drew a sigh of relief.

*

A Sunday Afternoon

One Sunday afternoon in December of 1941,
Chuck and I came into the house to find our parents close to the radio.

'The losses have been heavy,' the announcer was saying.

'What's happening?' we asked.

'The Japs have bombed Pearl Harbor,' my father said quietly. 'They sneaked in this morning. We're going to have to fight them.'

Living in the east and watching Europe, we had not been following events in the Pacific as closely. The United States opposed Japan's expansion into Southeast Asia and had embargoed steel and scrap metal shipments to them. Japan struck back while it was strong and America weak. What made the attack even more despicable in our minds was the fact that Japanese emissaries were in Washington to negotiate peace at the same time their aircraft carriers were slipping across the Pacific toward Hawaii.

The grim reports continued throughout that day and the next. Eight battleships and three cruisers had been sunk or damaged, 188 airplanes were destroyed, and over 2,400 men had been killed. The next day, newspapers showed sunken battleships at their berths, damaged buildings, and the smoldering ruins of airplanes on the ground. It had been a devastating blow. December 7, 1941, branded by President Roosevelt as 'the day that will live in infamy,' propelled the United States into war against both Japan and its allies, Germany and Italy.

I did not feel great concern at the time. Hawaii was far away and we had faith in our nation's ability to recover. A commonly held view was that the Japanese were poor fighters, possessed inferior equipment, and could be 'licked' in a matter of months. We took satisfaction in a popular story that the Japanese once faithfully copied the stolen design of an English battleship, not realizing that the plans had deliberately been altered to make the ship top-heavy. When the ship was launched it promptly turned turtle, and floated bottom-up in the water—or so the story went.

The years pass by slowly at age sixteen, so it seemed possible that the war could be fought and won before Chuck and I reached draft age in October of 1943. If not, we would serve without question. We had to do our duty—the nation must be defended, and Pearl Harbor had to be avenged.

We drifted slowly toward the vortex as the months passed. Red, white, and blue service flags began to appear in the front windows of village homes, a star for each son in uniform. In time the village was drained of virtually all of its able-bodied men between the ages of 18 and 36. Everyone was expected to take up arms, and those who did not—the physically unfit ' 4-Fs' and those in essential occupations—were looked down upon. 'Draft dodger' and 'slacker' were bitter epithets. 'Why aren't you in uniform?' older adults demanded of young men who appeared to be of service age. The question could have stemmed from patriotism or jealousy, or both. 'They're either too young or too old,' actress Bette Davis sang in a movie, referring to those who remained behind: 'They're either too gray or too grassy green—What's good is in the Army, what's left can never harm me.'

McGoosey Walsh quit school to join the Navy, where he became a radio operator on a submarine in the Pacific. Bob Burns' brother Ed entered an officers training program at Rensselaer Polytechnic Institute and became a naval gunnery officer. My older cousin, a plumber by trade, was assigned to duty as a mechanic in a P-47 fighter squadron. Eleanor Baker's brother entered an Army Officer Candidate School. Our school's music director was stationed in Washington, where he led a Marine Corps band and returned home often on leave, resplendent in full dress uniform.

In time, gold stars that symbolized lost sons, husbands, and fathers began to replace service flags in the windows. Chuck Eagle, the center on our football team, worked at night behind the soda fountain at Moriarty's Drug Store. The store also housed a Western Union office. When telegrams from the War Department arrived, it was Chuck's duty to deliver them to village homes after work. Mothers and wives fearfully opened their doors to him those nights. 'The Secretary of War desires me to express his deep regret,' the telegrams began, 'that your son or husband has been killed or wounded, or is missing in action.' The telegrams seemed to arrive far too often. Chuck hated the task. A total of 126 young men from our sparsely populated county were killed in the war, two dozen of them from our little town. Untold numbers were wounded or captured.

The wounded began drifting back. Pat DuPell, the big, strong, red-haired brother of one of our gang members, came home from the Navy badly scarred, nearly blind, and breathing through an opening in his throat. A depot of depth charges had exploded next to his barracks at an eastern naval base. We were shocked by his appearance. Word came back that Chuck LaFountain, a bright young classmate who had entered the Army Air Force before his graduation, had been killed in the crash of an experimental aircraft called a flying wing.

At the Sandy Hill Iron and Brass Works, machinists began making base plates for machine guns, then turned out heavy winches for landing ships. The firm proudly floated a Navy 'E' for Excellence pennant from its flagpole. Married and too old to be drafted, my brother Bill left the paper mill to spray paint the heavy tanks coming off a new assembly line at the American Locomotive Works in Schenectady.

Meat, coffee, butter, cheese, sugar, flour, and other foods became scarce. Our parents took their ration books of stamps to the stores, 'spending' points for a pound of butter or a slice of ham. Gas was rationed, as well. An 'A' card allowed the owner three gallons a week. A 'B' card enabled a driver to obtain a few more gallons if truly needed. The 'X' card was granted those in essential enterprises; Bill obtained one for his daily trips with other workers to the tank factory. At night, Chuck Eagle would take his father's car out to drain any remaining drops from gas pump hoses at closed stations. Hudson Falls High School canceled all track meets to conserve gas, but the baseball season went on.

A collection center for items vital to the war effort was set up near the fire station. Villagers brought in scrap metal, vegetable fats, empty toothpaste tubes, rubber tires, metal foil, silk stockings, flattened tin cans, and waste paper. *Lucky Strike Green Has Gone to War!* a cigarette company proudly proclaimed. I assumed that it was doing its part by abandoning the use of scarce tinfoil in its packages. Victory gardens sprouted; war bond drives were mounted; women wrapped bandages; older men volunteered to be air raid wardens. Wearing armbands and helmets and holding a page of silhouettes of German bombers, the wardens stood ready in case the Luftwaffe targeted Hudson Falls.

*

The saddest hours of the war occurred during the spring of 1942. The Axis powers—Germany, Italy, and Japan—were invincible. Their armies were spread across Europe, were approaching Egypt and Moscow, and ranged in the Pacific from Burma south to New Guinea, east to the Gilbert Islands, and north to the Aleutians. Axis navies were in command of the high seas. German submarines torpedoed American tankers within sight of the East Coast, and America's old P-40 and P-39 fighter planes fell quickly before Japan's excellent new Zero—so much for the belief that the Japanese could only copy designs developed by others. Nevertheless, it was inconceivable to me that 'our side' could lose. I was certain that someday, somehow, the Axis armies and navies would be halted and thrown back.

The tide slowly began to turn soon afterward. Japan's mighty fleet of aircraft carriers—the same ships that had launched the planes to attack Pearl

Harbor the previous December—was defeated in June at the Battle of Midway. British troops routed Rommel's Afrika Korps in the Libyan Desert and sent it reeling back toward Tunisia. The Soviets halted the Germans at Stalingrad after a ferocious struggle. American troops landed in Algeria. The long, hard, costly march to Berlin, Rome, and Tokyo had begun. We traced the movement of the Allied forces on newspaper maps, unaware that the salients and advancing lines on those pieces of paper were made at a cost of thousands of dead or wounded young men. Once again, Chuck and I thought the war might be over by the time we reached our eighteenth birthdays on October 12, 1943. It wasn't.

When that date arrived, *The New York Times* reported that the American Fifth Army, after making its way across North Africa, through Sicily, and into Italy, was inching toward Rome against fierce German resistance, hampered by rain, mud, and flood waters. Our Eighth Air Force in England was flying raids deep into Germany that were so costly in men and machines they had to be suspended, although that was not announced at the time. One mission, mounted against the ball bearing factory at Schweinfurt, Germany two days after my birthday, resulted in a loss of 60 aircraft out of the 291 that participated.

I registered for the draft after my birthday, ready to enter the service when I completed high school in January. There was no way of knowing at the time, but that delay of three months—from my birthday to my January graduation—later was to play quite an important part in my life.

The three months passed swiftly. I had been taking commercial courses in high school rather than college entrance subjects because I had no hope of attending a university. In the fall of 1943, I enrolled in classes in math and physics in the hope they would better prepare me for one of the armed forces. On weekend evenings, Eleanor Baker taught me dance steps at parties in homes with the rugs rolled up. I clumsily fox trotted to 'People Will Say We're in Love' and haltingly jitterbugged to Glenn Miller's 'String of Pearls' and Tommy Dorsey's 'Boogie Woogie.' By November, we had agreed to go steady.

Andy Doty, first row, right, and the crew of the "City of College Park," 1944. Source: Andy Doty.

CHAPTER FOUR

The Tail Gunner

(Notes to the heavy bomber pilots and commanders)

Duties of the Gunners
All gunners should be familiar with the coverage area of all gun positions, and be prepared to bring the proper gun to bear as the conditions may warrant.

They should be experts in aircraft identification. Where the Sperry turret is used, failure to set the target dimension dial properly on the K-type sight will result in miscalculation of range.

They must be thoroughly familiar with the Browning aircraft machine gun. They should know how to maintain the guns, how to clear jams and stoppages, and how to harmonize the sights with the guns. While participating in training flights, the gunners should be operating their turrets constantly, tracking with the flexible guns even when actual firing is not practical. Other airplanes flying in the vicinity offer excellent tracking targets, as do automobiles, houses, and other ground objects during low altitude flights.

The importance of teamwork cannot be overemphasized. One poorly trained gunner, or one man not on the alert, can be the weak link as a result of which the entire crew may be lost. —Duties and Responsibilities of the Airplane Commander and Crewmen, 1943[12]

***

Around the holiday time in 1943, some friends and I were in Glens Falls when the bus from Albany arrived. Two young men in leather Army Air

Force jackets got out, picked up their green B-4 bags, and stood waiting for the trip to Hudson Falls. We knew them; they had graduated from high school the previous June, and were home on leave after finishing gunnery school training. They were dashing in uniforms bearing colorful shoulder patches, silver gunner's wings, and fresh corporal's stripes.

The dramatic return of those men, as well as my early interest in airplanes, made me quite receptive when 'Muff' Nassivera, our football quarterback, suggested that we enlist in the Air Force rather than wait to be drafted into the Army. We would become pilots, of course; every boy worth his salt wanted to be one. I quickly agreed. The infantry held little appeal.

I told my father that I intended to join the Air Force. 'Do what you think best,' he said. There were few other choices. I don't remember telling Chuck my plans. I assumed that he would go into the Army.

Booklets that contained tips on ways to pass military tests were available in the 1940s. I bought one and studied it carefully. There were drawings of blocks stacked in uneven rows in a corner, and of interlocking gears. One had to calculate how many blocks were in the pile and the direction in which the last gear would be turned. It was rather basic stuff, but I did not want to take a chance at being rejected.

I rode the bus to Albany for the first time. The Air Force recruiting station was located in a downtown office building. After taking the written exam, I was interviewed by a young lieutenant.

'What's the equation for the area of a circle?' he asked.

'Pi R squared.'

'Have you ever driven a motorcycle?'

I knew what he was looking for: an adventurous future fighter pilot. 'No, but I loved open field running in football.' That should impress him, I thought.

'What's an isosceles triangle?' I was stumped. I knew it well, but for some reason it just wouldn't come. He nodded and said nothing. On the bus on the way home, I remembered that it was a triangle with two equal sides, of course. I went home feeling disappointed.

It made little difference. I was accepted, and told to wait for further orders after my physical examination and high school graduation. The examination took place in the National Guard Armory in Albany, a grim, old stone fortress of a building. Several of us boarded a bus to go down for the tests. The group included a man who was both our high school track coach and commercial studies teacher. He was married and nearly beyond draft age. We entered the armory, stripped down to our undershorts, and spent the day being probed, weighed, and measured.

At the end of the day I walked down a long stairway. A Marine officer was at the bottom, looking over the men as they descended. He caught my eye.

'Are you sure you don't want to be a Marine?'

'I'm sure,' I answered. I was patriotic, but not to that degree. I have since wondered what would have happened had I accepted that invitation, for the bloody amphibious landings at Saipan, Iwo Jima, and Okinawa still lay ahead.

When we gathered for the trip home, the teacher was beaming.

'How did it go, coach?'

'I didn't pass,' he said. 'Flat feet.' Despite the ig-
nominy of 4-F status, he was happy to have it.

Basketball season followed, as did long walks
with 'Bake' (for Baker) on crystal clear winter
nights. We held mittened hands and I stole frosty
kisses as we crunched over the snow. A week after
my high school graduation my first draft notice arrived. It was a mimeographed form letter from a
major in the headquarters of the Second Service
Command on Governors Island, with only my
name and the date filled in. It sent a chill through
me.

'Private Andrew M. Doty

*1. This is to advise you that you are being called upon
to active duty on or about 31 January 1944.*

2. Orders will be sent to you within the next few days.'

Soon after that, my induction notice arrived.
'Greetings,' it began. 'You have been chosen by a
board made up of your friends and neighbors to
serve in the armed forces of the United States of
America for the duration of the war. You will report to the Induction Center at Ft. Dix, NJ. on January 31, 1944.' It was signed by the elderly
chairman of our local draft board on behalf of his
elderly fellow board members.

Bake and I walked to her father's drug store that night and took our places in a rear booth. I showed her the two letters.

'They don't waste any words, do they?' she said.

'Not at all. They didn't even say 'please' report.'

'I'm glad that you have a few weeks left.'

Other than that, she said little. We were still in the formal stage of our relationship, and had not spoken of love. We did not ever admit how greatly we would miss each other. My time simply had come.

'I have a feeling this will take about two years,' I said as we walked slowly back down Mechanic Street.

'Oh,' she said. 'That long?'

The Waite Hose Company fire hall on Main Street was the scene of frequent farewell parties in those times. One was held for Chuck and me the week before we were to enter the military. We received some gifts and said goodbye to our friends. Chuck left the week before I did, bound for Camp Upton on Long Island. As his train pulled out of the D & H station he pretended to wipe tears from his eye, hiding his sorrow with humor.

The night before I was to leave I visited Bake at her house. We had known each other only a short time, but I cared for her and was sorry to say good-bye.

My mother and father watched silently as I packed my new toilet kit and stationery into a bag, along with a small Bible that my sister Ruth had sent me. What were my parents thinking? How it must have torn them to see their twin sons leave within a week of each other, but they did not say a word. It was our turn, and there could be no complaint. Thirty years later I fought off tears as my oldest daughter left home safely to attend college only one state away. How did our parents keep from breaking down as Chuck and I went off to war? Perhaps they did after we were gone.

The last day of January was bitterly cold. Mom, Dad, and I silently ate breakfast before Ken Howe arrived in the early morning darkness to drive me to Glens Falls to catch the bus to Albany. I said goodbye to them as quickly as I could. As Ken and I sat in his car waiting for the bus, a boy rode up on his bicycle. He was Gerry Ellsworth, a classmate who lived two miles outside of the city. He had ridden in to see me off, despite the frigid weather. I was touched by his thoughtfulness.

The New York Central Railroad station in Albany was an exciting place in those days. It had marble floors, hardwood benches, and towering ceilings. There was a USO area on a balcony where uniformed women volunteers passed out coffee to the servicemen. The station teemed with soldiers, sailors, and marines and echoed with their clamor and train announcements. It was the first time I had been there. I felt that I was entering the serious world of adults.

Alone on the train to New York, I saw my reflection in the window and wondered what would become of that young man. I wore the gray and white Hart Schaffner Marx suit I had proudly bought with my summer earnings, a tan shirt, and a wine tie. I was sad and apprehensive and excited. How long would I be gone? What lay ahead?

'Take Care of Yourself'

What lay ahead, indeed? Sixteen million men donned uniforms in World War II; the experience of leaving home for the first time was exhilarating and terrifying all at once, especially knowing the possibility of being in harm's way was very real. Adulthood was coming on, like a quickening freight train careening towards the unknown.

The train sped down the banks of the Hudson River, past the old Dutch towns and cities, and into New York. We dove underground with a roar and emerged in cavernous Grand Central Station. The huge, vaulted area was crowded with hundreds of servicemen and women of all kinds and ranks. The Albany station that had impressed me so much would be swallowed up in this one. At Ft. Dix, the huge, multi-floor concrete barracks contained several loud, vulgar men, seemingly all from Brooklyn or New Jersey. I consoled myself with the fact that they were Army recruits, not Army Air Force. Then I remembered that my brother Chuck had gone into the infantry.

After arriving at Ft. Dix I took off my new suit, packed it in a box, and mailed it home. I traded it for more clothing than I had owned in my entire lifetime—duffel bags filled with khaki shirts, trousers, socks, and underwear; a heavy overcoat, gloves, a knit cap, and GI shoes. We shuffled past warehouse bins filled with metal mess kits, ponchos, and light helmet liners, tossing the items into our bags as we moved along. I also gained a new identity: serial number 42120238, embossed on metal 'dog tags' to hang around my neck.

A piercing bugle call on the barracks PA system shocked us awake early every morning that week. Knit caps pulled down over our ears, overcoats hanging to our ankles, we stumbled onto the dark, frigid company street. We fell into formation, slapping our arms, stamping our feet, our breath billowing out in front of us. Then came the first of many manglings of a name that goes far back into English history. But the hard-bitten master sergeant was not aware of that. 'Dotty?' the sergeant called. 'Duty?' 'Here!' I answered, before any more damage could be done. It was hard to understand how he—and his successors at later roll calls—could butcher a name so badly.

The indignities of military life have been well chronicled—hair shorn almost to the scalp, long rows of toilets with no partitions between them, 'short arm' inspections by doctors at our bunks at unannounced times, and demands of unquestioning obedience. Our individual identities were being stripped away. We received a battery of immunization shots, learned to count off and march in formation, and attended an irrelevant lecture on the dangers of venereal disease.

Our orientation completed, we boarded a troop train bound for basic training at Greensboro, North Carolina. As the miles clicked beneath the car, I speculated on how long it would be before the distance was retraced. We disembarked at the camp. Spread out on the red, sloping hills were row upon row of low-lying barracks. Squads of men marched along the streets, counting off cadence and chanting songs. As we formed up and moved off, the others shouted, 'You'll be so o o o r r y!' and 'Here come more gunners.' The latter was a shock; we thought we were destined for preflight training. The shouts were another touch of reality. Later on, we took pleasure in repeating them to the new batches of recruits we saw arriving.

The smell of burning soft coal will remind me forever of our six weeks at Greensboro. It came from the two iron stoves in each building, and clung in the wet air as we marched from class to class in our ponchos and helmet liners. We would sit on the hard floor of an empty barracks to hear lessons about poison gases, camouflage techniques, and carbine nomenclature. Our drill sergeant was a ruddy-faced Southerner who wore sharply creased trousers and shirts, and highly polished shoes. His cap was set at a precise military angle, and he insisted that ours be positioned exactly the same way. He stood straight and tall. He briskly herded us about, shouting commands and calling out the cadence:

'Hup, two, three, four
Hup, two, three, four
Hup, two, three, four.
You had a good job and you left;
You had a good job and you left;
Your left, your left, you had a good job and you left.
You had a good job and you left—your right,
You had a good job and you left—your right.
You had a good job and you left.'

The beat was strong and irresistible. So were the marching songs, which made long hikes about the base almost pleasant. We had become a unit, and actually enjoyed it at times. We struck up a steady rhythm as we swung along, singing '*I've Been Working on the Railroad*,' '*Into the Air, Army Air Corps*,' and '*Around Her Neck, She Wore a Yellow Ribbon*' (for her airman who was 'far, far away'). The second verse was quickly corrupted to 'around the block, she wheels a baby carriage.' Singing, marching, chanting, joking, and griping made our lives much more tolerable.

The sergeant was an Army career man who shaped batches of clumsy civilians into fairly respectable soldiers. He taught us to run through the manual of arms smartly with our carbines, to salute properly, and to don a gas mask in minutes. When we failed to measure up, he chewed us out unmercifully.

'What a piss poor excuse for soldiers y'all are,' he told us early one morning for some good reason. 'Y'all don't fall out on time, ya don't get the drill raht, ya don't salute raht, ya don't do nothing raht. We're gonna lose this goddamn war sure as hell if it's up to the likes a y'all.'

'That's a double negative, Sarge,' someone offered.

'What? What'n hell do you mean?'

'That we don't do nothing right—that means we do something right.'

'You do like hell. This is the saddest lookin' bunch that's ever come through here. I swear to hell we're gettin' to the bottom of the goddamn barrel. The krauts must be lickin' their chops to get at the likes a you sad bastards.'

A member of our squad was standing in the darkness in the back row. With his lips pursed and unmoving, he muttered, 'Blow it out your ass.'

'What? WHAT? Who said that? Who said that?' the sergeant demanded, glaring into the formation. He paced in front of us, staring at each man.

'Somebody's buckin' for a year a KP, and he's gonna get it. Who's the smartass? Who's the smartass?' There was no answer.

'All right, you guys—twenty-five push-ups, ev'ry goddamn one of ya, raht nahw.'

We dropped to the ground to do as he said, but we were smiling among ourselves. Even a touch of revenge felt good.

A Greensboro boy would come into the barracks at night to sell newspapers. He was often met
by a chorus of cries.

'Here comes another rebel,' someone called out.
'Nail everything down!'

'Grab your wallets, men.'

'Don't let him outta sight.'

The boy strode down the long aisle between the
double bunks, looking straight ahead. 'Fuck-in'
Yan-kees,' he said, drawing out the words with a
marvelous drawl.

Our turn came for KP. [6] Innocent as a babe, I
showed up at the mess hall on my assigned morning. The older hands on the base disappeared mag-
ically into jobs that lasted only through each meal,
ladling out oatmeal or scrambled eggs. I ended up
at a huge sink, washing pots and pans by hand. The
sun rose on the far side of the building as I stood
there, and it set behind me as I scoured. I was at
the sink most of the day. Just when I thought those
of us who remained were finished, an officer came
into the kitchen, tested the silverware with a glove,

---

[6] *KP duty*-'kitchen police' or 'kitchen patrol,' enlisted men performing menial
kitchen tasks under supervision, like peeling potatoes, washing dishes, etc.

and ruled that it was so greasy that it had to be washed again with vinegar.

Mail call was the high point of each day. We went down to the mail room and waited to hear our names, or renditions of them, called out. 'Yo,' we shouted, and picked up our letters. There often was one from Bake, for we had begun to write frequently. I saved her letter for last and looked for some sign that she cared for me. She generally signed them 'Love.' Later, it was 'All my love' or 'Much love.' 'SWAK'—Sealed With a Kiss—began to appear on the back of the envelopes, along with a lipstick imprint. I was pleased by that show of affection. After a while, she sent me a photo of herself, auburn hair falling to her shoulders. I kept it in my box of writing materials and studied it often.

Pay day saw long lines of airmen waiting in front of a table. An officer sat with a log book containing our names and serial numbers. As we stood there, a soldier glanced at the sky.

'Looks like it might cloud up and rain,' he said.

A big, black sergeant stood behind me. 'I don't care if it cloud up and shits,' he said. 'Ah'm gonna stay here and get my money.'

That night men gathered in a corner of the barracks to shoot dice. Some walked away with fistfuls of bills. Others had lost all, or most, of their monthly earnings, and soon were borrowing from their friends. I did not understand how they could be so foolish.

We set out one day on a twelve mile hike to a rifle range, carrying carbines, packs, and gas masks. It was a long, hot trip. As we neared the range, tired and sweaty, a Jeep roared past, releasing a cloud of tear gas. Eyes burning, we fumbled for our gas masks and swore vigorously at the disappearing vehicle. It was a good lesson, but we failed to appreciate it.

At the range we lived in tents, ate from mess kits, and spent the days firing rifles and pistols at targets. We were eighteen years old. Stretched out in our cots at night, we could hear far-off train whistles and were homesick.

*

Back at the main camp, we took tests to find out if we could enter preflight training. The end of the war in Europe was in sight, so fewer cadets were being chosen for the lengthy program. Only one man from our group was selected. I was so ashamed that for days I could not bring myself to write home that I would be going into gunnery school instead of preflight classes. We packed our gear, shouldered it all, and marched off to the railroad tracks and a waiting train. Our sergeant shook our hands and wished us well.

'Y'all are going to do okay,' he said. 'You shaped up good.'

We boarded a 'cattle car' troop train that contained rows of bunk beds. I liked the arrangement; instead of Pullman berths that forced two men to share a wide lower bunk, there were rows of individual bunks on floor-to-ceiling steel legs. In between the bunks were wide aisles. We could move about freely in the open areas, and nap or read on our bunks during the day. No serviceman will ever forget the smell of the smoke that wafted back from the engine, or the grit that sifted through cracks and covered everything.

Standing patiently in the long chow lines with our mess kits, we were jostled by the movement of the cars. Looking out the windows, we were introduced to the poverty of the rural South. As I watched the shacks and small towns of Georgia, Alabama, Mississippi, and Louisiana slide by, I realized how fortunate I had been to grow up in our river valley village. The railroad crossing arms would be down as the train sped along the drab main streets, bells ringing as we shot past, the men waving and shouting at the girls as the girls waved back. Sometimes the train would halt in the middle of a town; the most adventuresome men would race to a nearby store and run back with all the beer they could carry before the train moved on.

We were on our way to the air base at Harlingen, Texas. The school was near the Gulf Coast, just above Mexico. We arrived at night, picked up our bedding, and retired. I awoke in the morning to find myself in a world unlike any I had ever seen. Suddenly it was summer—there were palm trees, soft, warm breezes, and suntan uniforms. High in the cloudless skies, four engine bombers droned continually on their training flights.

Our six weeks of gunnery school was a fascinating experience. There was no KP or other drudgery; we were a privileged class being readied for war. It was a grand adventure, still unrelated to the deadly aerial battles then taking place over Europe. Our instructors told us about the piercing cold in a bomber at high altitude, about the damage that anti-aircraft fire can inflict, and about the way bullets were deflected by the shielding on the front of an attacking Focke-Wulf fighter, but it did not really sink in. Much of that was due to the matter-of-fact way in which the information was presented, without reference to death, wounds, or downed crews. I had a distinct feeling that one of our instructors in particular, a staff sergeant who had flown twenty-five missions with the Eighth Air Force over Germany and looked older than his years, was sparing us the worst details. He held himself apart, and I sensed that he felt sorry for us.

One day at a range where we learned to fire machine guns, I asked an older ground attendant if he had ever flown. 'Are you crazy?' he answered. 'I've seen them wash too many of you guys out of a crash with a hose.' It was a sobering statement, but we laughed when I repeated it that night in the barracks. We were seated in an auditorium another time when an officer casually told us that a third of the men in the room would be killed, wounded, or taken prisoner. I felt sorry for the others, for surely nothing could happen to me. Youth is optimistic, feels indestructible, and sees life as infinite. Thus young people ride bicycles blindly around corners, drive cars too fast, and fight wars.

I wondered how they would teach me to kill another man. I hated fist fights, never hunted animals, and always tried to be kind to others. What would they do to change my nature? The answer is easy—they simply give you the training, the equipment, some indoctrination, and the opportunity. You can either shoot back, or regret it. And of course you could not let your buddies down, or be seen as cowardly.

Whatever was needed, we worked into gradually. There were slide shows of German, Japanese, American, and British aircraft. We called out the names of the Zeros, Spitfires, Me-109s, Lightnings, Nicks, P-47s, P-51s, and Focke-Wulfs as they flashed by. As a model builder and an airplane freak for so many years, I found it all very familiar.

Then came a turn with guns that fired a stream of BB pellets at a model airplane that moved on a track across a painted canvas sky. What adventurous boy could resist that game? It was good, clean, harmless fun. We peppered the model as it emerged from behind a 'cloud' and sped across an open expanse. Later we went out to a skeet range, where we fired shot guns at circular clay pigeons as they were catapulted in front of us. Leading the black saucers by a radius or two, we shattered them by the hour. There must be a stratum of broken birds several feet thick at that site today. We graduated from the stationary skeet range to the back of an open truck that circled an oval track. Catapult stations were located at various points along the route. We stood in the back of the vehicle and took turns firing our shotguns at the skimming targets as we drove along, compensating for both the movement of the truck and the trajectory of the birds.

One morning we were marched to a large classroom building. Inside was an area that contained several metal-topped tables. Mounted on a pedestal at one table was a large, black, lethal-looking machine gun. An instructor stood in front of us, his arm resting on the gun.

An armorer working on a .50 M2.
Credit: browningmgs.com.

'Men, this here is a .50 caliber, Browning M2 machine gun. It is a belt-fed, recoil-operated, air-cooled weapon. It can fire twelve to fourteen rounds a second, maximum, but that would burn out the gun barrel fast if you kept it up for long. So don't ever do it. Instead, we rapid-fire forty rounds a minute, in bursts of six to nine rounds, at five to ten second intervals to save the barrel. Before you're done, you're gonna learn this baby inside out and backwards. If you don't, it could be your ass, and I don't mean maybe! So listen careful.'

We did just that in the weeks that followed. The .50 caliber was a brute of a weapon, heavy, accurate, and rapid-firing. It weighed eighty pounds, and could shoot half inch diameter bullets more than four miles with a muzzle velocity of 2,900 feet a second. Its most effective range was up to 600 yards.

Day after day, we took the gun apart, learning the name and function of every piece. I removed the rear buffer plate, examined the buffer discs, released the driving spring rod, and withdrew the shiny steel bolt assembly. I could not help but admire the smooth, beautifully machined unit that pulled the rounds steadily into the gun, slammed them into the breech, fired, recoiled, ejected the clips and cartridges, and then repeated the process. We were shown how to keep the gun oiled and in good repair, and how to clear malfunctions. The day finally came when I could put on a blindfold, dismantle the weapon, spread the parts out on the table, then put them all back together. I smiled with satisfaction after the job was completed.

A machine gun firing range was located in the sand dunes near the Gulf Coast. Rows of .50s were mounted on steel pedestals, facing targets half a mile away. Holding a bucking gun by its two handles, I sent a torrent of bullets into a target area, creating geysers of sand and dust. The noise hammered my ears and the brass cases spewed into the air as long belts of ammunition were devoured. I did not let myself think about a similar stream of enemy slugs that someday could come flying back in my direction.

The next step was a visit to a large hangar at Harlingen that contained heavy wooden platforms. Mounted on them were the electrically driven nose, ball, and tail turrets that were found in B-24 Liberator bombers. Each turret contained two .50 caliber machine guns. We learned how to operate each of the turrets, swinging the units from side to side, and the guns up and down. The nose and tail turrets were like tiny greenhouses perched out on the edge of nowhere. I felt highly vulnerable sitting in them, surrounded only by thin, clear plastic.

The Sperry ball turret hung below the fuselage of both the B-24 and the B-17 Flying Fortress to protect the underbelly of the bombers. The turret was a metal and Plexiglas 'goldfish bowl' about three feet in diameter. It called for smaller men who could curl up inside for long periods of time. The B-24 ball had to be raised from its position beneath the plane so that the gunner could enter. The turret then was lowered into place. We practiced the routine on the platform. The ball would be brought up, secured, and the hatch opened. I would climb in, the hatch would be closed overhead, and the ball would be eased downward. Today, the memory of the practice gives me claustrophobic shivers; at that time, it was simply another command to be obeyed.

In still another classroom an instructor described the famous Air Force clock system for reporting the positions of attacking aircraft. 'Twelve o'clock' was directly ahead of the bomber, 'three o'clock' was off the right wing tip, 'six o'clock' behind the tail, and so on. Accordingly, a fighter closing in at 'seven o'clock low' was to the lower right of the tail gunner, and one at 'twelve o'clock high' was approaching the pilots from above.

The instructor held up a model of a German Me-109 fighter. 'Suppose I'm a German sittin' out here like this at three o'clock, checkin' you out and gettin' ready to come in,' he said. He positioned the model as if it were flying parallel to the front row of our class, the nose pointing to our left. 'Here's what to look for. You watch his inner wing tip like a hawk. If the guy is really serious, the wing will tilt up, and he'll come sweeping in and drop back toward the tail of your plane, like this.' He tipped the wing up and let the plane fall off to our right, the nose pointed steadily at us.

German ground crew pushes Me-109 onto tarmac, fall 1943, France. Credit: Bundesarchiv, Bild 101I-487-3066-04 via Wikimedia Commons.

'That's called a pursuit curve. It holds the fighter right on target every inch of the way. If the guy is a little chicken—sometimes they are—he'll dip the inner wing down and cut around behind you, like this.' He showed us how the fighter would bank sharply down and away to its left.

'That's a fly through. It means that his fire will be scattered and much less accurate, like a hose sweepin' across a lawn instead of being pointed straight at you all the time. You'll like that. And for God's sake, don't waste your ammunition on a fighter flying alongside you way out here, doing no harm! Hold your fire until he starts coming in. You're going to need every round you've got!' With those heartening words, we were ready to take to the air.

*

Several AT-6 training planes awaited us on the flight line at Harlingen one morning. They were low-wing, single-engine aircraft with an open cockpit in the rear. A thirty-caliber machine gun— the 'little' brother of the fifty—was mounted behind the cockpit. We were handed leather helmets, goggles, parachute harnesses, and parachutes, and told how to use them. A sergeant gathered us around a trainer. He told us we would be flown out to the Gulf, where we would fire at targets as we flew low over the water.

North American AT-6C-NT Texan trainer, 1943. Credit: USAF, public domain.

'Two things,' he said, holding up his fingers. 'One, don't shoot the tail off the airplane. If you do, somebody's going to be mad as hell, including the pilot. Second, remember to space your bursts. If you don't, you'll burn out the barrel, and then I'll be mad.'

Several of my companions flew first. Some returned swallowing hard, or with less color in their faces. When my turn came, I put on my equipment and climbed into the rear seat for my first airplane ride. The bored pilot sped out to the runway, paused as briefly as a bird on a bush, then roared into the air. Looking down at the countryside, I was exhilarated. The houses, barns, and cars were small toys far below. We continued toward the Gulf. Suddenly the plane banked, dropped, and swooped across the shallow water. I fired at the floating targets, taking care to do as I had been told. The bullets tore into the water, coming near a Mexican fishing boat that had strayed into the area to pick up stunned fish. A man dove overboard, not knowing that I had no intention of hitting the boat. We repeated the run, then returned to the base. In retrospect, the main objective of the flight may have been to see if we were fit to fly. If we managed to hit the water, did not get sick, missed the tail, and spared the gun barrel, we passed.

We began flying in different kinds of bombers as the pilots practiced piloting, the navigators navigating, the bombardiers bombing, and the gunners gunning. We donned fleece-lined helmets, jackets, pants, gloves, and boots and clambered into an old B-24 Liberator bomber. It roared down the runway, lifted from the ground, and slowly climbed upward. After a time, we put on our oxygen masks and plugged the long hoses into the ship's system.

Standing beside an open waist window some 25,000 feet in the sky, I marveled at the clarity of the air, the brilliance of the sunshine, and the vapor trails that formed long streamers behind our plane. Flight at those altitudes in those days was an adventure requiring heavy clothing and oxygen masks. Today it is commonplace to fly comfortably six miles above the earth in pressurized cabins.

High above Texas one April afternoon, a B-24 ball turret was raised, and the hatch opened.

'Your turn,' our instructor said to me. 'In you go.'

Sperry ball turret, retractable model. Credit: browningmgs.com.

I settled myself into the compartment and connected my oxygen tube and intercom line. The hatch was closed and latched above me. The twin fifties and I were pointed straight down at the ground, thousands of feet below. The turret was slowly lowered into the sparkling air. Using upright hand levers that pivoted in all directions, I leveled the turret and rotated it so that I could look all about. Overhead was the fat underside of our bomber and its big, oval twin rudders; around me was the vast sky. A camera was mounted in the turret to record simulated attacks by friendly fighters. One appeared from below—an old Bell P-39 Airacobra, coming straight on. I fixed him in my gun sight, pushed the firing buttons on top of the levers with my thumbs, and 'shot' him with my camera. It was an exciting moment.

Between flights we went to classes, learned survival techniques, and studied our manuals. I remember sitting in the lighted stairway of our barracks one night, reading a lesson after the rest of the building had been darkened. To 'wash out' of gunnery school would have been a terrible disgrace, far worse than missing out on preflight training. If I failed I could be sent to the Air Transport Command, where I would spend the war safely loading freight into cargo planes instead of flying missions over enemy territory. That was a fate to be avoided. The boy who never hunted animals now was willing to shoot at other men— or would be chagrined not to be shooting at them. I had not hardened or developed a killer instinct; I was simply responding to the pressures of the time.

I did not feel fear while suspended below the bomber, nor did I question the assignment. I should have; the turret was top-heavy, and could swing violently if not locked into place inside the airplane as I was sliding in or out. And if the ship's electrical system was knocked out, the ball turret could not be retracted. Worst of all, there was no room in the ball for a parachute. One was totally dependent upon the crewmen above to raise the turret, secure it, and help one get out, in order to put on a parachute. It occurred to me that if my bomber was aflame and spinning to earth, the crewmen above might well decide to save themselves rather than lose time retrieving me. How many ball turret gunners plunged to their deaths in World War II in the same fetal position in which they had begun their lives? Their casualty rate was high. Despite the problems, I continued on, and was destined for duty beneath a bomber when our training period came to an end. I had inherited my parents' stoicism, or their optimism, or both.

Our daily calisthenics exercises saw acres of lean, tanned men, wearing white shorts and black sneakers, swinging arms high and legs wide in chanted unison. Watching them, I speculated on the thousands of other young men at other bases around the world who at that same moment were preparing in the same way to do battle against their enemies.

'Look!' someone called out as we were returning from our mess hall after dinner one evening. He pointed to a B-24 with a smoking engine that was swinging low over the base, racing toward the landing strip. We stopped to watch the bomber bank sharply downward and drop from sight beyond the barracks. Soon a pillar of black smoke rose high in the sky. As I lay in my bed that night I imagined myself in the place of that crew in their terrifying plunge to earth. Later we learned that the bomber had leveled out to land and burn, and that everyone had escaped unhurt.

Soon, we took a battery of tests, received our silver wings and corporal's stripes, and were ready for assignment to a combat squadron. We were rolling out of gunnery schools across the south and southwest every week by the hundreds, ready to join the shiny new bombers that were steadily flowing off their own production lines.

Andy Doty went back to 'Hometown, USA' again on leave, and on his return to base he was assigned to the crew of a new bomber, the B-29 Superfortress, destined for the skies over Japan. It had been developed secretly and was well suited to the demands of the Pacific theater: long, overwater missions without fighter escorts. Before shipping out to the Pacific, he returned home one last time.

Once again, the two weeks vanished in a flurry of visits, movies, high school basketball games, and trips to the drug store. I picked up Bake at her house on those frosty evenings, and we walked briskly down Mechanic Street to the corner of Main Street to catch the bus to Glens Falls. The bus was crowded, its windows coated with steam or frost. A man gave up his seat to Bake, and I stood proudly beside her in the aisle, swaying slightly as I held onto an overhead strap. As the bus moved along, its lights showed high snow banks on either side of the road and dark clusters of people waiting in the cold at the bus stops ahead. We were on our way to Glens Falls to see 'Since You Went Away' at the Paramount Theater. It starred Jennifer Jones and Robert Walker as young lovers in wartime. Bake and I held hands in the darkened theater and identified with the two characters.

We ended the evening in the Baker family's warm front room, where we waited for her parents to go to bed after we had finished our ice cream ritual. When they were gone, Bake sat on my lap in a large, blue easy chair. Soft dance music, broadcast late at night from a hotel in New York City, formed a romantic backdrop. We kept the radio low so that we would not disturb her parents beyond their closed door. But after a time, Mrs. Baker's call emerged: 'Eleanor!' Once again it was time for me to leave. I walked home in my heavy overcoat, cupping my ears in the cold, running to slide across patches of ice in the street.

The farewells this time were much harder, for we all knew I was going overseas. Again I left Bake early the night before departing, and went through the routine of packing with my parents watching. Ken Howe drove us, Agnes, and Bake to Albany in a Buick that held three people in the front seat. Mom, Bake, and I sat in the back. It was a sad ride, but we tried to be cheerful, talking about anything but the future.

Standing on the slushy pavement in front of the railroad station, we said goodbye. I hugged Mom and shook Dad's hand. He had been taking nitro-glycerin tablets for an angina problem for years and puffed after the slightest effort. I looked into his eyes and wondered if I would ever see him again; I imagined him wondering the same about me.

Dad was not given to long statements. 'Take care of yourself,' he said. 'I will—you, too.' We did not embrace, for men did not do such things in those days. I wish I had, for I never saw him again.

I gave Bake a brief kiss, picked up my bags, and disappeared into the station.

*

Andy Doty survived 21 combat missions in the Pacific late in the war, detailed further in my first book, The Things Our Fathers Saw: Voices of the Pacific Theater. *He returned home in December 1945 and pursued higher education. His brother Chuck also survived the war, and went to work in the mills like their father. Andy and Eleanor Baker married in July 1950.*

*

Andy Doty

I think we shall never see the likes of it again. The nation was fully united and mobilized in a popular military effort. The youth of America was under arms, generally willing, and often eager to serve their country. Young men who had never traveled more than fifteen miles from home fought land, sea, and air battles in every quarter of the globe.

Richard 'Dick' Varney, flight engineer, first row second from left, and the crew of his B-24 Liberator. Source: Richard Varney.

CHAPTER FIVE

The Flight Engineer

Richard 'Dick' Varney was born in 1911, and was already an 'old man' when he was drafted at age 32. Mr. Varney lived on the corner of the block where I grew up, with his wife Anne and two children. He always had a smile on his face and a loving twinkle in his eye when I saw him; his wife Anne came into the house and minded us as young children when my mother started to work as a school nurse-teacher. When I started sending my students into the community to do interviews with veterans 40 years later, two of my students happened to meet him at a garage sale and got to talking. Though he had been a part of my own family's life for decades—he was even my youngest brother's godfather—I had no idea that Richard Varney had been in the war; he flew 28 missions in the B-24 Liberator. He gave my students a wide-ranging interview in his home in December 2003. Here he is, at age 92, talking to two seventeen-year-olds, and passing advice and his take on the current state of the world with the same smile and sparkle.

***

Duties of the Flight Engineer

Size up the man who is to be your engineer. This man is supposed to know more about the airplane you are to fly than any other member of the crew.

He has been trained in the Air Force's highly specialized technical schools. Probably he has served some time as a crew chief. Nevertheless, there may be some inevitable blank spots in his training which you, as a pilot and airplane commander, may be able to fill in.

Think back on your own training. In many courses of instruction, you had a lot of things thrown at you from right and left. You had to concentrate on how to fly; and where your equipment was concerned you learned to rely more and more on the enlisted personnel, particularly the crew chief and the engineer, to advise you about things that were not taught to you because of lack of time and the arrangement of the training program.

Both pilot and engineer have a responsibility to work closely together to supplement and fill in the blank spots in each other's education. To be a qualified combat engineer a man must know his airplane, his engines, and his armament equipment thoroughly. This is a big responsibility: the lives of the entire crew, the safety of the equipment, the success of the mission depend upon it squarely.

He must work closely with the copilot, checking engine operation, fuel consumption, and the operation of all equipment. He must be able to work with the bombardier, and know how to cock, lock, and load the bomb racks. It is up to you, the airplane commander, to see that he is familiar with these duties, and, if he is hazy concerning them, to have the bombardier give him special help and instruction.

Your engineer should be your chief source of information concerning the airplane. He should know more about the equipment than any other crew member-- yourself included.

You, in turn, are his source of information concerning flying. Bear this in mind in all your discussions with the engineer. The more complete you can make his knowledge of the reasons behind every function of the equipment, the more valuable he will be as a member of the crew. Who knows? Someday that little bit of extra knowledge in the engineer's mind may save the day in some emergency.

Generally, in emergencies, the engineer will be the man to whom you turn first. Build up his pride, his confidence, his knowledge. Know him personally; check on the extent of his knowledge. Make him a man upon whom you can rely. —Duties and Responsibilities of the Airplane Commander and Crewmen, 1943

***

Richard Varney

I grew up during the Depression. I remember that day in 1929 [when the stock market crashed] very well. I was about 17 or 18. I had been working for two years; I went to work at fifteen years old with working papers. My parents, God bless them, they grew up in an era when school was not that important. You went to work as soon as you were able to help the family. I don't think you people understand what I am saying or what that means, but it meant a lot. But I wish that I had gone to school. I did later on, but I made it in life without [a formal education]. I had to do it my way. I worked at the sawmill on Haskell Avenue in Glens Falls; it's not there now. I also started playing at dances in a band when I was 17 and did it for a long, long time; it was a lot of fun. It was quite necessary then because the wages then weren't what they are now. I took lessons for a little while on the violin, but I played by ear from then on. I also taught myself to play the alto and tenor saxophone, which I still have, incidentally.

You have to realize that when I went to work at the Imperial factory, later, if you weren't late or forgot to ring in and out, you got 40 cents an hour. Can you imagine that? You worked 40 hours, you got sixteen dollars a week! Now on this, you had a family to support—it isn't like what it's like today. In the Depression era you could buy a home for 1,500 dollars. You couldn't hang a door for that now! Money was something you didn't have, but you didn't feel deprived in those days because nobody else had any money. No, you probably had one change of clothes, maybe one pair of shoes if you were lucky. You didn't wear them in the summer because you didn't want to wear them out. I'm not exaggerating, because you just didn't have the money. You made do. You didn't eat a lot of prepared food, you [improvised and] cooked your own. You ate a lot of things... [Have you ever had] dandelions? We used to go and pick them. Clean them, cook them, you make do. You just didn't always have money with those kinds of wages.

*

On December 7, 1941, I was working at the Imperial Color paint factory in Glens Falls. It was a shock—I was outraged naturally, because it was a sneak attack. But it was not unexpected; believe me, we had been heading towards it. In fact, in my opinion we were already in an undeclared war; we were actually in it because we were supporting England. We had been giving them everything they needed; from then on it was just a matter of time before we all got into it. But Germany and Japan declared war on us first.

I was not a kid; I was thirty years old at the time. I was married and I had no idea what the future was going to bring for us, because I did not know what they wanted to do. I don't think anybody relished the idea of going to war; nobody does. But nevertheless, I think we had a level of patriotism at that time that we won't ever see again; certainly we don't have it now. Everybody was behind it, the whole situation, at that time. I don't think you heard anybody wondering whether we should go in or not, because we were in. In retrospect it was so long ago now, a lot of the details are not as sharp as they should be maybe, but I can remember most of it.

*

I was drafted in April of 1943, I think. Then we went through God knows how many schools, how much training, to prepare us for it.

I took my army basic training in Miami Beach. It was tough duty in Miami Beach. [*Laughs*] After that we were assigned to air mechanic school, and there I was trained for the B-24 Liberator. I was being trained as the aircraft flight engineer, and my job at that time was everything mechanical on the plane. It was the flight engineer's responsibility, so you were taught everything about the airplane. Then after we graduated from there, they sent us to Panama City for air gunnery. After that we went to various places and to Westover Field, and from there our crew was formed. Now this crew, when it was put together, was the first time that I had met most of these people, the enlisted men I met. Then we went to Walker Air Base in South Carolina, and there we met our pilot, copilot, navigator, and bombardier; from then on, we were a unit—we stayed together, we trained together, all our practice missions and everything. Then we went to Langley, Virginia, and from there we took radar training. And that was the last duty in this part of the world—from there we flew to Goose Bay, Labrador, and then to Iceland and from there to Wales. We flew all the way over. Now as a unit, we stayed that way. And then when we got there, we were assigned to our bomb group. And there we went through even more training—that's all you ever did, you train, train, train, and train.

*

'There Are No Heroes'

The B-17 crews were the glory boys. The B-24 flew faster, carried more bombs, and flew higher, but the B-17s were the glory boys. We didn't name our planes like they did. We had ten to a crew in the 24s, yes. Originally they had a ball turret on the bottom but when we got over across the ocean they took that out and they put the radar transmitter in the bottom, where the belly turret was. That left the engineer free to do everything mechanical, and the assistant engineer flew the top turret [gun] in my plane.

Finally we were scheduled for our first mission, to Hamburg. It was a vital mission, in the sense that Hamburg had all their oil refineries. And without that, they couldn't fly, they couldn't have gasoline, they couldn't have anything, so you could destroy it because it would certainly limit their supplies. It was a very important mission. And because of that they concentrated their [fighter] aircraft and anti-aircraft guns to protect it. So that's a target I really remember, believe me.

I've seen planes go down, naturally. And the only things you'd look for were how many 'chutes came out of it, because when an airplane gets spinning, you couldn't get out. Sometimes because of centrifugal force, the spinning of the plane would kill you, because you couldn't get out. As I said before, I never got hurt. It was always the other guy. And the frame of mind that you have is something that most people can't understand—you can see this happening, but it's not you. It becomes an impersonal thing; it has to be, because you would go crazy if it wasn't. Not that you didn't have sympathy for the people, but still, it wasn't you. I don't know how to explain it. But there are no heroes, contrary to what people may think. It's like a job. I don't think there are any heroes up there, because you're just doing your job, you have to—you either did, or you didn't come back. You don't have time enough really to be scared a lot.

*

Our missions were all over. They were over the Rhineland, yes, sure. And Cologne, Dusseldorf, whatever you can think of. And we hit them wherever they were—we bombed as far as Austria and Czechoslovakia; in fact, we even hit Berchtesgaden, which was Hitler's retreat.

I was looking at the calendar and today is the date, incidentally [December 16], that the Ardennes offensive started, the day when Hitler tried to break through to split the Allies. They were going through the [U.S.] First Army. They did go through pretty well. And we stopped them at Bastogne. Have you ever seen that movie about that?

Well, that's where General McAuliffe was the commander there. The Germans had them pretty well surrounded and beaten. The German commander asked for his surrender. Then General McAuliffe made the very famous remark [*laughs*]—he says, 'Nuts,' the General did, when asked to surrender. That's all there was to it. That actually happened. And that was of course the time when Patton was racing across France to relieve Bastogne, and he got there. But in the meantime, we're bombing. We couldn't get off the ground for about a week when that started because we were socked in with the bad weather, so we couldn't take off, we couldn't land. And of course it didn't bother you once you got in the air because we didn't have to see the ground to bomb, because we bombed by radar. The cloud cover didn't matter, but you did have to land. So we couldn't get off the ground. But when we did, we just bombed everything in sight.

Most of the missions we flew were around 20,000 feet, and believe me, in the winter time at that altitude, it's about minus 70 degrees. That's cold. But we did have heated suits, heated clothes.

And of course, under those circumstances, we still had our job to do. As an engineer, I had duties at the time. I had to check to make sure the generators were synchronized, I opened the bomb bay doors, and I transferred fuel. All of these things were part of my job. I won't speak for the other people; they had their own jobs. But that is what I did.

*

'Something Always Goes Wrong'

Interviewer: Did anything ever go wrong during your job?

Did anything ever go wrong? [*Chuckles*] Oh, something always goes wrong. Yes, I remember one time when we got ready on the 'IP,' which is the Initial Point, where we start the bomb run to the target—I forget where the mission was to— well, they loaded the bombs all right. But there's a propeller on the back of it, and when you drop the bomb, the wind screws the propeller off. When that propeller comes off, that bomb is armed; it won't go off otherwise. But when the group crews load them, they're supposed to put a safety wire through it, in each thing. Well, somebody on that mission [*laughs*], they didn't put the safety wires in. So when I opened the bomb bay doors, the wind hit them, and I called the pilot on the intercom and I said, 'I got news for you, we got 10 thousand-pound bombs here that are now armed. The propellers are all off.' Any piece of flak coming through would hit the nose of them and... [*Makes the sound of an explosion*] that would be all she wrote, you wouldn't find anything! It didn't, though. But that's one time I sweated a little bit, I can tell you. [*Chuckles*] You couldn't fix anything. We were on the 'IP.' You couldn't take evasive action, you couldn't do anything, and we're flying right through that flak. But when they dropped the bombs, it was fine.

That was one system that they used—the other system, that's visual bombing. They had two other systems; they had one where you bomb by radar, and the other, I forgot what they called it, but they used radio signals [radio navigation]. What they would do was pick a point, say, in England somewhere, and put a directional beam. And you would fly along this leg [*motions with fingers*], and this one would maybe be giving you signals like 'Da-da-dit. Da-da-dit.' And then this other one over here would be, 'Dit-da-da. Dit-da-da.' So as you came closer, they joined all of a sudden and that was your target. You didn't have to see the ground. As soon as you hit those signals together, you dropped because you were over the target. Does that make any sense to you?

Flak

I learned more about the German anti-aircraft than I did about anything else because that was the only way you could defend yourself against anti-aircraft. Oh yes, we picked up holes, sure, flak holes. They used their 88s, they called them, and at different levels, and they generally fired in bursts of three. Each battery of anti-aircraft was three guns, usually. The first gun would be [set for a range of] 18,500 feet, and another one would be at 18,700, and so on; three. They're like steps. And they would try to bracket you with the target, and they had so many of those batteries at some of our targets! When they started firing, you would have thought there was a thunderstorm up there, you know what I mean? Our protection was a skin of a piece of aluminum about that thick, and that was it [*Holds two fingers together closely*]. And those planes were all aluminum, except for the engines, of course. But it didn't provide much protection. We did have flak suits, flak vests they called them. I always used mine to sit on because that's where the flak was coming from. [*Chuckles*] But they were very heavy, very cumbersome. And of course the gloves were heavy too. But I never lost it, I never lost an engine. I did lose the oil out of one when we landed because there was a hole in the oil reservoir, but the pump in it was strong enough so I didn't lose the engine in the air. No, I made sure the engines were all right before we went up.

As I said before, I don't make that much of that because there's not many heroes up there. You're doing your job, that's all. But for flying personnel, we had the highest rate of casualties than any branch of the service, because there's no foxholes up there either, no place to hide, but [we were lucky]. Out of our original crew of ten, we only lost two. There was a bomb group that was short a co-pilot and a tail gunner. And we weren't scheduled to fly that day, so they assigned them to that other aircraft, from the other group. And they got shot down. They didn't come back. But, outside of that, there's not much I can tell you. You didn't do too much worrying because it's something that you were trained to do, and you had to do it, and you're busy and taking care of the duties of the job. You didn't have much time to think about anything else. No, I don't think we always wondered—of course, it crosses your mind naturally, why wouldn't it? When you look out the side window and see a plane going down, it isn't you, but naturally you're going to wonder about it, you know… But as far as that, that's all there is to it. I mean, the way the job was—what, in retrospect, what I did like about the air corps was that despite the hazards, if you went over and came back, you did have a place to sleep. You weren't like an infantryman sleeping in a foxhole! You ate in the mess halls; you did get your hot food. But outside of that, as I said, I don't think there were many heroes flying up there. I can't say I worried too much—because what are you going to do? If you don't like it, are you going to get out and walk?

You're going where the plane goes, that's all there is to it. And that's it. But I can't say I got to take much credit for that. The only thing you can take credit for is being able to function under those conditions. You take 70 degrees below zero and you've got murderous work, and if you take your gloves off, it wouldn't be for two minutes and your hands would be frozen.

As the air crew, of course, we couldn't afford to get sick. But one time I went up with a cold, and I was stone deaf for a week when we returned. You see, you could take a balloon at ground level and it'd be about that big around [*puts hands together showing a small width*]. And you tie it out there in the plane where you can see it; when you get up to 20,000 feet that balloon is that big [*shows with hands a much bigger width*]. The air pressure is so much less, but the air pressure inside the balloon stays the same because it can't escape, and that's what happens to you when you have a cold. Your ear tube—your Eustachian tubes—you can't clear them, so you can't balance the pressure in your outer ear, so what it does is it stretches your ear! That happened to me and you can't turn back and it's very painful—you can't turn back because you can't abort the mission for that! That happened to me, and that's why I am having difficulty hearing you today, probably. They grounded me for a week until I could hear again, then I sat through missions. And then the stupid commander at that time, when I couldn't fly missions, they had me out there at nighttime manning machine guns to guard the base! That wasn't a good thing. In the wintertime in England it is damp and miserable, cold, and they have a longer night. People don't realize that, but it's true. But what are you supposed to do? It's like everything else—you either do your job, or else. Every member of that crew has a job to do, and he has to do it because everyone depends on everybody else.

Interviewer: Did your heated suit ever malfunction?

[*Chuckles*] There isn't anything ever made by man that didn't malfunction at some time, but not very often. Not very often, because you were careful to test them before you went out. If you had any brains, you tested it. And your oxygen, you had to have oxygen. We went on oxygen at 10,000 feet, and from 10,000 feet on up, we stayed on oxygen. Otherwise, hypoxia is a horrible thing. If you didn't have oxygen at 20,000 feet, you'd pass out never knowing it. It's amazing; you wouldn't even know it. You'd just go to sleep and that would be it, if anything ever happened to your oxygen supply and you didn't know it. But like anything made by man, it is going to malfunction occasionally. We didn't have the technology in those days that you have now.

*

Incidentally, sometimes for a mission the only warning you got was when the C.Q. in charge of quarters would come along and shake you about 4:00 in the morning. That's the way my day started, although we may not take off until 8:00. But we went and got our breakfast. We went to our briefing, where they explained where the target was and how we were going to get there. They explained the route they picked out, to eliminate as much flak interference as possible. And they told you all this sort of stuff. If everything worked right, we were back by 1:00 anyway— if you came back.

After the morning briefing, I pre-flighted the plane, checked it out all over. Our crew assembled and we got into the plane and took off, and we went up and circled around until we got all the other elements of that particular group together. So we would fire a color-coded flare and these other planes then would see that and they would come and join us. When we got all assembled and took off over the Channel, then we really started climbing to our altitude. From then on, nothing else mattered, because you were busy.

*

We were the lead crew from our seventh mission on. I don't feel we were doing anything heroic or anything like that. We were doing our job, but the job had risks. Statistics ruled.

There was another mission that I remember when we were establishing a bridgehead across the Rhine.[7] The front was only about a quarter-mile wide. Two hundred and fifty Liberators were sent up for this mission with no bombs, but we had wicker baskets filled with ammunition and

---

[7] *a bridgehead across the Rhine-* On March 7, 1945, the 9th Armored Division found the only intact bridge remaining across the Rhine River at Remagen, which the Germans had neglected to destroy. For ten days American troops poured over the bridge into the German heartland before the damaged Ludendorff Bridge finally collapsed. Miller, Donald L., *The Story of World War II.* New York: Simon & Schuster, 2001. 496.

supplies and food, and one thing or another. And we flew that mission over the Rhine at about 500 feet in the air, right down in the deck. And they were throwing rocks at us, we were so low! [*Laughs*] And we were the elite crew in that mission. We had everybody and anybody important in the squadron who wanted to go on that mission, all the 'big wheels.' So we could have a full colonel as a copilot, or something like this, because all the brass wanted to go, you know? We dropped these baskets of supplies in that perimeter, but they were so low half the time the chutes didn't fully open. They'd hit the ground and they'd start bounding across, and we would see people running for dear life every place we could look. I remember that one. We lost 25 planes in that mission because before we could even turn, we were over the German lines. And they were throwing everything at us! Fortunately I was in the lead plane so they'd shoot at us, but it would hit the plane in the back of us, I imagine. I remember I wasn't too concerned about it at the time. That's part of history, that bridge at Remagen. We did take that bridge—the ground troops did, but I guess we had a hand in it.

*

At the debriefing after the mission, the first thing they did was they gave us about three ounces of Irish whiskey; the beautiful part of that was we had six members of our crew who didn't drink. I always brought my canteen with me and they took their whiskey and we poured it in my canteen. I shouldn't tell you that, but it's true. [*Chuckles*] Incidentally, the bombardier became an Episcopalian minister. His name was Marshall V. Minister, and he became a minister!

They wanted to know everything that we saw in the flight. How heavy the flak was, how many fighters were in the air, anything that had to do with anything, but they were more concerned with the flak than they were about anything else. And, well, they should have been, because I think we lost more planes to flak than we did with anything because you couldn't defend against it. But they wanted to know everything about the flight—they had officers debriefing in one group, and the enlisted men in the other group. They got every opinion on what happened, and that's what they used to plan the next mission.

Interviewer: Do you recall your feelings when FDR died?

FDR? He was a great president, great president. Now I see they got some jerk who wants to take his picture off the dime and put Ronald Reagan's on it. Yes, that's what these [politicians] are trying to pull now. And what they're doing today is ridiculous, and I'm not going to get into that, but anybody that can read ought to know what I am talking about... I get disturbed. I find it hard to watch—why are we doing it [Iraq War, 2003]? How long are we going to be there? Do you see the end of it? I can't understand it. We've seen troubles over there for over 2,000 years, so what makes [the president] think we can change it? You can't. I don't know what the answer is; I don't know when the end of it is going to be, either. I do know there's going to be a lot more people killed before it ends.

Interviewer: What do you think about Truman's decision on dropping the bomb on Japan?

Well, I don't think it was necessary at the time because Japan was already beat, and so was Germany. But I never knew of any weapon that was ever made that wasn't used. It probably did save a few hundred thousand American lives because they wouldn't have had to invade the Japanese mainland, which would have been costly—so for that part of it, maybe. But I think that we could have done the same thing with conventional bombs, because, actually, they had no defense against the B-29 anymore. No, I don't think it was really necessary—but I don't think anybody ever made any bomb that they didn't use. When they developed that, there were a lot of worries about it—some scientists were even afraid that it would set the atmosphere on fire, with the hydrogen in the atmosphere and one thing or another. They never knew what it exactly was going to do, but they did it anyway. Now what do we have now? Now it's proliferated all over the world, and we can't stop it. Why did Truman use it? I don't know. Thought he was going to save some people, and I guess that's what he did. We were the only ones that had it. We thought we were, but we had a lot of people in this country that sold us out. They gave it to Russia, some of our own patriots. If there's a buck in it, they'll do it. I hope that answers your question.

*

'The Guy Who Will Kill My Son'

There was a British lieutenant colonel I was talking to in London. That's the period when they were bombing London with the V-2s. That was the rocket bomb; they went up into the air and came down. [*Motions with hand*] A big sign on the building fell down. I sit there looking at it, and this colonel is looking at it.

'Boy, they got that one.'

'Yes', I said, 'it happened nearby the day before, so it was weakened, so it finally fell on a bus.'

He says, 'Tell me, Yank, what do you think about this anyway, when you're dropping your bombs?'

I said, 'I don't think anything about it. I never see it; it's impersonal to me.' But I said, 'I know that we probably killed a lot of innocent people. Women and children, they didn't do anything.' I said, 'I kind of feel sorry for them.'

He said, 'Why?'

I said, 'My God, they didn't do anything!'

'No, but you want to remember something: out of their bellies will come the guy who will kill my son 20 years from now.'

They had 20 years apart, World War I and World War II, so he had no sympathy for them at all. That's the way the British felt about it. Of course, they took a lot more punishment than we did; remember, they got bombing and everything else you can think of. We didn't get that in this country. This country never had that. And our attitude would change a lot if we ever did, believe me. And it could happen today. With the kind of technology we have today, there's no place in this world that's out of range. And we're not exactly loved in this world, and we did that to ourselves. We can't run the world. I don't want to tell you my politics, but...

*

I was in Liverpool Street Station in London when they announced that the Germans had surrendered. I was just coming back from a three-day leave. So I got right off the train, turned around, and got right back to London and stayed three more days. [*Laughs*] I knew I was going to catch hell, but I did it. So they took care of me when I got back to the base; they asked me if I had a good time. I said, 'Yes.' [*Laughs*] Every day from then on, for two weeks at 4:00 in the morning, they had me flying with every pilot there was, up in the plane. They kept me going, I'm telling you. I didn't say a word. I shouldn't tell you that, but it's true. [*Laughs*]

We loaded our planes up with ground troops, people who didn't fly, non-flying personnel. Did you know that it took seven people on the ground to keep one man in the air? That was the ratio. So the people who flew were actually 12 or 13 percent of the fighting force. But these people on the ground who serviced our plane, who loaded the bombs, rebuilt the engines, all this sort of thing, they never flew. So after VE Day we loaded as many of them as we could get into the bomb bays, and we flew them at 500 feet in the air up the Rhine Valley so they could see the different places that we had bombed.

'Cologne Cathedral stands intact amidst the destruction caused by Allied air raids, Germany, 24 April 1945.' Source: U.S. Department of Defense. Department of the Army. Office of the Chief Signal Officer. Public domain.

We could see the railroad tracks all twisted, and at Cologne, the only building that had a roof on it was the cathedral.[8] Everything else was destroyed, it seemed—all the way up the whole Rhine Valley.

---

[8] *The only building that had a roof on it was the cathedral*-After the 8th Air Force's last combat mission in late April 1945, planners were working on a May operation called 'Trolley,' *'to provide all ground personnel with an opportunity of seeing the results of their contribution in the strategic air war against Germany.'* One GI remarked, "The remarkably statuesque Cologne Cathedral was still standing with very little, if any, obvious damage to it... right directly across the street from it, one could see that the Cologne train station and rail yards had been completely and literally obliterated from Allied bombing! I am certain each of us privately wondered at the time (and perhaps even now) just what 'message' of war which this scene offered." Source: WW II Trolley Flights Overview, www.b24.net/trolley-missions-overview.

The ground crews had a chance to see what their bombs did. Of course, a lot of them got airsick, because at just 500 feet it's pretty rough, because the plane bounces all over the external draft and one thing or another. So I had given each one of them an empty ammunition can, and they asked me, 'What for?'

I told them, 'You just keep it with you—pretty soon you won't have to ask me, you'll know.' [*Laughs*]

*

'I Don't Brood About It'

I was relieved when Germany quit; I felt pretty good, but that wasn't the end for us. That was only the end for the European part of the war. We were still at war with Japan, of course. So I went from there; finally we came back to this country. We landed in New Hampshire and then they transferred us to Fort Dix, then from there we went to Sioux Falls, South Dakota, to continue our training, in preparation for going to Japan, to the Pacific theater. See, in my original training, my graduating crew was split right into two, and half of us went to the European theater, and the other half went to the Pacific theater. So now, we were waiting then to see if we were going to be called to go to the Pacific theater, but the war ended when I was in South Dakota. That was VJ Day, and then it was a matter of time trying to get out because they were demobilizing so fast that they didn't have enough bases. I went to Lincoln, Nebraska, stayed there for a while. I went to Victoria, Kansas, stayed there for a while. Finally I wound up in Maryland, and I was discharged from there. But it took quite a while even after that to get out.

I liked Truman as president. He was very direct, and very honest, which is a rare commodity today. He didn't lie to us. Certainly what we have now lied to us for the reason for going into Iraq... Pardon me, I don't know what your politics are, but I'm just telling you what I think.... Why would we get into something with no idea how we're going to get out of it? We didn't learn our lesson in Vietnam? We had no business in there, either. Those people didn't do anything to us. Nothing! That attack on September 11 had nothing to do with Iraq. The people who did that were Arabs; they were from Saudi Arabia, and it's one of our friends! They're friends as long as we got the bucks to buy the oil. I don't know. This world's a mess right now. I don't know where the end of it is, and you young people are the people who have to grow up in this. And I hate to think what is going to happen now.

*

It's not a very exciting thing, not to you. It was to me at times, but I have to tell you just like it is. I'm just telling you that I don't feel that air combat was such a personal thing. It only gets personal when you're flying through flak or got another plane coming at you or something—then it gets a little bit personal. So, like I say—what are you going to do? So I don't pretend to be a hero; I just did my job, and I was good at my job, too. I made it a point to be, because I wanted to learn everything about that plane that I could. [When I entered the service] I never expected to fly. I thought I'd be a mechanic at my age. Instead of that, I wound up over places; I'll never know how, but I did. I was in pretty good condition physically, I guess. Not very exciting, but that's the way it is.

I don't brood about it, I don't miss it, but I can remember most of it. What is different about it so much was the attitude of the people. It isn't like Vietnam, where you had people taking to the streets protesting a war or one thing and another. These are the things that I remember. It was quite an experience. I'm glad I went, but I'm not going again. Besides, I'm too old for that stuff now; I couldn't take it.

I have my problems—physical problems, naturally. I have such a high blood pressure now, I have to watch my diet; I see food, and I eat it. [*Laughs*] That's my diet. I figure I got this far doing what I want to do; I think I can go the rest of the way. Thank God I'm not senile, though. I lost my wife in '82; I was married to my wife in 1936. Oh, I wrote to her every day [during the war]. Every day. Oh yes, she was a wonderful girl. She was too good for me, and I've been living alone here since then. You could probably tell that just by looking around. You want to know what time it is? [*Motions to his collection of cuckoo clocks on the wall, laughs*]

*

Interviewer: Do you have any questions we could answer for you?

Your project, I think it's good. [I hope] it will get people an idea of what went on in those days. I don't think that it will make much of an impression, because it's not the way people think today. As I said, I don't think we'll see the level of patriotism that we had in the 1930s [and 40s]. I just don't. When you get to be my age, you look at a lot of things and wonder, you know? Of course, I've seen a lot in my lifetime, way back to the time of Herbert Hoover, and well before him. But I never saw anything like what we have got now. You think this invasion of Iraq was a good thing? Can you think of any reason for us being there? I mean, honestly. You're the people who are going to have to live with this, not me... It's not what you think. I don't really have questions except that I hope I have given anything you need; have I helped at all?

Interviewer: Yes, we appreciate it a lot. Thank you.

Well, you're nice kids. I wasn't going to do this, believe me.

Dick Varney passed away on April 28, 2008, just shy of his 97th birthday.

Richard Alagna, World War II.
Source: Richard Alagna.

CHAPTER SIX

The Ball Turret Gunner

I found Richard Alagna living in Saratoga Springs, New York, just to the south of 'Hometown, USA.' At 91, he was excited to hear of my interest in his story; he invited me down for a drink. 'You ever hear of the movie actor Jimmy Stewart? He was my commander.'

Richard Gregory Alagna was born on November 16, 1925, and was attending college in Brooklyn, New York, when the news of Pearl Harbor reached him. My wife and I went to visit with him and his wife.

'Did you know that my father served in the Navy, and then the Army? In World War I and World War II? He wasn't around much; I was an only child, and my

mother raised me; she was a strong woman. She signed the papers for me, and said, 'Don't do anything stupid.'

Richard was anything but stupid. He went to Brooklyn Law School after the war on the GI Bill, passing the bar exam in New York. Only after that did he go for his undergraduate Bachelor of Arts degree! I asked him why.

'I just wanted to learn. I basically had gone into the Army at seventeen and a half years old. After the war and law school, I didn't really have a major; I just took classes, all kinds of subjects I was interested in. I racked up 132 credits in college; they kicked me out because I had too much.' Later, he also became a highly regarded painter and collected art.

He asked me about my world travels; I mentioned I had been to Germany. He said, 'Me, too. Actually, about 20,000 feet over it, dropping bombs.'

This interview was recorded in 2002 when he was seventy-seven years old. He served aboard the B-24 Liberator. I asked him if he kept in touch with his crew.

'No. I think they are all dead. I'm the last one.'

***

The Turret Gunner
Without the men who invented the turret, today's great bombing missions would be impossible. For without

turrets, the bomber would be almost as helpless over enemy territory as an ordinary transport plane without a single gun.

The modern power turret-driven by electricity and mounted inside the bomber-was developed after many experiments in the 1930s and proved its worth in action in the second year of World War II. Its effect on air strategy was spectacular. At last the bomber-heavier and slower than the fighter plane-could really fight back. For turrets-little blisters of Plexiglas or safety glass, bristling with caliber .50s, swinging around to meet enemy fighters no matter where they come from-enable the bomber to match the enemy slug for slug in an air battle.

The top turret swings in a full circle; its guns move up and down from straight out to nearly straight up; it protects the whole top of the plane. The lower ball turret swings in a full circle and points its guns anywhere from straight out to straight down; it can fight off any attacker who comes from below. The tail turret throws out a big cone of fire toward the rear, and the nose or chin turret a heavy cone of fire straight ahead.

The turrets are spun around, and the guns raised and lowered, by electric motors or by hydraulic pressure systems run by electric motors. All the gunner has to do is hold on to the control handles of his guns and move them to steer the turret; the mechanism does the rest.

Armor plate or bulletproof glass will protect you as much as possible-though your best defense, like a good boxer's, will still be the offensive power packed by those caliber .50s.

If the turret power should ever fail, you will usually have a MANUAL SYSTEM for operating it by hand cranks. Some turrets even have foot pedals which enable you to fire the guns while using both hands to crank the turret into position. This is an important emergency protection; use it to keep your guns pointed at enemy fighters even though your fire cannot possibly be so accurate as when the power is on, for a motionless turret is an invitation for fighters to attack.

Even if the guns are out of order, keep tracking the enemy; if you can't hit him, you may at least scare him away. —Air Crewman's Gunnery Manual, 1944

***

Richard G. Alagna

The Funny Things

I like to tell the funny things that happened. I got into lots of trouble. Every time we went some place, they wanted me to do something I didn't want to do, like stay. [*Laughs*] But I never went AWOL in my life. I [just] didn't like the Army, I didn't like playing soldier.

I recall [the bombing of Pearl Harbor] was a Sunday morning; I was born in 1925, so I was still a kid, pretty young. Quite frankly, I didn't know where Pearl Harbor was. I think that everybody knew that we were going to go into a war, and it was as simple as that; I think the government and Mr. Roosevelt prepared us for that.

I enlisted [soon after]. I always wanted to fly; that was my goal in life. I wanted to be a bird, just fly in an airplane. I read all about the exploits of the World War I aces, and that's what I wanted to do. I was seventeen and a half when I graduated from high school, and I wanted to fly in naval aviation—the Navy flyers, Marine flyers were the best. They had to be very good because you had to be able to land a plane on nothing, on a boat that is going up and down. [*Makes wavelike motion with hand*] Then I found out that I had 20/20 vision in one eye and 20/30 in the other eye and none of the flying units—Army, Navy, or Marine—would take me. I was real depressed about that.

Then they came around with an exam called the 'A-12 exam,' and if you passed this examination you were qualified to be an officer; you had the mental ability to be an officer, which was minimal, as I would learn. They would send you to college, and this is where I have the big bone of contention with the government—which doesn't always tell you the truth, and everybody knows that. But I didn't know that at seventeen and a half years old, because I played it straight. They said they would send me to college, and I distinctly remember being given a choice of [studying about] political affairs, government—you know, what's going to happen when we take over a country, what are we going to do there, and so on. I had a great liking not just for flying but also for history and political science, and later I became a lawyer.

So I took the [officer] test and I passed. I managed to convince my mother that this was the thing to do, and she signed for me. I graduated high school and took another exam and was admitted to day session at Brooklyn College, which was a bit of an honor. I was only there a month or so [when the Army] papers finally came through, and I was to be sent to Alfred University. I did not know where Alfred University was, but I knew they had bells up there; they would wake you up and put you to sleep with bells.

When I got up there [to upstate New York] with all these other seventeen-year-old kids, they handed me some books and they handed me a very strange instrument, which turned out to be a slide rule. Now I don't understand mathematics, or whatever it is called. 'Two plus two' I get, [but other than that, you lose me]. They told me I was to be an engineer. I said, 'This is not what you told me.' They said, 'You're going to be an engineer.'

This was a reserve program. I was not sworn into the Army at the time, but I took the oath of allegiance. We plodded along, and I did not want to be an engineer; I didn't understand it, just hated it. I should have had prerequisites for some of the courses that they gave me, and I played catch-up like you wouldn't believe. It was very trying, even though I have a little grey matter. So we grumbled and mumbled our way through, and then we got good news—the Army Air Corps was lowering their eye requirements, so that if one eye was 20/30 they would take you into their flying program. I was in seventh heaven, and there were approximately twenty other kids with me who were in seventh heaven! You would think that the commander of this unit, who was a major, would be delighted to think that twenty young kids are willing to go out and fly. He was furious! We had gotten this information from a second lieutenant who had crashed and was on limited service. He had told us about this deal and that we were all pretty smart boys and that if we wanted to, we could take the air cadet test. Twenty of us went to the major and said we wanted out; he was furious. One boy said he wasn't going to go to classes anymore, so the major had him marching up and down, up and down. We all took an oath among us that we'd all fail, which was very easy for me because I hated what I was doing. I didn't have to study anymore, right?

We went to Fort Dix and we went en masse. Everybody who was in our unit went down there. The kids up there who had already passed their courses were razzing us—they said we were foolish, this and that, 'stay in the program.' Well, did they ever make a mistake, because the program they were in dropped dead right about then and there. They did not go back to Alfred University, they went into the infantry!

We were the boys they didn't know what to do with; we couldn't take orders. We were all very rebellious, bright boys; it was hard to push us around. The twenty of us passed the exam, not one of us failed, and they gave us a little card that said, 'Welcome to the Air Corps.' We went to our little barracks in Fort Dix.

I have to digress for a second because this is kind of important. I was bitten by a dog when I was very young, and I had the rabies injections with a big hypodermic needle. It was not a shot in the arm but a needle that would go into the wall of your stomach. Men would hold my arms and it was very painful. I don't like pain. So we're at Fort Dix and we get our [first set of] injections, and I don't like injections because I keep thinking about needles, and I get very upset. Anyway, we fall out into the street, and some of the guys who had passed the test were sent to Greensboro or someplace, and some guys were sent to some other place, and I'm waiting for my name to be called and it hadn't been called, about five or six of us still milling around. If you were there for a quarantine period you could get a pass. I got a pass, and where did I go? I went home, naturally.

I got home and my mother said to me, 'You don't look good.' My mother had been in training as a nurse. I said, 'I don't feel very good.' I was perspiring. She called the family doctor, and he came and he said, 'He has the measles.'

He said, 'I can't treat him, he's in the Army.' He made a phone call and they sent an ambulance. I went down in the ambulance. I don't think they let me sit up; they made me lie down. I got the chills and all kinds of nonsense, and they took me to Staten Island. They put me in a dark room and they told me I had the German measles; I think the quarantine period was fourteen days. So there I am, in the hospital. They promised that they would send a message to Fort Dix. They said I was cured. I asked, 'Can I go back home?'

They said, 'Absolutely not, private, you must go back to Fort Dix immediately.'

I went back to Fort Dix. Now when you get back on an Army post, the first thing you do is show them your papers, which I did, and then you sign a book that indicated that you got in and the date—this is very important. Signed the book, went to where I was sleeping; naturally all my gear was gone now, so I had to get more stuff, blankets or whatever. All the fellas who I had been with had left; they're gone, they're on their way, flying planes, they were killing Germans, I don't know. [*Laughs*] The weeks dragged on, they never called my name. Every day I would go out and stand in the street.

By the way, I was now a barracks chief. When I was in Alfred University, it was a cadet program. We had military procedure, how to write communiques, how to read the book. We knew the Army regs, we were officer material, and we were going to be officers of some sort. I knew how to march, how to do all the fancy nonsense. So when the new guys would come in, I'd teach them how to make beds and all kinds of things, where to go and all that. Come the weekend, I go home, got a pass, come back, comes the weekend, I would get a pass, go home, come back. I'm in Fort Dix, nobody's bothering me, I'm a king. Except the problem was, if you miss the [scheduled sequence] of injections, you have to go through them again. There was no way that I was going to have anybody stick a needle in me. I finally decided that this is ridiculous, and I began to ask, 'How about me? When am I going out?'

They said to relax.

I wandered down to the medical unit, and I said, 'I think it's time for me to get the second series of shots.'

They said, 'Who are you?'

I said, 'I'm Richard Gregory Alagna, 12228219.' The serial number is exceptionally important, because if you don't know it you can't get off the base. I have forgotten everything else, I sometimes have to look up my own zip code, my telephone number, but I will never forget '12228219,' because you can't get a drink, you can't go play with the girls. Well, all hell broke loose! This officer came over and he started to scream at me. He said I was 'absent without leave.' I was not AWOL.

I said, 'I was in the hospital, they sent you a telegram. I was in an Army hospital, [and when I returned] I signed the book.'

He was real nasty, and he said to me, 'You're going out on the first shipment.'

I said, 'Where to?'

He said, 'What did you say?'

I said, 'Where?'

Understand, I had had three months of being a cadet; I realized that nobody tells you the truth, they knock you around, and you have to grow up awful fast.

He said, 'You're going into the infantry. You don't have any service records, we have no record of your passing the exam, and we have no record of you. When your service records catch up with you, they'll transfer you to the Air Corps.'

I said to him, 'May I talk to you man to man?' I was all of eighteen years old. 'You know in your heart that once the infantry gets me, they're not going to let me go. They're not going to transfer me after they teach me what to do in the infantry. I have this booklet.' I had this booklet that said I was an air cadet.

He said, 'Anybody can get one of those.'

I said, 'It's typewritten and I don't know how to type. Give me the [air cadet] test. I can take the test blindfolded.'

He looked at me and said, 'You really did pass that exam, didn't you?'

I said, 'Yes, sir, I did, and all I want to do is fly. I got a shot at it; you have to let me do it.'

'I will send you out in the first group to the Air Corps, and I hope to God you're not lying to me.'

'I swear I'm not lying!'

Here comes the fun and games. They send me out to the Air Corps without any of my permanent service records, my hospitalization stuff was lost, and I don't even remember if I went through the second series of needles. I didn't care at that point. I was with men who were thirty-eight up to forty-two years old; they were going to be the laborers in the Air Corps—they were going to build the barracks, grade the roads, and do the menial things. Remember I was eighteen at the time. Every time I fell out, an officer would come by and say, 'What are you doing with these people?'

I would say, 'You don't want to know, unless you have my service records.' I would talk to everybody; anytime a captain, a major, anybody, came by, I'd plead with them, 'Find my records, I'm supposed to be on the other side of the field taking air cadet training!' I wrote letters for these men, I listened to them cry at night. They had never been away from home. One man had a funny story; he and his son both went down to the draft board— his son was rejected, and he went in.

Finally the major called me in and said, 'I've got some good news for you and some bad news for you, private.'

I said, 'Let's hear the good news, sir.'

'We've got your service records and you are an air cadet trainee.'

I said, 'That's wonderful!' I was in seventh heaven; I'd already gone through basic training. The bad news was I think it was 47,000 cadets were now washed out, summarily; zap, gone, finished! They weren't killing enough of us, so they cut the program down.

I said, 'What does it mean?'

He said, 'Well, I've got a problem. We don't know what to do with you.' These air trainees were being sent back to their old units. They had transferred from the infantry or the ski troops or God-knows-what.

'But you've never been in a unit other than the Air Corps. How would you like to get back [in line] as a flyer? If you volunteer to be an aerial gunner, when you finish your missions and you come back, you can get to be a flyer. I will personally see to it.'

I'm listening to this guy and I'm saying to myself, 'Who the hell is he kidding?' Although I did know a navigator who finished his missions, came back into training, and became a pilot. It wasn't such a bad deal.

'Malfunction'

So I'm now going to fly. They sent me to the place to become an aerial gunner. You have to understand, I really did want to fly, wanted to see what it was like, wanted a taste of this. Because of my height, they said I'd become a ball turret gunner. They told me later that the tail gunners wouldn't go down in the ball. I had to gain a little proficiency, mechanical ability. If you recall, I said I can't add 2+2; that is, I don't like to. They made me learn the machine gun, which was the basic thing. There was a group of two flight engineers, two radio operators, an armorer/gunner, and myself. I was the only career gunner, I think it's called a '612' or something like that.[9] You had to learn how to field strip the machine gun, you had to be able to take the machine gun apart and put it together, and we were supposed to be able to do it blindfolded. I was always very rebellious and always liked to make a joke. I would put the machine gun together and there would be a couple of parts left over and the sergeant didn't like that.

I said, 'It looks okay to me,' because it's flipped in the case. 'Why do I have to do it blindfolded?'

He said, 'If you're flying a night mission and you burn out a barrel'—we had extra barrels on the plane, we could put them in—'you have to be able to do that.'

I said, 'If it's night time and [whoever is trying to kill me] can't see me and I can't see him, why do I have to do this?' My concept was if we just keep the lights off in the plane, he'll go away. [*Laughs*]

The gunner on a bomber is not supposed to be looking for trouble; he's supposed to make the trouble go away. [I had to keep doing it]; I went at night on my own time, and they gave me the nickname 'Malfunction' because I couldn't get the thing

---

[9] '612'-Military Occupational Specialty (MOS): MOS: 612 Armorer/Gunner

together. It's important that you know that I understand how things work, I just don't seem to
have the ability to hold on to a screw without
dropping it six times. I don't know the nomenclature of the tools that most men know, certain
screwdrivers and certain bits. I just have no interest in that.

*

Now I'll tell you about people. When you fire a
machine gun, it's not like a pistol or a rifle. It jumps
all over the place, and a lot of guys would be quite
frightened of it. Everybody had to fire this
weapon. They had them fix mounted on a tripod,
and they had a track that [a target] would go
around towed by a Jeep with a governor on it to
make the Jeep go around without anybody in it. It
would go around and around, and when it would
come by, you would shoot the machine gun. It was
a .30 caliber gun, and the first time I went out to
this range, it came by, I went 'bang-bang,' and a
cartridge exploded in the barrel, in the breech! I
had no glasses on, and I was hit in the face with the
cordite, and it caused little blood spots; some of it
was indented in my face, and when it kicked back

like that, I went right down to the ground. The sergeant came over—if I ever met him today, I'd kill that son-of-a-bitch. I mean it, because he said to me, 'What are you, a coward? Get up, clear it, and do it again.' I knew later what was wrong with the weapon, but I didn't know at that time. Naturally, everybody's looking at you, peer pressure, and I want to do this thing, so I started again, and it blew up again! This time when I'm on the ground, I saw a pair of saddle shoes and pinks.[10] The only ones that wear pinks are officers, and this officer said to me, 'Are you all right?'

There were little specks of blood on my face, and I said, 'Yes, sir, I'm fine, it happens all the time.'

He said, 'What happens all the time?'

I said, 'The thing opens up, it explodes, the bullet comes out all over your face.'

He said, 'This happened more than once?'

Well, he dressed that sergeant down. The sergeant came over and whispered in my ear, 'I'll kill you if you ever come back here.'

I could have lost an eye, could have lost both eyes! I didn't realize until later that [he knew] the

---

[10] pinks- 'Officers' pinks,' so-called for the pinkish hue of the stripe on their American uniform khakis.

gun wasn't put together properly. What possesses somebody to be that callous? I couldn't put my finger on it; I didn't know why this guy would do this, at the risk of having some kid lose an eye. He had a cushy job, not being shot at, some place in the States, Florida, Texas, wherever the hell we were. Why did he do that? I couldn't figure it out. I couldn't figure out a lot of things.

*

Cute story. I was still in gunnery school at the time, but we're sitting around not doing anything, not going anyplace. They said that they needed some volunteers—that's a bad word, by the way, as everybody knows. The deal was that if you pulled guard duty for a week, you'd get a pass to go to New Orleans. I said, 'Okay, fine, I'll do it.' They gave me a carbine; I checked it out. I was very good with weapons now, and I now got live ammo. I'm marching back and forth, back and forth, in the heat. There were some tents there, not too far away, about 100 feet, and there were some guys who had been flying Catalinas, they were doing submarine patrol down in New Orleans. I'm going back and forth, back and forth, back and forth, sweating like a pig. I can't see this nonsense about marching, because to me, all you had to do was stand in one place and you could turn your head and look back and forth, but that was what the Army wanted you to do. So I noticed a kitten, and the kitten was spitting at something. I got closer to it, and it was one of the biggest rattlesnakes I have ever seen; it was a doozy! The kitten is going to get bitten and die, so I'm calling the kitten, but the kitten won't come over. I figured I never missed anything in my life when I shot, so I pulled back the slide on the carbine, took aim at the snake. This guy in the tent sees me, and he's calling me a son-of-a-bitch because he thinks I'm shooting at the kitten! I pulled the trigger, nothing happens. I eject the bullet, do it again, and nothing happens. They're lying to me again! I then yelled for the sergeant of the guard. This snake is a goddamned big snake. I figured that if the snake gets into the tent area, they're going to have a hell of a hard time. The sergeant comes over in a Jeep, and I'm trying to figure how I can hit the snake, move the kitten off to the side; I'm beside myself. He pulled out his .45, but this guy couldn't hit a goddamned barn if he was sitting next to it. He pointed it at the snake and missed, shot three times.

'Sergeant,' I yelled, 'let me have the gun, I can hit the snake.' I could hit anything; I hit the target all the time. He got pissed, managed to kill the snake. Now I'm complaining about why my carbine wouldn't go off. I found out they had filed the firing pin so it wouldn't strike. What the hell was I doing with a gun that couldn't work? He got mad at me and he made me stay in the barracks. He said he was going to have me up on charges, and I didn't know what kind of charges he was referring to; I didn't do anything wrong, I tried to kill the snake. He couldn't shoot worth a damn. Maybe I said something, but now I'm in trouble and I don't know what it is.

I went into the latrine, and guess who's sitting there? The latrines have no stalls back then, and there he was, sitting there on the throne. He glared at me; I didn't say anything to him. He got up and left.

I relieved myself and I looked over to where he had been sitting, and he had taken off his heavy canvas belt that had his .45 on it. I was delighted because you can't lose your weapon, you cannot lose your weapon. I picked up the .45, and I said to myself, 'Richard, heave it into the jungle, no one will see you. Let him sweat to figure out where his .45 is.' Then another voice went off in my head, which said, Just because he's a son-of-a-bitch, you don't have to be one.'

I went over to where his office was, knocked on the door, and he snarled at me, 'What do you want?'

I said, 'I want to give you this.' [*Extends hands*] He went like this [*Moves hands to sides*] and realized his cannon was missing, his .45.

I said, 'You left it in the latrine.'

He realized that I wasn't such a bad guy, and he said, 'Forget about the charges, you're free to go back to your unit.'

I said, 'Wait a minute, how about my pass to New Orleans?'

He said, 'You kids from New York'—he was a Southerner—'you have a pair of balls on you that I can't believe.'

He gave me a pass to go to New Orleans; he laughed, I laughed. He would have been in a lot of trouble not to have had his weapon. I went to New Orleans and had a very good time. I went with another guy who was a gunner; it was fun, we had a fun time.

*

After learning how to strip and fix a machine gun and all that, I had to learn how to work the ball turret. The ball turret was an instrument of death, torture, the most ridiculous thing they thought of. It was self-contained, it was held on by a big ring, and on the B-17 it was permanently out of the plane. On the B-24 there was a shaft, and hydraulically you'd drop it and then you'd get in it. It was exceptionally tight—you could not wear a parachute in it; you could wear your harness but you couldn't wear the parachute. When I had to get in it, I always had to turn my face sideways and put my face down on the gun sight and then signal the guy above to slam the door, and invariably I'd get hit on the head with the door. It was not very comfortable.

Let me digress again. If you recall, I desperately wanted to fly. I'd been with men that were thirty-eight, forty years old, and our training was nothing, and I'd gotten fatter and fatter and lazier and lazier because I wasn't really doing anything; I was so badly out of shape that I was a good twenty pounds overweight. I was about 185 at the time. When we got to gunnery school and I'm taking the machine guns apart and all that, I had to play catch-up with the physical part. I was never much of an athlete when I was young, but I would run with everybody and do everything they did, except I just couldn't get over the wall. I'd hit the wall and my nails would scrape on the wall. I'd always get just my fingers up there. I'm short; some of these guys were six foot, and they could just bounce up and grab it and pull themselves up.

There was an officer who thought I was horsing around. I said, 'I'm trying,' and I hit that wall. He did catch me once going around it. When I was in high school the coach always yelled at me because they used to make me go around the track, and I used to go around, then cut across, and then go in the back and read a book. I was the kid who liked to read, and I didn't want to play any of their games.

On my own I went out at night after we did everything we were supposed to damn-well do and I
ran, losing weight. I even put crap in a knapsack to
try to lose weight. I think I got over the wall. The
officer was going to wash me out, but it got to the
point where he realized that nobody in their right
mind would hit the wall like I hit that wall; I would
have gone through the goddamned wall if I could
have. I couldn't get my hands up there! Forget
about going up the rope. I could not go up the
rope, but I did build my chest up; my arms were
pretty strong. Anyway, he passed me on that.

*

I wanted to fly, and now we had to get into a
plane, a B-17, and do our stuff that we were taught
on the ground. Underneath the seat of the ball turret was an oxygen tube. We wore an oxygen mask
with a certain length of tubing to connect to the
oxygen supply. We went up in a B-17 and they
outfitted it with long benches. My last name begins with an 'A' and I was always first, which was
lots of fun, because it would have been nice to
learn by watching the other fellow go first for a
change. [We're in the air] and I'm supposed to go

down into the turret, hook up to the oxygen, and I'm supposed to stay down there and then they'll tell me come on up. We're flying above the level at which you could breathe on your own well; you could get anoxia, get brain damage, and die. You get silly, too. I went down into the turret, put my head down, [had the hatch] slammed shut, but I was not breathing the oxygen, just breathing the air that was in there, pretty thin. I reached for the tube and I got it in my hand, and I can't make contact. I was breathing heavily and I'm nervous and I don't know how many minutes went by, but I do know that I can't stay there because I'll pass out, and frankly, I didn't know how they would then get me out from above. The sergeant was saying to me on the radio, 'Aren't you going to get it going?'

I said, 'I can't breathe, I can't connect.'

He called me a coward. I was mortified. I was really very upset.

I heard the pilot saying, 'Get him the hell out of the turret.'

I got out and I hooked up to oxygen in the plane and guys are looking at me kind of funny. The pilot orders the sergeant who's training us to go down and see if what I said was true. He said it was true. Nobody else went down in the turret. We landed, and the sergeant was a very good kid; he made all the men stand there and he apologized to me. It seems that some schmuck idiot jerk cut the tube too short. It had frayed, and no one was even thinking that the oxygen mask won't connect; some of these guys just didn't think these things through. That was the reason, and the sergeant apologized, and I felt pretty good.

Speaking of anoxia—stay in the middle and never volunteer, right? We go into the pressure tank and they simulate the altitude that you're going to go up to, and what the pressure is. The sergeant says, 'We need three volunteers.'

I thought, 'Boy, this is great, this time I'm in the middle.'

He says, 'You, you, and you,' and I was right in the middle.

One guy had to write with a pad and pencil, the other guy had to do something, I forget what, and I had to do exercise, because this will show how a guy will pass out. They started the simulation, you get giddy, you begin to laugh, because it's a great high. The lights got dim in the place, it looked like it was a rheostat, and I'm getting giddy and they slap an oxygen mask on me and give me pure oxygen. The other guy who was writing, his handwriting was going up and down, and he finally passed out and they gave him oxygen.

*

The Crew

I met my crew; now, the crew is very strange. The pilot was an old man. At that time I was nineteen or twenty, the pilot was 28 or 29, and that was very old. He didn't take the wire out of his hat, his garrison hat—there was a wire that if you took it out and crunched it, you got that fifty-mission Air Corps look. He had transferred from the infantry, and was Southern, and I don't think he realized that the Civil War was over.

The second officer was from Kansas; he went to the University of Kansas, and he couldn't fly worth a damn. He was probably the worst pilot in the Air Corps; he was obnoxious. The navigator was a nice guy, he was a couple of years older than I am, he was an accountant. He was a flight officer, not

an officer—that's the difference between an enlisted man and an officer; you're some place in
limbo, they gave you a bar with a little color in it,
some nonsense like that. We had a bombardier
who was afraid. He got us up to 30,000 feet one
time and said his bombsight didn't work and he
couldn't use it. We went back down; it takes a long
time to go up to 30,000 feet. It turns out he just
didn't plug it in. We went on a practice mission,
supposed to hit a target on an island surrounded
by water, surrounded by a federal reserve park. He
hit a farm; he was worthless! He didn't go overseas
with us. I thought he was stupid then; later on, I
realized that he just liked to walk around in an officer's uniform with a pair of wings. He always
wanted everybody to call him 'Lieutenant.'

The nose gunner was a delight. I don't know if
he had a high school education, but he was an engineer, he had mechanical ability. He loved to
smoke cigars. The radio operator was a million-
aire's son. They owned a big, well-known fish can-
nery. Jimmy was Catholic and he couldn't make up
his mind if he wanted to be a priest or marry a girl.
He showed us a picture of the girl and it reminded

me of the center for Notre Dame. [*Laughs*] On the very first mission—and this is one of my anti-Catholic stories—Jimmy took his Saint Christopher's medal and he hung it in the cockpit, and the navigator had a fit because the pilot couldn't fly the plane correctly because it demagnetized the compass. There was good old Saint Christopher, leading us around in circles. [*Laughs*] Needless to say, that medal wasn't used on any more missions.

The engineer, his name was Brockmeyer; he looked very young but he was competent at what he was doing. He could fix anything on the plane, did all the magic things. He was a slight kid and he was a wise guy. Once he picked me up in an automobile and said he had hot-wired it. I got out of the car instantly; this kid had stolen the car!

The armorer/gunner, Neil, was a nice guy. Neil was from Connecticut and Cornell. Most of the kids on the crew were college men. He was in advanced training and I could have killed him, I hated him for this. He had it! He was in advanced training for flying, he was the cadet officer, and they gave him his orders to go to heavy bombers, to fly multiple engines. He wanted to be a fighter pilot, as we all did; we all wanted to be Eddie Ricken-backer.[11] He got to a guy who wanted to go to bombers; he wanted to make a switch [to fighters]. He must have said it in a loud voice because the Army brass got wind of it and they washed him out. You don't tell the Army what to do. He ended up in heavy bombers. [*Laughs*] But when I heard his story, I nearly died because I was just dying to get my hands on the controls of the plane, though I did fly the plane once or twice, but just when we were in the air. I liked him; he was a very nice guy.

The tail gunner was a ski trooper; they were go-ing to send him back, and he became a tail gunner. He was from the University of Chicago; we had Harvard, we had college men on the crew. The only two non-college kids were the nose gunner and the engineer.

Westover Field

We were in training and we're up at Westover Field [in Massachusetts]. We're flying very old planes; these were not the ones we flew in combat.

---

[11] *Eddie Rickenbacker-* Medal of Honor recipient and America's top fighter ace in World War I with 26 kills, 1890-1973.

Now we had some old planes in combat, but these were bad planes. While I was there, one kid from the Bronx, nice kid, said to me—I was looked upon as a guy who had the training before, and I could handle some of the officers by giving them what they wanted—he said, 'I can't take it.' He said every time he got into the plane he thought it was going to blow up, and he couldn't go near a plane again. I told him it's not a disgrace because we're supposed to be in a team, and if a unit can't function together, you're not helping the guy next to you, and you're going to let him down when it's important. I told him to go see the commanding officer, which he did, and tell him exactly what he told me. Later, I met him at Fort Dix when I was being discharged. He ended up as a sergeant in the infantry; he saw hand-to-hand combat in the Philippines. The point I always made is that everybody had a point where they'd snap, where they just sat there and couldn't function.

Now I'll tell you about this great co-pilot we had. We're still in the States, and I'm down in the ball turret. In this turret, you lower it down, it comes out the belly of the plane, you have to jump down in it, open it up, get in, and it's all hydraulic and electric. I'm listening on the interphones and I don't hear anything except the engines. It's deafening, by the way, flying in a four-engine bomber. There are some portholes, and I had my hands on the handles to make my turret turn, and it wouldn't go. It was dead in the water. I looked up in the portholes and I saw some of the guys running around and I thought I saw one of the guys put on a parachute! Normally we just wore chest chutes and the parachutes were kept separate, because it was an additional weight you had to stand up with.

I turned on the radio and tried to speak and I couldn't hear my own voice—if you can't hear your own voice, it's not coming through your headset, ergo, something's wrong. I realized that now I had to go back to my training, that there's a way to get out of the turret. You cannot drop out of the ball turret when it's in the air, but there were some cranks and you could manually crank the turret around and it would come up to where you could get out. Your memory has to be 'A' perfect because you had to then lock it. If you didn't lock it, when you got up to get out, it would spin and you would lose your legs. Thank God the sergeant who trained me told me that. I did exactly what he told me to do, and that's what comes with training. Training is a very important thing; you must do what you're supposed to do, what you're trained to do, and improvise when you have to. So I locked it, got out, pulled myself out of the well. Everybody's got their parachutes on! I put my parachute on. One of the guys said, 'We have lost electrical power.' The plane will still go, like an automobile, because the gasoline is flowing into the engines. The pilot's going crazy; the engineer is running around trying to figure out what the hell is wrong with the damn thing. He had rung the 'get ready to bail out' bell, and that's what I saw through the porthole, but I didn't hear it; there's no bell in the turret. I immediately thought that there should have been a bell in the turret or that somebody should have taken a wrench and whacked on the shaft three times or whatever so I would know to get out!

Now don't forget, this story is about the co-pilot. The co-pilot's supposed to be in charge of the

gunners, that was his job. He was supposed to co-
ordinate things that we were supposed to do. So
they got the problem fixed, the music goes back on,
the radio's on, everybody's happy. Up comes the
turret; I'm not going down there again, not that
day. Now I can't tell other guys what to do, I don't
have the rank, but I was slightly pissed at them.
They had to think for themselves, because when
they say, 'get ready to bail out,' they're going to
go—they're not going to come and hold my hand.

We landed, and the first thing I did was walk up
front, and I said to the co-pilot, 'They rang the bell
to get ready to bail out, but there's no sound in my
turret. I would like you to instruct the gunners
back there to give me some kind of a signal when
that happens, so I can get out.'

This is what the son-of-a-bitch said. 'When I
bail out, I'll wave to you as I go by.'

He was a big football player; I'm five foot seven
and a half, but I'm from Brooklyn, and you don't
say things like that. I grabbed him. You're not supposed to touch an officer, it's against the rules.

I turned him around and said right to his face,
'As God is my witness, if I get my guns around fast

enough, I'll blow you out of the sky, and if I get down on the ground, I'll hunt you down and I'll kill you.'

I let go of him. Now I've got a problem, because you don't touch an officer and you don't threaten him. I went back to the barracks and told one of the guys from another crew what happened.

'I'm going to be called up, I'm going to go see the commanding officer.'

He said, 'No you're not, he's not going to say a word. Did he say that to you? Will you say that to the commanding officer? He's not going to say a word.'

So he didn't say a word, I didn't say a word, I don't think I ever spoke to him unless he asked me a question. We put in a system where you bang on the turret.

*

They always had to test your ability to function as a gunner, and they would put film next to your machine gun and it would film through your gun sight. We had very special gun sights, a Sperry invention. It had a line [*draws imaginary horizontal line with index finger*] and you had to do all kinds of

crazy things. It was very unique. You had to rec-
ognize the aircraft you were firing at, it had to be
a certain length, et cetera, and you'd set it in
quickly into your gun sight, which is actually a
computer. Then you had to cross it. You did everything—you did it with your feet, with your
hands, it was quite a complicated thing but allegedly it was very accurate. The first time [all the
gunners had to use it], I'm down in the ball turret.
One of the gentlemen, I'm sure it was an officer,
used the relief tube. A relief tube is a funnel, and
you would urinate into this funnel and the urine
would go out the plane and it would come back
and splash over the turret. Now a little urine is not
going to hurt you, but it colored the entire area of
the turret where my gun sight would function. I
had a problem, because they brought this plane up
and they wanted me to shoot at the target, and I
couldn't very well shoot at it, so I used my finger
and I went like this [*waves index finger in air*], and
I made some film [for them]. When we went to
the briefing, everybody had good grades, and they
said, 'The ball turret gunner is very creative, but

we figured out it had to be his finger because we played it over and over again.'

Up we go again, and I told them in the front of the plane, 'Don't use the funnel until I'm out of there.' Well, they did it again. This is no joke because we had to go up pretty high and we had to be on oxygen. You piss on me once, you piss on me twice, the third time you don't get a shot at it.

The third time I heard the co-pilot say, 'I wet my leg, my leg is wet!'

The pilot said, 'What do you mean you wet your leg?'

'I had to use the relief tube and it's been cut.'

The pilot said to me, 'Did you cut the relief tube?'

I said, 'Me, sir? Not I, sir.' I cut it. [*Laughs*]

When we got the film back for that run, I got a commendation, which made me very happy because they used my film for a training film.

The tail gunner was a character. He had a knife; he was Jewish and he always carried a knife. My father was Roman Catholic and my mother was Greek Orthodox. I joined the Protestant Church because I was fed up with all the fighting in the family about which church I should belong to. In the barracks one time, a drunk came in and he called me a dirty Jew.

I got up, and one of my crew members grabbed me and said, 'You're not Jewish.'

I said, 'Fuck him.' The point of the story is that anti-Semitism permeated the Army and all of our lives back then, and it just wasn't very nice.

*

We hadn't gotten overseas yet. At that particular time I bought a fountain pen, a Waterman, guaranteed for life, and it broke. [*Laughs*] I was very superstitious, most guys were superstitious. And then there was the fire [on the plane].

Everybody on an aircraft had to be trained to do somebody else's job in case they got sick. My nickname was 'Malfunction,' so they made me the assistant engineer—perfect, right? For example, they taught me how to transfer fuel, which is very important on a plane, even though I had absolutely no concept of where the fuel went [after it was transferred]; it just made the engines go around. I also learned to stand behind the pilot when we would land, and I would call off the air speed because you had to land at a certain air speed or you were in deep trouble. Back then there was always someone standing when you landed a plane, I don't think they do that anymore. But then my job, what the engineer did, I would then leave, go past the turret gunner, radio operator, drop down into a well with a catwalk where the bomb bays would go to the back, and I would go forward. At that point, everybody in the nose of the plane is out. That would be the nose gunner, navigator, bombardier; three people would be out. There was a machine there like a lawn mower, which had a pull, and it was called the 'putt-putt,' for want of another name. It provided the auxiliary power to run the generator on the aircraft so that you'd have electricity. When the plane lands, the nose wheel opens up; this was a B-24, and the wheel goes down and all the papers in the front of the plane would be blown all around the place. It was not my job, not that I'm saying 'not my job, I don't do windows,' but I had no knowledge that this was an important factor. It was up to those people that had their loose papers, whether they were maps or anything like that, to have them secure. So you pull the string and the machine starts. I pull it and it belched fire! On an airplane, like on a boat, fire is not a nice thing. By the way, I heard a story that one guy got a Congressional Medal of Honor, at least the story went, because he pissed on a fire, which I thought was a very cute story; I don't believe it. Anyway, I put the fire out with my hands, and when I got it out, naturally I wouldn't turn the machine back on because I still didn't know what the hell was going on. I went up and I screamed that there was a fire, and the radio operator, Jimmy Broderick, jumped down, took a fire extinguisher, and completely encased the machine in [fire retardant].

We were now traveling on the runway. The pilot rang a bell when he heard 'fire,' and the nose gunner went out the bomb bays and luckily he didn't get killed; he went into a rolling position—we had on leather suits and stuff like that. Well, it turned out that what had burned was a comic book—I have no idea whose comic book it was, but it had blown and caught in that machine! I think I told you that my pilot wasn't a very forgiving person—he accused me of having the comic book. I didn't read comic books. I was into reading whatever books I could carry, but I didn't read comic books. I was slightly incensed that I was accused of starting a fire on a plane. This man would accuse me, if it was raining outside, that I had ruined the day.

I'll tell you more about the navigator. We're in Westover Field and we are told that we're going to go on a night mission to Ohio, with no radio and only wing lights on. We had to navigate our way out to someplace in Ohio and practice bombing something out there, without actually dropping bombs. I [tried to convince] the pilot that it wasn't necessary for me to go on the trip. It's a night mission; there's nothing a gunner can do in the back. He said, 'You're flying!' So on the way back we get to the area of Westover Field and we drop down. He dropped his wheels down, and we gunners were supposed to use flashlights and look at the wheels to see if the pins came out, because if the pin didn't come out, it meant that the landing gear was not locked and it would collapse on landing. It's dark and I'm looking out and I've got the headset on, the wheels are down and locked, and the pilot said to the navigator, 'Are you absolutely certain that's Westover Field?'

The reason he asked is that there was an airfield at Hartford; I believe there was a Navy field there.

The navigator said, 'I'm reasonably certain.'

The pilot then pulled the plane up, and everybody went on their ass, and then the fight started.

He said, 'What do you mean? If I land the plane on a commercial airfield or a Navy field, I will be the laughingstock of the Air Corps!'

I look out the window and I said to the pilot, 'I know where the airfield is.' That's when the second fight started.

The navigator said, 'He's only a kid.' He was right, I was nineteen; he must have been about twenty-one or twenty-two, so really we're all in that category of being infants.

'You are going to listen to him?'

The pilot said, 'He said he knows where the field is.'

We're practically at treetop level now, and I told him what direction to go—straight ahead, to the left, to the right—and I said, 'The airfield is directly ahead.'

He made the signal, the lights went on, and we landed on our field.

The pilot came over, and he said, 'How did you know where the field was?'

I said, 'I followed the bus route.'

Any flyer will know that old-time flyers used to do sight navigation, and you would go down and read railroad crossings, and that's just what I did. I knew where the movie house was, and in Springfield, I'm positive that it's still there, is a good restaurant, the Student Prince, good sauerbraten. The navigator wouldn't speak to me; I guess he didn't want to be put down.

Then there was the time we went on another night mission in Springfield, and as I told you my job was to look out the window and see if the wheels were up or down or if anything was wrong on the plane. We had windows in those old planes that lifted up. I had my Class A uniform on; it was the only way you could get off the post. I looked out this window and I was blinded, couldn't see, and I had a mouthful of gasoline! I fell to the floor, I was really in pain. I don't remember if I threw up or not.

The other gunner said, 'What's wrong?'

I said, 'I can't see, I'm blind, there's a gasoline leak!' Gasoline was just gulping out of the wings! He passed the word on; down we went, we landed.

I was sitting there, there was a canteen of water, somebody either put water on my face or I had washed my face, so now I could see. It turned out that when they fueled the plane up it wasn't level, it was at a tilt, and they put too much gasoline in. The mission was off. I unzipped my flight suit, put on my hat, and my pilot said, 'Where are you going?'

I said, 'I'm going to town.' He did not appreciate that; he thought I set that whole thing up because I had a pass to go to town.

Passes—it always annoyed me that the officers could go wherever they wanted but the enlisted men could not, so we created our own passes. We got a book of passes and we were under the impression—which was wrong, I found out later in law school; I thought that if you signed a phony name, it meant nothing. I remember once I was stopped by an MP [checking passes] in Times Square, and he said, 'Captain Midnight?'

I said, 'Yeah, that's my name' and got away with it. We would do things like that.

It's been often asked of me if flying was voluntary. Nobody would believe me when I said it was, you did not have to fly. At any time you could have just gone in and said, 'I'm out.' That wouldn't mean you'd be out of the Army, you just didn't fly. Where they would send you, God only knows. They'd send you some place; the Army wasn't going to let you go.

Ken Carlson, first row second from right,
and the crew of 'Myrtle the Flying Turtle.' Credit: Ken Carlson.

CHAPTER SEVEN

The Navigator

Kenneth R. Carlson was born in 1921 in New York City. As a boy in the Great Depression, he spent his summers at Glenburnie at the Lake George Camp, the northern fringe of the communities surrounding 'Hometown, USA.' He called me at home one evening, shortly after I had returned from swimming near there.

'Tell me about yourself, your family. I myself was from a middle-class family, but we were lucky in that I was able to attend what was probably the best private school in New York City. Incidentally, my tuition in grade school in the '20s was $250 a year; today a kindergarten slot is $45,000. I had a terrific education, even though I had to fight my way through the Irish gangs on 69th Street when I came back home from school.'

He tells me that the man who cuts his hair was an eight-year-old boy in occupied France. He would look up, see the twin tails of the B-24 Liberators coming or going to attack Germany, and wish them a silent prayer, hopeful that one day he would indeed be free.

'I think what you are doing is very important. I still go to speak to the students here a few times a year; when we got out of the service, I joined the 8th Air Force Historical Society here in New York and vowed to speak to kids. At 96, I'm still keeping that commitment. Years ago the Smithsonian put out a book, High Honor, *of inspirational stories with World War II veterans, myself and twenty-nine other fellows. Get the book, but I wouldn't try to contact any of the other fellows. I'm the last one left.'*

The interview was recorded in 2003 when he was 82. He served aboard the B-24 Liberator.

***

Duties of the Navigator

Navigation is the art of determining geographic positions by means of (a) pilotage, (b) dead reckoning, (c) radio, or (d) celestial navigation, or any combination of these 4 methods. By any one or combination of methods the navigator determines the position of the airplane in relation to the earth.

The navigator's job is to direct your flight from departure to destination and return. He must know the exact position of the airplane at all times.

Pilot and navigator must study flight plan of the route to be flown and select alternate air fields.

Study the weather with the navigator. Know what weather you are likely to encounter. Decide what action is to be taken. Know the weather conditions at the alternate airfields.

Inform your navigator at what airspeed and altitude you wish to fly so that he can prepare his flight plan.

Learn what type of navigation the navigator intends to use: pilotage, dead reckoning, radio, celestial, or a combination of all methods.

Determine check points; plan to make radio fixes.

Work out an effective communication method with your navigator to be used in flight.

Synchronize your watch with your navigator's.

Miscellaneous Duties

The navigator's primary duty is navigating your airplane with a high degree of accuracy. But as a member of the team, he must also have a general knowledge of the entire operation of the airplane.

He must be familiar with emergency procedures, such as the manual operation of landing gear, bomb bay doors, and flaps, and the proper procedures for crash landings, ditching, bailout, etc.

After every flight get together with the navigator and discuss the flight and compare notes. Go over the navigator's log. If there have been serious navigational errors, discuss them with the navigator and determine their cause. If the navigator has been at fault, caution him that it is his job to see that the same mistake does not occur again. If the error has been caused by faulty instruments, see that they are corrected before another navigation mission is attempted. If your flying has contributed to inaccuracy in navigation, try to fly a better course next time. —Duties and Responsibilities of the Airplane Commander and Crewmen, 1943

***

Kenneth R. Carlson

I'll never forget where I was when I heard [about Pearl Harbor]. My father had died in 1939 unexpectedly when I was 18. The only asset that we had was a brownstone home on 73rd Street and Lexington Ave. So I had my mother and grandmother to support and we lived in a 4th floor tenement, a walk-up. It was Sunday, and I was in the front room listening to the radio. Being a former athlete, I was listening to the Giants football game, and during that game there was an announcement that the Japanese had bombed Pearl Harbor. Even though I'd had a great education I wasn't sure where Pearl Harbor was. As a matter of fact I thought it was in the Philippines. So that's how I found out, and that's where I was. With no television, we had to wait for radio reports and read about it in the newspaper the next day. So it really didn't make that big an impression on me at that moment; I had no idea of what the magnitude of this bombing was until a day later. I felt this was unbelievable, because although I was well educated and was aware of the problems we had been having with Japan over the last few years, I felt that this could not have happened.

I decided to enlist. It took me a couple of days to think it all through and to read and to see newsreels and see what really had happened and the damage that had been done, what was really going on and how it related to the war in Europe. We declared war on Japan, and they were negotiating in Washington when the surprise attack took place. Two days later Germany declared war on the United States. That made my decision to go to war. I picked the Air Corps, I guess, because my father had taken me to see Charles Lindbergh take off when I was seven years of age, to fly across the Atlantic. Being Swedish-American like me, he was a hero figure to me. And with my education I understood all about Billy Mitchell and the power of the Air Force and how it was going to be the future of any war. So in my own mind, I decided the best thing I could do was to become a fighter pilot and shoot down the Japanese who had attacked us. So two days later, I enlisted in the Air Corps, [even though I had never flown before].

When I enlisted I was just about to be married; I was 21 when I got married. But the Air Corps did not call me until January 1943, so it was a little more than a year before I was called to active duty. The reason for that was that they had very limited training facilities. So in January 1943 I got on a train with orders to report to Nashville, Tennessee, which was a reception and classification center. When I got there they took away my civilian clothes and gave me my uniform, which was two sizes too big. It was a GI uniform because at that time you enlisted as an Army private at $21 per month until you were accepted as an Air Corps cadet. That meant that you had to qualify as a pilot, a navigator, or a bombardier. Though I qualified to be a pilot, based on my gifted mathematical skills they wanted me to be a navigator. I didn't want to do that because in my own psyche I was set on being a fighter pilot and shooting down Japanese. But they told me I would have to wait six to nine months to get into pilot training, whereas if I accepted navigator training I could go immediately. So I accepted navigation.

I had no feeling for bombers and I had no idea where that was going to take me. They sent me to San Marcos, Texas, which was a navigation school. It had just opened, located between San Antonio and Austin. There I underwent six months of navigation training. In August 1943, I was commissioned a 2nd lieutenant. From there I was sent to Boise, Idaho, where the crew would be assembled; when I got to Boise I found out who my pilot was. He became my best friend and was just an unbelievable pilot. He was a small guy; his parents were from Czechoslovakia and his father was a bartender in Hollywood, California. All he wanted to do was fly, and his instructor was Jimmy Stewart, the actor. He didn't drink, he didn't carouse, and he was single. I met the rest of our crew and we were sent to a new air base in Mountain Home, Idaho, south of Boise. It had the longest runway in existence, and that is where we did our crew training.

From Mountain Home we were assigned to Wendover, Utah, a little town one hundred miles west of Salt Lake City at the end of the salt flats right on the Nevada border. We lived off base in this place called the State Line Hotel. On the Nevada side they were drinking, gambling, and doing anything they wanted, but on our side, because of the Mormon influence, it was ice cream sodas and going to bed early. This is where we learned to operate as a bomber crew. Wendover later became the secret training base for the crew that dropped the atomic bombs on Hiroshima and Nagasaki.

The scary part about training in those days was that so many of us had [been brought up] to do things individually, but were hard-pressed to learn how to work together. We lost a lot of airplanes through poor maintenance, false navigation, and pilot error into the surrounding mountains of Nevada, so we experienced losses right there in training and we understood that not everyone was going to go down because of enemy fire. After we completed that training we were then sent to Harrington, Kansas, where we would pick up our own airplane and fly it to wherever it was ordered to fly. In Harrington the thing I remember most was sitting in the room while the pilot, Joe Roznos, signed a piece of paper that said he was responsible for a B-24J, which was a four-engine Liberator bomber. The J signified that it was a later model, which had a turret in the front with two machine guns instead of just two flexible machine guns that the navigator shot. He signed a paper for $250,000 worth of government property and that we would return it, and the question was, what if we don't come back? [*Chuckles*] They said, 'Don't worry about it.' When we picked up the plane, said good-bye to our wives or girlfriends (five of us were married and five were single), we were given orders to fly it to West Palm Beach, Florida, to Morrison Field. When we got there our passes were taken away and we were confined to the field, awaiting orders to see where we would be sent. At that time we were all hoping that we would be sent to the South Pacific and that we would be killing Japanese. When we got down the runway and opened our orders, we were sent on a southern route; our final orders indicated that we were to report to the 8th Air Force, which was headquartered in England, so we knew then that we were not going to be killing Japs—we were going to be killing Nazis.

The trip over was an unbelievable experience. As navigator I had to plot our southern route, which took us into Trinidad, then Brazil, and over to Africa. It took us 45 days because there were weather delays all along the route. This was the first time that I had ever left the U.S., the first time this city kid was about to see the world. The thing I remember most when we got to Brazil, where we saw three different towns before flying to Africa, was the tremendous poverty, disease, and filth. Young people were walking around naked; they were going to the bathroom in the streets, and had diseases such as elephantiasis, which I had never heard of.[12] So that was a big shock. When we left Brazil it was the moment of truth for me as navigator, using celestial navigation.[13] We had no radar or radio or anything like that. We would see if

---

[12] *elephantiasis*- symptom where parts of a person's body swell to massive proportions.

[13] *celestial navigation*- ancient science of finding one's way by the sun, moon, stars, and planets and the visible horizon, using a sextant to measure the angular distance between two visible objects to establish a 'fix' on a location.

I could navigate our way across the South Atlantic, which was eleven hours, and arrive where we were supposed to. So that memory remains a very dramatic one for me, of being alone in the nose of that plane with my sextant; I felt so alone and so at peace at the same time. The stars were so bright over the South Atlantic Ocean! I had this tremendous worry about knowing where we really were when I looked down at that ocean. So when I would plot these fixes that showed where we were according to the stars, that's when I found that we were not on the course that was planned. So now the moment of truth was, do I accept that as fact and correct it, or do I pretend that maybe I didn't shoot the stars correctly and stay on the course? I decided to do what I was taught, and that was to correct the course based on the star sightings taken. After doing so, eleven hours and some odd minutes later, on the far horizon there was Africa, and there was Dakar, and we were on target! We landed and everybody thought I was just terrific. Five of them thought so because they couldn't swim, and all they could think about was that we were going to run out of gas before we got to Africa!

There again it was the poverty. There were young people who were pimping their sisters, preteens almost, to make a living off of those who were passing through there. They were sailors and soldiers, Americans, British, or Dutch. Leaving Dakar, our next stop was Marrakesh, which took us over the Sahara Desert and over a mountain range called the Atlas Mountains. We flew through them and into Marrakesh, which was in a beautiful area of Morocco. That trip I will never forget either. I plotted the course, and, it being daylight, I went to sleep. When I paid more attention to where we were and looked at the maps, it seemed to me that we weren't really where we were supposed to be. This was not looking at the stars—it was looking at the mountains and fixes on the map. So I found that I had made a mistake. Instead of taking the deviation between true north and magnetic north, adding it, I had subtracted it, so I was basically twice as far off the course as I should have been! So I didn't notify anybody else and made a correction and the correction worked, taking us into the mountain pass through the Atlas Mountains and into Morocco. So once again my navigation was working, what I had been taught was working, and I was becoming relatively confident. The last leg was to go from Morocco up over Portugal, the Atlantic, and on to Prestwick, Scotland. That was a long flight, and gas was a factor. It was uneventful until we got to Prestwick, where there was fog and drizzle and it was difficult to get clearance to land. One plane in front of us ran out of gas and crashed, but we landed okay and that was it.

They took our plane away from us, and that we didn't expect. Then they put us on a train and sent us to a reassignment center for the 8th Air Force in England. So we lost our plane, which we had named 'Myrtle the Fertile Turtle.'[14] That was our first disappointment. The plane that we thought was going to be ours for our missions was not going to be ours. When we got to the center where

---

[14] *'Myrtle the Fertile Turtle'*- Mr. Carlson came up with the name. 'The reason I did it was that people were talking about wives or girlfriends, but our pilot was Joe and he didn't have a girl or a wife and he wasn't interested in doing that. So I said, 'Let's give it a girl's name.' The B-24 is a very slow, lumbering thing, like a turtle, so I said, 'Let's call it Myrtle the Turtle.' The 'fertile' part came from the plane's ability to carry the biggest bomb load of any of the four-engine bombers.'

crews were assigned to established bomb groups, we waited and finally got our assignment. We were assigned to the 93rd Bomb Group. We were sent to a little town about twenty miles south of Norwich in East Anglia, which is where most of the heavy bombers were stationed. They were all within about a 50-mile radius around Norwich in the northeastern part of England. It was easier for them to form up and go out on a mission together. When we got there we learned two things. First, that our airplane was an old airplane that had survived 25 missions. At this point in the war, late 1943 to early 1944, if you completed 25 missions you were promised that you could go home and become instructors for new cadets who were learning about combat.[15] We did the math at that point and we were losing airplanes at the rate of 5 to 10% every mission. The actual math worked out that most people either got killed, wounded, or captured by their eighth mission. So we got this old airplane called the 'Judith Lynn' that had no nose turret. It just had the two flexible machine

---

[15] *if you completed 25 missions*-the required number of missions for bomber crewmen went up to 30 missions in the spring of 1944, and then to 35 missions after D-Day in the summer of 1944.

guns, one on either side, that the navigator used, or the bombardier if he wasn't at the bombsight. But it had been a lucky ship because it had completed 25 missions. So that was our first shock, that we had an old airplane.

We were in the 93rd Bomb Group, which, by the way, was called 'Ted's Traveling Circus,' because it had moved from England to Africa, where it had made raids on the Romanian oil fields at Ploesti, then back to England, and back to Africa again. This takes me up to what I guess was the moment of truth, which was our first mission.

'Your First Mission'

Your first mission is one that you never forget because it starts with a wake-up call. People talk about how we got a wake-up call at Pearl Harbor or on 9/11. A real 'wake-up call' began in the 8th Air Force with a hand on your shoulder while you were sleeping on a little cot in a cold Quonset hut. A hand shakes you and someone says, 'You're going to fly today' and you have to get up. So it's 3:30 a.m. and you get up and go to a cold stove and try to find water to shave, because you have to be clean-shaven in order for the oxygen mask to fit closely when you are up high in the air. So your wake-up call starts with a soldier waking you up, shaving, going to eat breakfast, and then going to a briefing room. By this time it's 4:30 to 5:00 a.m. [*pauses*], and there you are, locked in in a secret way, and the map is in front of you and uncovered [*makes sweeping gesture with hand*]. The commanding officer and intelligence officer show you where you are going and what the route is. So now you find out what your first mission is, which in this case was Nuremberg, which was far inside Germany. That was where the war trials were held later, but it was also near an industrial city with factories that made ball bearings. So this was our first mission. You get up, get dressed, and put on your electric flying suit, and heavy clothes after that. The navigators go to a special briefing where they plan their course. Then you go to your airplane. You are in your airplane by 7:00, and you look for the weather. It is normally rain or drizzle, or snowing, as it is never clear in the morning in England. You wait to find out if you are actually going to take off, because many times the operation is what they called 'scrubbed.' If it never takes off, it is scrubbed; if it takes off and then the whole mission is called off, it is called 'aborted.' So you are waiting to see if the mission is scrubbed and never takes off. There was nothing worse than having a mission scrubbed and knowing you were going to go back and have to do the same thing the next day. So, we took off. On that first mission [you get a feel for] the power, and it makes you feel terrific. A B-24 starts down the runway, and it only gets halfway down the runway when another starts down the runway, and then your plane starts down the runway, so at one time there are three B-24s on the runway, one taking off, one halfway, and one starting out. This sense of power that you have, going down that runway with four tons of bombs, is quite overwhelming. From there you work your way through the clouds and come up above, and there is an airplane up there with a big yellow body on it with zebra stripes. That is the plane you are going to form on. It doesn't go with you; it just circles up there until you get into for- mation and ready to go, and then you are on your way over the Channel. And this sense of power really is overwhelming. You are happy that you made this decision, and you see all the hundreds and hundreds of bombers that you have with you. And you have air cover. In those days it lasted for 50 to 100 miles over the coast, and then they run low on gas and have to return to base, and then there is no air cover. That is when the German fighters of the Luftwaffe would begin to attack the bomber formations as they came in. Then you begin to see the losses of your power because you look and see planes on either side of you being shot, being on fire, going down. Or you feel that yourself, which we fortunately did not on our first mission; we did not feel any hits directly. But I did see planes going down that were in formation with us. So the mission was long and it was successful. We hit the target, everything worked, we came back, and we landed. It was a very powerful experience.

When you come back, however, the letdown is tremendous. There is nothing to look forward to except doing it again, and you don't really want to do it again. You wanted to do it, and you did it, and it was terrific, but knowing that you have to do it another 24 times, knowing what you have seen, is not something you look forward to. So in between missions, one of the paradoxes is that you are at death's door and the next night you are down at a British pub drinking yourself silly because you are not going to have to fly the next day. You are with other fliers, British, free Poles, and you are having a great time. So from that experience you learn that maybe today is the day you are going to live or today is the day you are going to die. Most people drank a lot when they weren't flying. Alcohol became pretty much a way of life for people in the Air Force who were not on missions. I won't bore you with other missions, but we were on the first three raids on Berlin. March 6, 1944, was referred to as 'Bloody Monday' because we sent 600 airplanes up and 69 did not come back. That was not the worst experience I had because our group was not damaged. A lot of groups were, so we were very fortunate. But on our eighth mission we were sent to Freiburg in southern Germany, near the Swiss border. And it was there, just as we were going over the target...

Flak

Let me tell you a little about flak. I have carried this with me ever since, because this is what flak looks like [*digs into jacket pocket, pulls out a jagged flak fragment about the size of two fingers*]. This is a piece of flak from a German 88mm artillery shell, which is fired from the ground and explodes at 25,000 feet, which is where we were flying. It is designed to destroy the plane or the engines or blow up the gas tank. And on my eighth mission, just as we were flying over the target, through these black clouds of exploding shells that you had to fly through, and just as the bombardier released our bombs, I hit the salvo handle, a handle right next to the instrument on the navigation table. That would release the bombs in the event that the bombsight did not release the bombs. The second the bombardier says, 'Bombs are away,' the navigator hits the salvo handle so if any bombs did get hung up, they would automatically go when you hit the salvo handle. So as I hit that handle this piece of flak nearly took my right arm off. And all I felt was no pain, just the feeling that someone had hit me with a sledgehammer. I felt total peace. It was the most unbelievable experience I'd ever had in my life. I didn't talk to God or see God, but I had absolutely no fear.

I looked down and there wasn't much left of my right arm; I saw it hanging there. I called the pilot and asked him to send somebody down to put a tourniquet on. Meanwhile I was checking instruments, because now we were on our way back and navigating was part of what I had to do, and I was still capable of doing it; I had no problem with it. The radio operator came down, took one look at it, and fainted. So I called again and the engineer came down. He revived the radio operator and sent him back with his portable oxygen mask. He then put the tourniquet on and stayed with me for the three or four hours it took to get back to base. An engine was on fire. Joe put the fire out and we lost a second engine. He brought it back, we landed, and I was brought to the hospital. They repaired my arm. I was on the operating table for eight hours. I didn't wake up for 72 hours due to an overdose of Pentothal, which was the drug they used in those days.

Ken Carlson holds up the flak fragment
that nearly took off his right arm.

While I was in the hospital, our plane had 150 holes in it [to be patched up], and the crew was given a leave to go to London and relax. Joe came in and brought this piece of flak to me. [It had been lodged] in the instrument panel, and it had a piece of my wire suit and my blood on it. So it took part of my arm and then went on to demolish part of the instrument panel. Joe said to me, 'Sorry you are so unlucky, Navigator. We're going to miss you,' because there was no way I was going to fly again.

They came back from leave to fly the repaired airplane on the next mission, and they flew and they never came back. The crew next to them saw them explode, just like the Space Shuttle did on my 65th birthday. They were officially declared missing; [only] one parachute was seen coming out. For years I assumed they were missing rather than the fact that they were killed. About two years later, the government declared them killed in action. But up until about four or five years ago, [it was assumed that] there were no bodies ever recovered, because there was no indication otherwise. Then, through a German internet source, I discovered that they had been found by the Germans and were buried in a small German-occupied cemetery just north of Paris, but there were only body parts and one piece of wing that had a star on it. That was their identification. So they [turned out to be] in a cemetery in a little town northwest of Paris.

That was the end of my combat career. My arm was repaired by a doctor who, by fate, I met thirty years later. When my hand began to contract again I was sent to an orthopedic man. As I was sitting across from him he was questioning me about where this had happened, and he was the doctor who originally had put my hand back together again. He was the only doctor in that hospital, which had just opened the week before I was shot.

'The Nine Old Men'

When I came back from combat I was sent to a rehabilitation center in Pawling, New York. There we had the company of people like Lowell Thomas, the famous commentator, and Tom Dewey, [the former governor], and Norman Vincent Peale, who came over and played softball with us. So here we were with missing legs and arms, and we were called the 'nine old men.' This was the wonderful part of convalescence, and they were great people.

From there I was sent back to San Marcos as an instructor. All of us there would devote our time and energy to trying to tell people that what they learned in school would take them only so far. That what they needed to learn in combat was how to operate under conditions that were not classroom. That's how we made most of our contribution to those people before they were sent to Japan.

*

When President Roosevelt died, I was an instructor in Houston on special assignment. Having been a 'peacenik' before the war, I would never have gone to war unless we were attacked by Germany. I had studied enough about World War I and understood there was no way in the world that America should get trapped in another European war with France and Britain, who had allowed Hitler to build himself into a dictator over ten years. So I was always an 'America First' person; Lindbergh was one of my heroes, saying, 'Let's talk of America first,' and that is [originally] what my politics were.[16] Pearl Harbor changed all that. When I went to war and served Roosevelt, I was doing that coming from a family where my father thought Roosevelt was the worst thing that had ever happened to America, because [to my father], the free enterprise system was going to go down the pike. I would have tremendous arguments with him. I would say, 'Look, the banks are closed and the Republicans have not done a thing, and this guy is doing something!' I had a fondness for FDR, so when he died I was relieved because I was aware of the fact that he was a very ill man. I

---

[16] *'America First'*- Founded by Charles Lindbergh and others in 1940, the America First Committee opposed any U.S. involvement in World War II, and drew the ire of FDR, who was portrayed as pushing the U.S. into the European war. After Pearl Harbor, Lindbergh recanted his stance.

remember thinking, 'Thank God that he lived to the point where he knew the war had been won.' And he did know that, and I knew that. And I learned to have a tremendous respect for Harry Truman, who I didn't know anything about prior to Roosevelt's death.

I think all of us who had been in combat felt that Harry Truman did the right thing, [when he decided to use the atomic bomb]. I was aware of the fact that Einstein, one of my heroes growing up, said that you have no idea what you are doing when you set off this weapon, that it is beyond anyone's wildest imagination. I still think that, politically at that point in time [to invade Japan], it would have been unconscionable as to the number of Americans that would have been killed, knowing that [the Japanese] would have fought, as they did in the islands, to the last man. And I had to put it all into perspective. And this is the thing people, including my own children, who are in their fifties, don't understand—when we dropped bombs on Berlin and other cities, I understood that not only did we hit our target, we also killed hundreds of thousands of women and children. But at the same time there were nights when I sat in a bomb shelter in England with a woman and her child right next to me while Germans were dropping bombs on England. So I saw it both ways. I was in a bomb shelter seeing the horror those women were going through and remembered that Hitler had been doing this to England for a year without any real target—he had just leveled London and Coventry. So in doing what I did, it seemed that what I was trapped into had nothing to do with soldiers. It had to do with civilizations and cultures, so whatever it takes is what a president has to do. So I thought that Harry Truman made the right decision, one that I would have made. And I would have taken the bomb [to the target] had I been the navigator. I would have had no problem delivering the bomb.

*

I had enough points to get out, so in September of 1945, I was sent to Fort Dix, New Jersey, and that was the end of my Air Force career. I resigned my commission at the beginning of the Korean War; I felt that I was no longer young enough or capable enough to keep up with the modern technology to be of use to the government in Korea.

[After the war, I did not go to reunions.] I had lost my crew and it was something I didn't talk about for many years. I had no desire to go back and share memories with crews that had survived. It wasn't until much later that I decided to do this book for reasons that it would be helpful to young people in understanding what World War II was like. Not so much understanding it in its entirety, but how it affected individual people's lives. It wasn't until then that I had any real reason to try and recapture people who had been there. Then I joined what is called the 8th Air Force Historical Society. And through that I have maintained contacts at both the national level and at the local level in New York City. I found that very rewarding.

[I think my time in the military affected me] in a very dominant way. People talk about religion and believing in something; the moment of truth comes to you. I was raised and schooled in the Christian church. I don't go to church anymore, but I do have the faith that came to me when this piece of flak hit me. There was just no question in my mind that I was coming home, and that I was going to be safe and go to work and just do the job that I had to do. It is a feeling that has stayed with me all my life. So, from that standpoint, there is no fear. So many people today seem to be afraid of so many things. The fear of doing things or fear of failing has never been with me since I left the service. I have continued to look at my own life as one of missions, a series of missions and not just adventures, and it has worked for me.

Meeting the Enemy

After the war I was lucky enough to be able to open my own business on Madison Ave. doing advertising, marketing, and public relations. I started with Milton Bradley, the game company, and helped make them very successful. And for my second client I had the opportunity to make a presentation to BMW motorcycles and cars. Here was a German company and 33 other organizations were making [potential sales] presentations. I flew to Munich to meet the director of BMW. In talking with him after making my pitch presentation, he asked me where I was during the war. I said I was in the 8th Air Force bombing Germany. He said he wanted to show me what we did to

Munich. He drove me out to a park and he said they had to bulldoze all of Munich out here and raze everything. So I pulled out my piece of flak and asked him if he knew what that was.

He said, 'Jah, German 88.'

I said, 'This went into my right arm and almost took it off, and another one on its next mission went into my airplane, and my whole crew blew up.'

He looked at me and said, 'You see this missing earlobe? American .50 caliber machine gun bullet.'

From that moment on, we would drink together and he would say, 'We should have been on the same side. The Russians were the enemy.'

But I reminded him that they had a little guy with a mustache named Hitler.

Then he said, 'What could we do? We had Hitler and you had Roosevelt.'

See, in his mind it made no difference; to him, in either case we had to do what our leaders said. Anyway, he became a good friend and I did get the account. I became very successful. I drove the first BMW that came in from Munich for $2,300, drove it to Maine, wrote the marketing plan, and you know the rest.

Later, in working on a consulting job with the game company Milton Bradley in the 1970s, I had to go to Tokyo. In another marketing company I met a man who told me he was the last kamikaze pilot. I said, 'What do you mean, you were the last kamikaze pilot?' It was the last day of the war, and he was on a suicide mission to crash his plane into an American ship. Halfway there he decided he didn't have enough fuel and turned back. He said he got back, and the war was over. He was seventeen! So I had met the head of BMW who had been an SS trooper, and had met the last kamikaze pilot during my business career.

It has been a fun trip. In 1972 when I retired from business, the war then had become the war on drugs. By 1972 it was a problem in all of the high schools in New York or Maine, or wherever. President Nixon had declared war on cancer and then a war on drugs, so most of my effort has been talking to people in the school systems and helping young people in finding some kind of career guidance. That is my current war. When I work with young people in the school systems, both public and private, I try to use the book *High Honor.* I talk further about the drug problem and why the war on drugs is so vital to the future of this country; that word 'honor' is difficult to define, not just in reference to World War II, but easy to understand when read in relation to what the Founding Fathers said when they signed the Declaration of Independence. The final sentence said, *'And for the support of this declaration, with a firm reliance on the protection of Divine Providence, we mutually pledge to each other our lives, our fortunes, and our sacred honor.'* My chapter is entitled 'Borrowed Time,' and in that chapter there is a photo of me and my crew taken in 1943. [*Pointing out crew*] Frank Caldwell was the bombardier, from Anderson, Indiana; 'Johnny' Johnson, the co-pilot, from Houston, Texas; Joe Roznos, the pilot, my greatest friend, from Hollywood, California; 'Wally' Waldmann, waist gunner, from Houston, Texas; Hal McNew, waist gunner, from Montana; Ed Miller, tail gunner, from Wyoming; Frank Dinkins, the engineer; John Rose, 'Rosie', our ball turret gunner—he could shoot a squirrel, or a German fighter pilot, from his shoulder or his waist, it didn't make any difference; and Cleo Pursifull, our radioman. He is the one that came to help me and fainted. And he failed to go on that last mission. He had just had enough.

The thing that haunts me is that I can't put a face to the guy who replaced him. He was an eighteen-year-old Jewish kid named Henry Vogelstein from Brooklyn. It was his first and last mission. And when you think about it, an eighteen-year-old boy was put as a replacement in a crew that he did not know; we were an all-Christian crew. We all had our little New Testament that the Air Force gave us, and he would have been given an Old Testament. He made his only mission with a crew of strangers. Now that's bravery!

We all want to be free, but very few of us want to be brave. For all of us to be free, a few of us must be brave, and that is the history of America.

Earl Morrow, first row, far left, and his B-17 bomber crew. 1944.
Source: Earl Morrow

CHAPTER EIGHT

The Pilot

Earl Montgomery Morrow was born on June 27, 1921, in West Pawlet, Vermont. His father, a school-teacher, decided to take up farming across the border in Washington County, New York.

Earl first came on my radar when he called me up twenty years ago, having heard of my interest in World War II veterans and their stories. 'I just had to call you and ask—why are you doing this? Why are you interested in our stories?' Later, he would be a frequent visitor to my classroom, and I even got to introduce him to the granddaughter of the man who liberated him, General George Patton. I would also be invited to sit with him and two other B-17 veterans at his dining room table as they reunited after many years to swap stories of the day they were shot down and about their prisoner of war experience, to be detailed in the sequel to this book.

This interview was recorded in 2009, when Earl was eighty-eight years old, in the rural farmhouse he grew up in, B-17 memorabilia and photographs adorning the walls.

***

Duties of the Pilot

Your assignment to the B-17 airplane means that you are no longer just a pilot. You are now an airplane commander, charged with all the duties and responsibilities of a command post.

You are now flying a 10-man weapon. It is your airplane, and your crew. You are responsible for the safety and efficiency of the crew at all times--not just when you are flying and fighting, but for the full 24 hours of every day while you are in command.

Your crew is made up of specialists. Each man--whether he is the navigator, bombardier, engineer, radio operator, or one of the gunners--is an expert in his line. But how well he does his job, and how efficiently he plays his part as a member of your combat team, will depend to a great extent on how well you play your own part as the airplane commander.

Get to know each member of your crew as an individual. Know his personal idiosyncrasies, his capabilities, his shortcomings. Take a personal interest in his problems, his ambitions, his need for specific training.

See that your men are properly quartered, clothed, and fed. There will be many times, when your airplane and crew are away from the home base, when you may even have to carry your interest to the extent of financing them yourself. Remember always that you are the commanding officer of a miniature army--a specialized army; and that morale is one of the biggest problems for the commander of any army, large or small.

Crew Discipline

Your success as the airplane commander will depend in a large measure on the respect, confidence, and trust which the crew feels for you. It will depend also on how well you maintain crew discipline.

Your position commands obedience and respect. This does not mean that you have to be stiff-necked, overbearing, or aloof. Such characteristics most certainly will defeat your purpose. Be friendly, understanding, but firm. Know your job; and, by the way you perform your duties daily, impress upon the crew that you do know your job. Keep close to your men, and let them realize that their interests are uppermost in your mind. Make fair decisions, after due consideration of all the facts involved; but make them in such a way as to impress upon your crew that your decisions are to stick. Crew discipline is vitally important, but it need not be as difficult a problem as it sounds. Good discipline in an air crew breeds comradeship and high morale, and the combination is unbeatable.

You can be a good CO, and still be a regular guy. You can command respect from your men, and still be one of them.

Crew Training

Train your crew as a team. Keep abreast of their training. It won't be possible for you to follow each man's courses of instruction, but you can keep a close check on his record and progress.

Get to know each man's duties and problems. Know his job, and try to devise ways and means of helping him to perform it more efficiently.

Each crew member naturally feels great pride in the importance of his particular specialty. You can help him to develop his pride to include the manner in which he performs that duty. To do that you must possess and maintain a thorough knowledge of each man's job and the problems he has to deal with in the performance of his duties. —Duties and Responsibilities of the Airplane Commander and Crewmen, 1943

***

Earl M. Morrow

I went to school in Hartford, New York, and I graduated in 1939 as the valedictorian. It was a small class; I think there were 19 of us or something like that. I stayed around for a year and took postgraduate courses and tried to pick up some of my grades a little bit, and then I went to Iowa State College, studying mechanical engineering. I got through the first year there and I started the second year, and that Sunday, when Pearl Harbor was hit, I sat there and listened to that on the radio, and I made up my mind right there and then that at the end of the semester, I was going home and getting in the service.

As soon as the semester was over I got out on the road and hitchhiked from Iowa State and made it in three days to the farm up here in New York. Back then, people would pick you up. [*Chuckles*] I got home and told my dad what I was going to do, and my dad informed me that I wasn't going to do that—I was going back to school! He was the director of the Selective Service for Hartford, and he told me he knew the rules and regulations, and he informed me that he would have to sign it, for me to go in the service, and he wasn't going to do it.

'I'm Not Going Back'

I was 20. Dad was the kind of man that, well, you did what he wanted. Put it that way. But this was the first time that I [went against his wishes] and told him that I wasn't going back to school. So I went down to Schenectady, and got a job at General Electric as an apprentice machinist, and I enjoyed it. The instructor picked me and another guy up and we were doing real serious work on the lathe in the machine shop. But the day I turned 21, I went down to the Armory in Albany and I applied for the Aviation Cadet Program; there were thirty-some of us that went in that morning. Six of us out of the thirty-some got in and the rest were rejected. They told me, 'Be down to the railroad station ready to depart on Wednesday at 0900.' This was on a Friday. So I went home and told my family what I had done, and Mother was all upset.

I told her, 'Look, there was one boy in that group who was athletic, played every sport that there was, and they found he had a heart problem and he could drop dead at any minute. I'm one of the few that got through, and I'm healthy, and I'm going!' And that made her feel better.

The next day I got my orders to report to the draft board, and Dad couldn't do it, so I had to go to Granville to their draft board. So I went over there and I told them what I was doing and I showed them the paperwork, and they didn't do anything except tell me 'Good luck!' Wednesday morning came, and Mom and Dad took me down. And one of my little girlfriends went with us. Walked into the station, and a guy in uniform had a pack of manila envelopes, and he walked over to me, and he said, 'You have 30 people you need to get down to Fort Dix in New Jersey.'

And I looked at him and said, 'Why me?'

He said, 'Because you had ROTC in college.'

Well, I got them there, but I don't know how. [*Chuckles*] We had to change trains down in New York City, and I got all thirty of them there and delivered the papers to the proper people, and that's the way I entered the service.

There were delays with the Aviation Cadet Program, so they sent us over to Aviation Field on Long Island and gave us a .45 automatic, showed us how to use it, and put us on guard duty. I had never fooled around with guns—Dad and I had a little rifle I shot once in a while—but they gave us pretty good instruction on the .45, and we'd go out there at night and you couldn't see your hand in front of your face, it was so dark out there. And they said, 'If you hear movement or anything at all that's not right, you holler 'HALT' three times, and then shoot!' And so I killed a cow one night. [*Chuckles*] It was just outside the line—I hollered 'HALT!' three times, and it didn't stop! But there were some fellas that actually shot people trying to come over the fence, and what happened was they were tried, found guilty, and fined a dollar and shipped out. I made up my mind early on that I wasn't going to be shipped out of this Aviation Cadet Program. So I was real careful, and eventually they shipped us out and sent us down to Nashville, Tennessee, on another train.

'You Did The Right Thing'

We're still in '42. And I'm down there, and that's where you get classified whether you go as pilot, bombardier, or navigator. And everyone wanted to be a pilot, of course, including me, and I made it, and they shipped us out of there to California. And this was a real enjoyable trip, because the train didn't go straight to California. It would go south, and then it would go north, and then it would go south, and so if the Germans were watching, they wouldn't know that this was a troop train and they wouldn't know exactly where it was going. And it took about seven days to get out there, so I got to see a whole lot of the U.S. on that trip. Once we were there, we went through pre-flight school where you took courses in theory of flight, weather, meteorology, and so on and so forth. Then about January 1, I guess it would have been in '43, I got my first flight. I had never been in an airplane before in my life, and this was a single-engine, open cockpit, and the instructor was sitting in the front seat, and they showed us how to start it.

The second day after I had been up twice, the instructor told me I would never make it. I asked him why, and he said, 'You're afraid of the airplane.'

And I asked him, 'Well, can't you do something about it?'

He said, 'With your permission, we'll make or break you this afternoon.'

I said, 'Fine, let's go.'

Man, I've never been afraid of an airplane since. We did everything that an airplane can do in that airplane. We rolled, we looped, we dove, we flew straight up and then let it fall back down, and then he went down and actually landed on a big truck going down the highway, just touched the wheels down to the truck long enough and let it sit there a few seconds! And then we found a farmer down there, and he threw a hammer at us and it went over the top of the airplane, so you know how low we flew! And within two days I had soloed on the airplane.

I think I had about six hours total [in the air] when I soloed. And we had class work and we had flights. We did night flying, we did day flying, we did short landing, and I learned in a hurry! The first time right after I soloed, I'm out there flying by myself, and here comes a thunderstorm, came right up on me, sitting right there, and I said, 'What do I do now?', and I looked around and I spotted another plane with two people. That told me that one of them was an instructor, so I got right on his tail and stayed there and we went into another landing field. And he said, 'What are you doing following me?'

I said, 'Look, I just soloed; I didn't know what to do. I saw two people in the plane, and I figured one was an instructor and I figured he knows what to do, follow him.'

And he said, 'You did the right thing.'

I got through the primary training and then we went to Chico, California, for basic training, into bigger airplanes, enclosed cockpits now. The instructor sits behind you and you sit up front; a bigger airplane, it's got more power. It's a fixed gear, though, a P-13, and it's a real nice airplane. Now I got a little more of formation flying, quite a lot of night flying, and a lot of maneuvering, precision flying, so on and so forth. I got through that. But I couldn't get through lazy eights the way I should have been doing them.[17] The instructor had me out there, and we were working, and we were just about to do the lazy eight and smoke started pouring up into the cockpit from underneath the plane, and he said, 'Get back to the field!' So I turned around, and we flew back to the field and I had a good landing even with all the smoke, and he said, 'If you can fly under those conditions, you've passed.' From there we went down to Marfa, Texas, and got into a multi-engine, five or six passenger aircraft with retractable landing gear. And this is where I was really learning to fly now; I had a whole lot more to handle. The day we got down there we had a hail storm and all these planes had fabric wings, which got all torn up. My last day there a new plane came in; it was really nice to fly around in, an airplane you could do things with. This was at the end of June, exactly six months from when I first got in an airplane, and I got my wings and a rating as a 2^d Lt. They sent us down to Roswell, New Mexico, and had me doing takeoffs

---

[17] *lazy eights*- changing combinations of climbing and descending turns at varying airspeeds used to develop and demonstrate the pilot's mastery of the airplane

and landings and in a B-17; I had never even seen one before in my life! But after two months I was qualified, but instead of sending me overseas, they sent me up to Las Vegas to fly gunners in training, which was a real plush deal. When you come out of the B-17 training, you're listed as a 1st Pilot. I was a 1st Pilot all the way through, but up there in Las Vegas there would be times I would be sitting in the co-pilot seat. We had a lot of fun up there training gunners—you'd get 10 or 12 guys on Monday morning and they'd never been on the airplane before, so we just flew around and got them used to flying. The next five or six days would be real serious—they would be towing targets behind airplanes, and they had to shoot and hit stuff, and they had cameras so they could tell if they were hitting it or not. We had a lot of fun— we would go and fly down in the canyon, and go into Death Valley and fly below sea level, and let them see what the countryside looked like, and so on and so forth. Then all of a sudden they picked five crews to go fly some new B-17s down to Tyndall Field in Florida, so now the only people that I had on the airplane were a co-pilot and a flight engineer.[18] We flew from Las Vegas down somewhere in Virginia or somewhere—I forget where it was—but before we landed there, we really dragged it down below because my co-pilot's hometown was nearby, and we flew real low over there. We saw people were running out of their houses and falling on their face, because they were wondering what the heck [the roaring of the multi-engine bomber was]! After we landed, that night we went to see his family and we stayed over there. Then we went over to where he went to school, and one of his teachers saw him and said, 'I was on the third floor when you went by, and I was looking down on you!'

From there, we went down to Tyndall Field and we trained gunners down there for a while. We couldn't get Pullman railroad car to get back to Vegas straight away, so I eased up there up to the farm in New York and visited my folks, and then got out to Vegas. From there, I got my overseas orders, and I went to Kansas to get my crew. All the pilots who went there got new crews; it was people coming right out of school who had just gotten their

---

[18] *Tyndall Field*-on the Gulf Coast of Florida, it opened as a gunnery range. and school in 1941.

wings. I now had my crew, and I was really happy with them—they all seemed like a really great bunch of guys. There were four officers, myself, the navigator, my co-pilot, and the bombardier, and the rest of the crew had a staff sergeant rating, enlisted men. I got all my enlisted men off to the side on the first day where no one could hear me, and I said, 'I don't ever want one of you guys to salute me, unless there's someone standing over there expecting you to salute me, then you do it.' I never once had a problem with discipline, and I think the guys really appreciated me doing that. When my officers found out about it, they fell right in with it, and we never had an issue.

We started training, hard. We did night flying, long distance flying, we did high altitude and a lot of formation flying. We were practicing dropping bombs and doing navigating flights, and one night we had something break on the instrument panel, and hydraulic fluid just came flying out into my lap. The boys had an idea, and we took our para-chutes and put them up under the pilot and co-pi-lot seats, where we could reach them easily but they would be safe. But those parachutes got soaked with hydraulic fluid, so we had a situation where we had a very flammable fluid all over the aircraft and I decided we had to get this thing on the ground. Luckily there was an emergency field up there right close by, in one of the middle states, but they didn't even have a radio there, so we had to call our home base in Louisiana and they had to call on the phone to the emergency landing field. It was just a field with a flare on each end of the 'runway.' We got the flares spotted and came in really low, and at about fifty feet off the ground a light turned on just below us in a house! So I gave it full power and we went around again; we went over the house again and got it down on the ground. We went to a hotel where we could sleep, and they said they would send parts up to us the next day. There were small crowds gathered the next day because it was a small town, so everyone came out to see us—we showed them through the aircraft, but we covered up the bombsight because that was secret, so the boys were telling the people to buy war bonds. That morning a stripped-down B-17 came in—there were no guns on it—and it made three passes over the field in daylight before it finally landed. A major was flying that and he had been in combat, and he came over and said, 'Who the hell landed this thing in here at night?' It was probably the best thing that could have happened before we went overseas, because after that the crew had absolutely no concern whether Bill and I could fly that thing or not—they didn't have to worry about [our abilities], which helped a lot. Shortly after that we got on a boat with all of our equipment, and we get in a boat in New York, and a whole fleet of boats go across.

Now that was '44. It was about two weeks in the boats going across. And the closer we got over there, I began to get a little nervous about what are we getting into over there. Especially when one of the guys mentioned about submarines being in the area. But it was a really nice trip over there, because we were on what used to be a French luxury liner—but they pulled out all the luxury, and put in all the bunks. They kept all the crew, and I've never eaten so well in my life—three and four course meals, every meal. It was great. [*Chuckles*]

'People Were Shooting At Me'

We got over there and we got in a couple of days of training. The first mission I went out on, I sat in the co-pilot's seat and I was with a crew that had been out there for quite some time. I saw all these little puffs of black smoke, and I was wondering what it was—I figured it out real quick that people were shooting at me! We sustained some battle damage to the airplane that day, but we got back okay. The missions I was on were all over lower Germany, in the 457th Bomb Group, out of the little town of Glatton, close to Peterborough, probably about 40 miles or so north of London.

I had my own airplane, but in 17 missions I flew it three times. The rest of the time they were putting it back together. The boys named it 'SHAD'; I had gotten married just before, and I had skinnied down to just a shadow of what I was, so it was short for 'Shadow.' [*Chuckles*] For my second mission, I had all of my crew, except I had an experienced co-pilot in the right seat. So we had a little battle damage on the plane, but what was bothering the crew were those short runways in England. The bombardier and the navigator had stayed down in front, but that was the only mission they stayed down in front on. We were carrying heavy loads, you know, and I had been told not to let the crew sit in the nose, but to sit in the back. You had to use every inch of the runway. We moved them back after that. We always left one man home, because there was a gun in the radio room that they had taken out, so they figured that the radio man could always get out and get on the gun.

I don't remember too much about these missions specifically, with the exception of three. Once we were going pretty deep into Germany, and on the way in, we lost the number one engine and it must have been a fuel pump or something, the way it just quit on us. So we were going in light on the power and feathering it in, because we only had the three remaining engines. We were in a formation of probably about a thousand airplanes and were in a squadron of twelve airplanes, in a group of 36 planes. We had to keep working on staying in the formation—you have to use full power just to stay in it if you're on the outside, and low power if you're on the inside.

My co-pilot was going to make this bomb run on this day. We came down in altitude, and just before we dropped our bombs, we got a direct hit on the number three engine! I went through the feathering procedures. What I mean by that is, you shut the engine down and then set the propeller blade parallel to your flight, so they're not creating a windmill and drag. I shut everything down, but we started windmilling. So now we had to get out of the formation, because there's no way we could have stayed in. Luckily we had been able to drop our bombs and get rid of them.

The dome of the number three engine started to get red-hot, then white-hot, and the engine started to break apart; pieces of it started flying into the aircraft and coming through the thin skin on the aircraft. So Bill and I decided to put the plane into a dive and then pull up to try to break the propeller free.

We dove twice and we lost a couple thousand feet, and I said, 'Look, Bill, we can't lose any more altitude, we're going to just have to leave it as is.'

That engine was still windmilling. So number two was running and number four was running, but number one is feathered and number three is out. We were now losing altitude all the way, and we had to come across occupied Belgium to make it home.

The Germans were shooting at us all the way, so we were turning every ten seconds; our fighters stayed up above us and covered us in. We had a spot about a mile and a half wide to come out of Belgium over the English Channel—there was a swamp or something there, and if you came out over the swamp, there were no guns there. My navigator brought me out right over that spot dead center, and we were flying real low now, heading for home, but we have got to get over the Cliffs of Dover when we get across the Channel. Now just as we got out over the Channel, we lost the number four engine! Unbeknownst to anybody, the Germans had flak barges out in the Channel, and they knocked out number four... It feathered; we had one engine running, two feathered, and one windmilling, so we weren't doing too well.

So now we're over the Channel and we're throwing everything out to lighten the weight. We threw the guns out. We all had flak suits and we dumped them, and everything we could throw out. And we finally got over the Cliffs of Dover, and right in front of us there was a field, and a plane was in front of us! I told the engineer, 'Throw him a flare!', and the plane got out of the way. And I got it safely down on the ground, and the guys were getting out of the airplane, kissing the ground, running around and stuff like that. I couldn't even get the plane off the runway with one engine! By the way, my bombardier had professed to be an atheist but he became a good Christian after that, and he was one until the day he passed away.

The boys got out and they started counting up the holes in the airplane—we had well over a hundred holes in the airplane. Most of them were small holes, but one of them was as big as a bushel basket. And there wasn't one of us who was scratched, but the medical people showed up and they grounded us right there, and they said, 'You boys are going to a rest camp for a week.' So we went down to some place in southern England; it was old and a real big place where they had a lot of bedrooms. The Red Cross people were running it and we had to come to dinner every night in Class A uniforms; other than that, we could wear what we wanted. They had bicycles you could ride out in the country with, and so on and so forth.

The Final Mission

Earl and his crew rested their nerves. When they returned to base after a week of much-needed relaxation, they were briefed on the next mission—a heavily defended target that would test their abilities yet again and end in disaster.

We found out we were going to Merseburg, which is a synthetic oil plant, and it was a rough one. And when you went down to breakfast in the morning and you got fresh eggs, you knew it was going to be a rough mission. If you got powdered eggs, you knew it was going to be a 'milk run,' but I never did get one of those milk runs.

This was my 17th mission. So we knew we're going to Merseburg—we've been there before and we know it's going to be rough. We took off and we got over there, and there was [heavy cloud cover over the target area]. We dropped our bombs on what we thought was the synthetic oil plant, and then there was some mix-up—I don't think anyone really knows what happened for sure, but for whatever reason after we dropped our bombs, our group was going one way [*gestures towards the right with one hand, points towards the left with the other hand*] and the rest of the strike force started turning the other way! Nine hundred and some airplanes turned right, and thirty-six turned left, and which ones do you think the German fighters were going to hit? They picked us, and they pulled our fighters, who were supposed to be protecting us, off in a dogfight.

I told the guys, 'Keep your eyes open, we are about to be hit!' And sure enough, they came down in groups of fifteen right behind us—I never saw a fighter at all—and they started pumping 20mm rounds into us. After they started to run out of ammunition or whatever, they would just peel off underneath our planes.

The crew told me my rudder, my vertical stabilizer, was gone. I could hear the shells exploding in the back of the airplane and I could feel the hits, but we never saw the fighters from where we were in the front—I'm flying formation, that's my job. The next group of fighters came in, and I saw about six or eight feet go off my left wing, and again I could feel the shells exploding in the back. The third group came, but kind of missed us. The fourth group came in, and we got two 20mm rounds right in the cockpit beside my co-pilot.

I didn't know if he was hurt real bad or what, but now the plane was on fire, so the top turret gunner came down and grabbed the extinguisher and he put the fire out. We thought it was out, but it flared up again, so now the only thing to do was to get out. I rang the 'bail-out' signal, and I reached out and grabbed William out of his seat, yanked him out. I didn't know whether he was hurt bad or what. The top turret gunner bailed out and went down.

I got out of my seat, grabbed Bill, and started down the gangway. But I felt the airplane climbing, and I thought to myself, 'If this thing stalls out, and starts falling down backwards, no one is going to get out.' So I crawled back up—I didn't get into my seat, but just pushed the controls forward enough to get the nose down. So I went back down to jump clear, and Bill was sitting down there with his feet hanging out. I just put my foot in the middle of his back and kicked him out—and then I sat down there and rolled out, and just as I dropped clear, the plane exploded! I could hear it and feel it, but did not see it; when you jump out like that, your eyes automatically close. You're jumping out and you're moving 160 or 170 mph, so your eyes aren't going to stay open.

'How to bail out of the Flying Fortress.' B-17 training manual, U.S. Government. Source: www.cnks.info/b17-flying-fortress-interior

So now I was out there in the clouds, and I'm thinking, 'What's going to happen if I rip this cord and I get pulled up into everything, with the updrafts in these clouds?'

I was falling and had the wind on my face, trying to look down, so when I broke out of the clouds I could know how far I was above the ground. I figured I was above ten thousand feet when I broke out, but in fact I was well below that when I did break out—I was pretty close, and I ripped my cord [*motions across his waist with his hand*] and the parachute worked perfectly, and I swung over one or two times and I was on the ground. I almost stayed on my feet, but the chute dragged me and I went over on my behind.

Prisoner

I was trying to get out of the chute as fast as I could, because about thirty feet away were three women with pitchforks coming toward me and they weren't friendly, so I had to get out of that harness as fast as I could. I had a .45 strapped against me. I didn't take it out, but as they got closer I unbuckled it, and they backed off. I was real close to a road so I ducked down onto this road below me and ran up to the other side and started to cross this field. And German civilians were coming with rifles, so I just sat down and put my hands up.

We had been told to get under military control if we could, [as soon as possible, if there was no opportunity to escape]. Men, women, and children came up to me; the women were spitting in my face and the little kids were throwing stones at me. I saw a guy in the distance that I thought looked like he was in uniform, and I tried to tell them that was where I wanted to go, and I pointed. I couldn't speak German, [although I think the kids at least knew some English]. I got knocked down three or four times before I convinced them I wanted to get over there. The Germans then took me into a small town and the first person I saw from my airplane and crew was my tail gunner. He was so glad to see someone else from the plane, because, you see, he came out of his turret, way at the back end of the plane.

The tail gunner had got out, and he told me that the escape door was gone. Now little Joe Salerno was the waist gunner and he was a little eighteen-year-old kid. He was standing there [as the plane was going down], my tail gunner motioned for him to go out, and he shook his head, 'No.'

That's not Joe; Joe wasn't afraid of anything. When the tail gunner told me that, I realized what Joe had done. He was in the waist gun and Bob Koerner was in the ball turret, and they had this agreement that if Bob was in the ball turret, Joe would wait until Bob got out, and Bob didn't get out, and Joe just lost it. And we think that because the main door was gone, that possibly the radio operator might have gotten out.

Later, while we were on the ground, I was informed by some Germans that one of my 'comrades' was bleeding, but they wouldn't let me go to him. I got the feeling that it could have been my radio operator. But those are three boys who were killed from my crew.[19]

I didn't see my co-pilot until three or four days later. They had us in [what seemed to be the] backyard of a house for some time. The count in our squadron was twelve airplanes, and we lost nine that day. Now that's 81 men, and I only saw thirty-something of us alive.

---

[19] *three boys who were killed from my crew-* Radio Operator: Charles Lindquist, Ball turret gunner: Bob Koerner, Tail gunner: Joe Salerno. Source: American Air Museum in Britain, www.americanairmuseum.com/aircraft/11772. Mr. Morrow states that Salerno was on a waist gun at the time of this last mission.

The two Germans [who took me into custody] must have been on sick leave, though they both had rifles. One had a patch over his eye, and the other had his arm in a sling. They took me and another one of our boys who I never knew before; his name was Jerry Silverman.[20] They put us in a car and we started cross country; we had no idea why or where we were going. I didn't realize that Jerry was Jewish. They drove about 10 minutes and then the car quit. They got out, opened the hood, pulled the wires, cleaned them out real good, and we went another 10 minutes. Now at the next stop one of these guys turned around and he wanted my pilot wings. He reached out and started to touch them, and I slammed his arm down on the seat!

Jerry was sitting over there yelling at me to give them what they want, saying, 'You're going to get us both killed! Just give him anything he wants.'

But you see, what I had been told before was that if you stand up to the Germans, you'll do a lot better than if you cater to them. So I'm just playing

---

[20] *Jerry Silverman*-I met Mr. Silverman, the lead navigator for this raid, when he came up to visit with Earl's bombardier Sam Lisica and Earl in 2001. Their B-17 PoW reunion is a main focus of the sequel to this book.

the game—that's not the way I really am—but I got away with it, I slammed his arm down on the back of the seat.

So they got out and cleaned their plugs again and we went on to the town, so their families could see that they had captured us. That night they took us out and put us in something like a one-room schoolhouse, and there were two guards there for about thirteen of us. One of the guards would take a couple of us and go into town to get food; we had a little kid's wagon. I might be pulling the wagon, and the other guy would be back there pushing the wagon, and we would argue with the guards. When one of us was arguing with the guard, the other was sticking everything he could in his pockets for the other guys who were sick—we were manipulating the guards the whole time, so we could get the food for the guys who were really in bad shape. One boy, a tail gunner, his back was broken in three places; one of the other pilots had his head severely burned going out of his airplane. I don't know what actually happened to these people who were hurt so badly.

We stayed there about three days, and they brought my co-pilot in to me while we were there. He said that a farmer and his daughter had picked him up and hid him for a couple of days, but they got scared and they turned him in. He was not bleeding, but he was in bad shape.

The Germans wound up moving us out of there on a train and I don't know where they took him, but they moved the rest of us to Frankfurt to an interrogation center.

I think the reason we got away with [our uncooperative behavior toward our guards] was because they were under orders to make sure we got to interrogation—the Germans wanted us over there badly, so they could find out what was going on. So we rode this train and we got into Frankfurt, and we had to run/walk from one end of Frankfurt to the other side to catch another train to take us out to the interrogation center. Now I never saw a full building standing; everything was shattered in that town of Frankfurt. We got over to the other station, and there was a little while before the next train, and there was a good-looking German gal there, but she got a rioting crowd rounded up in a hurry, ready to come after us. The guards finally locked us down in a room in the basement because they couldn't hold the crowds off.

Eventually the train came in and it was just a short ride to the interrogation center. We were there about three days and we gave nothing but name, rank, and serial number. About the third day in, the interrogator said, 'Well, if you won't tell me, I'll tell you.'

He proceeded to tell me things that I didn't think my parents even knew. He told me that when I was in fifth grade, I was sent to the principal's office! They knew that our bombardier had made major, which we didn't know. They had [an intelligence] system and they were working on it a long time, and the only way I can figure out how they got this information is my folks would be sitting up there on the farm, and the college kids would come through selling magazines. Mother would invite them in for dinner, and then she'd sit there and talk to them all afternoon. I think that they were spies—that's the only way I can figure out how they got this information, but I didn't think my dad or my mother knew that I had gone to the principal's office for a little offense like going down the slide headfirst; they seemed to know everything. But I just told the guys, just don't talk; name, rank, serial number, and that's it.

The third day there, they pulled us out and put a gun on a train with us. We went to the town of Sagan, southeast of Berlin. That was the camp—if you saw the movie 'The Great Escape,' that's the camp that the movie took place in. And all the time that we were in there, we were working on escape deals. But the commanding officer in there made rules—we had our own government in there, and if you wanted to escape, and you had a plan, then you took it to them and told them what it was, and then the whole camp would work on it. And they made it a court-martial offense to try and escape on your own. There were two or three escapes that went on when I was in there, and one of them failed because of exactly what I said. There was a [guard] tower with search lights and machine guns on it, and then they had a barbed wire fence and a warning fence inside of that. You didn't go over the warning wire, never. So it was winter, and we had eleven guys dressed up in clothes they had made out of white sheets, and they were hiding in the latrine, and they knew there was a space right under that tower that [the guards in] the tower couldn't see. So they went out that night and got out clean and free, and made it out. But two other guys decided they were going to try it, and they got caught. So immediately the Germans were looking for a count, knowing that some were gone. So these other guys totally screwed up the deal for the eleven that got out.

[They got recaptured], but what happened to them, I don't know.

When you first get in there, no one will talk to you until someone identifies who you are. They figure you might be a mole or a spy. I ran into my roommate from basic training, and he okayed me and then I okayed the rest of my crew.

These were all officers in the camp I was in. The enlisted men went to another camp somewhere else, and they were staff sergeants, so the Germans couldn't make them work. But we were in there and we were in barracks. And my barracks commander was Colonel Gabreski, you've probably heard of him—fighter ace in World War II, and then a jet ace in later wars; he passed away just a short time ago.[21] But every evening they would put us out on the parade ground by the barracks, and the old German major commander from the camp would come around and give the 'Heil Hitler' salute and [Colonel Gabreski] would give the accountability report: 'One's in the hospital,' so on and so forth.

Death March

[It got to be January 1945], and we began hearing guns; the Russians were getting close. Around January 10, I didn't know exactly what day it was, but one morning they routed us out of there. There were ten thousand of us in that camp, and one o'clock in the morning they rousted us out of there and put us out on the road, running. They had guns and they had dogs, so when they said, 'Run!', you ran. Blizzard, thirty degrees below

---

[21] *Colonel Gabreski-* Francis Stanley "Gabby" Gabreski, January 28, 1919 – January 31, 2002. He was the top U.S. Army Air Force fighter ace over Europe in World War II, with 28 kills before surviving an accident that made him a PoW. He was also one of seven pilots who went on to 'ace' status in Korea as well.

zero, and we would run ten minutes and walk ten minutes, run ten minutes, and at the end of the hour they would give us a five-minute break. And this kept up all day, and somewhere on the route down there machine guns started going off, and I just dove into a snowbank until things quieted down—never did find out what it was about.

Now they put the word out that if we fell out for any reason, they would run us through with the bayonet. And as we left the camp they ran us through a warehouse and threw us a Red Cross parcel that had food in it. Well at thirty below zero we didn't have gloves and couldn't carry it, so I just busted mine open and stuck everything I could in my pockets, drove my hands in there, and pro-ceeded on down the road.

We had a break at 5:30 in the morning; I had a clean pair of socks in my pocket and I thought it would be a good idea to change them, so I did, but while I tried to change them, my shoes froze and I couldn't get my feet back in. So I had to try to walk around for a while to heat them up enough until I could get my feet back down in.

We started walking again, and it was still dark, and, well, I was just so tired I figured if I just sat down I'd fall asleep and that would be it—I just felt like I couldn't go any further. So I sat down.

We had two guys who were up and down that line; one was a Lt. Col. West Point graduate. The other played football for Penn State—big guy, Polish guy, and we couldn't pronounce his name so we just called him 'Smitty.' And Smitty got to me, and he's just slapping the daylights out of me and cursing at me, 'Get your 'blankety-blank' up and get moving!'

I thought to myself, I have to get up to get away from him, so I got up and started moving again. Well, then they brought my bombardier, Sam, to me, and Sam was completely out of it. He had no idea where he was or who he was, so they wanted somebody who knew him to take him. I got well in a hurry—I snapped out of it because now I had to take care of Sam. And you'd be surprised how well it worked. So I grabbed Sam by the shoulder, and we kept him going down through [that part of the ordeal]. We stopped again, and he looked up at me and he said, 'I know who you are. You're the best damn pilot in the world!'

I never let him forget that—I told him later that when you're really down and out, the truth comes out. [*Laughs*]

But if you think about it, it was Sam who really saved my life, because up until then I was just bound and determined that I just couldn't do it. When you see somebody else who really needs your help, it really makes a difference; when you have to do it, you just do it.

*

I can't remember the names of the towns anymore, but we got into a town and they put us into churches, and they were concrete floors and it was cold. The next morning the burgermeister of this town—we heard he had a son who was a PoW in the U.S.—he [appeared to] take over from the military. They had pottery factories there in that town and they opened up the drying rooms and put a bunch of us in there. We were warm! We stayed in there two or three days, and then we marched out of there, not too far, to a railroad station, and they put us in these little boxcars—fifty to a car, you couldn't even sit down. I still had my blanket, and two or three other guys had their blankets, and there were rings in the tops of the cars, and we managed to get five or six hammocks up to get some of us off the floor and make some room for the others. We were in there probably a day and a half, something like that, and we pulled into Nuremberg and went into a camp there.

Nuremberg was nasty, filthy, and dirty. We were there for a while. We'd walk into our barracks room and we'd see rats come running down the wall and walk across the guys who were sleeping. We got a cup of soup every day, and if it was bean soup there was a worm in every bean. I had seen my dad throw that kind of stuff out; he wouldn't feed his cows what we got. But if you're hungry you'd eat it anyway.

We had to get in a line to get water, and all we could get was a tin can, though we were probably in that line for an hour. I got bitten from head to foot by bugs, and swelling all settled in my feet, and I couldn't walk, I couldn't do anything. They put me in a barracks, they called the hospital, and there was an American soldier there, a doctor who was running the hospital. He put a hot water bottle on it overnight, and the next morning, they sat me up in the chair, and he said, 'Hang on,' and he had someone hold my shoulders. He cut a hole in my knee and squeezed out a cup of stuff.

He had penicillin tablets and he didn't know what they were because they were new, and he just stuck tablets in there. Would've done more good if he had fed them to me, but he put them in there and tore up a sheet and just wrapped it up.

He said, 'Now, we're going to move out of here in a couple of days, so I'll fix it up so you can ride in the train.'

I told him, 'No way!' See, we had a radio in the camp—the Germans knew we had the radio, but they could never find it—and you could get the BBC. We had the information now that our boys [fighter planes] were shooting everything up even if it had a Red Cross on it. We had seen it as well; we saw the Germans load tanks on trains and cover them in sheets with a big Red Cross sign on it so they could move them to the front lines. Our boys had gotten wise to that, so I wasn't going to get on any train at all. I'd rather walk. And afterwards, the doctors told me it was the best thing I could have done for my leg anyway.

[We had been in the camp near Nuremberg] for a month or so, and sure enough, the first day out, we got strafed by our boys. A couple of our guys got nicked, but they then flew right down the side of us, to see what we were and who we were. We just pulled our clothes off and made a big 'PW' sign, and from then on we had a fighter escort all the way down into Bavaria, and this was a four to five, or maybe six-day trip. By then we were actually bribing the German guards to stay with us, because there were SS troops in the area, and you didn't want a bunch of Americans just floating around down there, because those SS troops would just mow you down.

So we were bribing the guards and even the civilians then; I saw a bunch of civilian women attack our German camp commander and they knocked him down, and were knocking him around pretty good. Before we got down there to Moosburg, we could have just walked off if we wanted. I found some kids in one town and bought some eggs off them with a couple of cigarettes that the Red Cross had gotten to us—one of the home guards came out and followed me to make sure I left the town and didn't stick around, but by then the Germans were screaming and hollering, 'When are the Americans going to get here?', because they wanted the Americans to get there before the Russians did.

One night we stayed in a farmer's hay mound. It was nice and really clean hay. It was a nice place to stay. The war is still going on but the kids are out there playing, and you can see the kids' ribs. And I asked him, 'Why don't you kill one of your chickens and feed your kids?'

His answer was, it's a death penalty to kill that chicken without a government permit.

'He Saluted Me Back'

We finally got down to Moosburg; I guess all the PoWs in Germany were in there—I think that there was over 100,000 in that camp. It was a Sunday morning, and we knew General Patton was coming. We got the information on our radio. Matter of fact, they had it set up so that if the Germans were going to move us again, we would put sheets on top of the building and signal to a particular place. Well at exactly ten o'clock that Sunday morning, the first tank rolled over the top of the hill—the tank drove right through the fence, they didn't open the gate or anything, and behind the tank General Patton was standing up in the back of [a vehicle], pearl-handled pistols at his sides and all. [*Gestures where the pistols would have hung on his waist; chuckles*] And I threw him a salute, and he saluted me back, and he pulled off and made a little speech to us, and then he said, 'See you, gentlemen—I have a war to win,' and he pulled off and was gone.

Coming Home

We 'pulled spades' to see who would come out first. And my commanding officer of this area pulled out the ace of spades, and I came out on the seventh airplane. The C-47s or the DC-3s were coming in with supplies for Patton, and then they would load them up with PoWs and haul them out to France. So I came out early. We stopped in Paris to refuel, and while we were there I ate nineteen doughnuts! I was trying to get even more, but they wouldn't give me any more. They brought us to the place where they were bringing all the PoWs in, and they gave us a chemical bath. We threw all our clothes away, and they gave us enough pants and underwear and clean stuff to get on, and then they ask us if we would give up our quarters on the next ship going home. We figured they would probably put sick and wounded in those decent quarters, and then we would be in other quarters. So we weren't in the best quarters, and when we pulled out we were very disappointed because they had [given our quarters to] a bunch of British war brides. They got the good quarters, but I didn't care by then, they could have put a log under me and I would have ridden that home. [*Laughs*] But we came home, and came into Camp Myles Standish up in Boston.

This would have been May. There were a whole bunch of German PoWs in there, wearing brand-new American uniforms with 'PW' on the back of them. We ran after them; they had to get all the MPs after us and round us all up. We went in the mess hall that first night, and I'm right behind that big guy Smitty, you know, the one who was banging me around on the march. The Germans were serving the food. We're in line and they put a steak on each tray as we went through, and you're supposed to move forward. Smitty tells the guy, 'I want three more steaks!' The German shakes his head no, and that German went flying across the room! They got the brass in there, and they informed everyone that these guys get anything that they want. And a couple of days later we got on a train and went down to Atlanta, Georgia. From there they put us on a thirty-day leave, so I got a bus and went up to my home here and spent some time on the farm. After that, I went to Plattsburgh for a while and went to an Army hospital. Then I came back down here to try and get into the swing of things again, went down to General Electric again, where I was working before I went in the service. I didn't stay there but a couple of weeks—I don't know how we won the war from what I saw going on there, but maybe it wasn't going on during the war, but some of them in there were putting out the least amount of work—well, that's another story.

*

The Last Close Call

[When the war ended], the airlines wouldn't talk to us right away—they said we 'flew too rough.' But eventually they found out maybe we weren't so bad. So I flew a couple of years for a non-scheduled airline, which wasn't bad, but then I was gone all the time—you didn't know where you were going or when you were coming back.

I was living in Nashville. On one of the trips out we had a long layover or something in Michigan, so I caught a train into Chicago and talked to American Airlines, and they hired me. I couldn't have had a better job. I loved flying; I never had any big problems with American. I was in the co-pilot seat for eleven years, but that was because it was all based on seniority and right after I got in, they quit hiring for quite some time. But then, when I was flying out of Nashville, I wanted to get on the bigger airplanes, especially now with the jets coming out. Then I got to Chicago and I was flying co-pilot, but very soon I was flying captain. I flew the old piston airplanes for a little while and then I started working my way up—at the end, I wound up flying on the DC-10, a 289-passenger jet airplane. I loved it.

I had stayed about eleven years on a three-engine jet so I could be pretty senior. I loved the 727; it was a nice airplane. But then someone told me for retirement purposes you better get on a bigger airplane, so then I went to the DC-10 and I really enjoyed it. That 727, you could push the throttles up and roll down the runway to make the turn to line up, and then you'd take off. But with the 10, you couldn't do that; you had to line that thing up straight off because when you pushed the throttles up, it was going where it was pointed, with no turning at all. It would push you back in your seat, and I really liked that. But it turned out I had a close call on it. I took a flight from Chicago to Phoenix on a 10 and left it there, and brought another back to Chicago and went home and went to bed.

I got home at about six in the morning—it was a night flight. About noon my wife woke me up, and she said, 'You've got to get up and see the TV!'

I went in there, and a DC-10 airplane had crashed on takeoff at O'Hare Airport, killing everyone on board.[22] Worst accident they had ever had.

I looked at it, and I said, 'That's the airplane I flew last night to Phoenix!'

Now I had brought a different plane back. And shortly after that, the phone rang, and it was the chief pilot, and he said, 'Guess what!'

I said, 'I know, I flew that airplane last night!'

He said, 'I just have one question: What kind of landing did you have last night?' You see, right off the start they have to try to nail it to somebody.

I said, 'You call the co-pilot and ask him.'

The co-pilot was a young fella, and he had flown with me a lot on the 727, but never on the 10. We were coming in to Phoenix [on that same plane], and I thought, 'I better show this young fella something,' and I touched down and we never even felt the tires touch, we never even heard them.

He looked over and said, 'You can really slick them on with the 10 too, can't you?'

---

[22] *crashed on takeoff at O'Hare Airport, killing everyone on board*- On May 25, 1979, American Airlines Flight 191 from Chicago to Los Angeles crashed moments after takeoff, killing all 271 on board and 2 persons on the ground. It remains the deadliest aviation accident in U.S. history.

So that eliminated [any theory that the previous pilot had anything to do with the problem]. It turned out there were thirty-something airplanes with the same problem. The engine just broke off, but instead of just breaking off and falling to the ground, it broke off under power, and it came up over the leading edge of the wing, and tore off the lift devices, so the left wing quit flying and the right wing was still flying, and it [careened over and crashed right after takeoff]. The amazing thing is it could have happened on that airplane at any time, and I don't know why it didn't happen when I flew it. But it made me wonder if that had happened to me, what would I have done? I think I probably would have done better than they did. I had a really good chief pilot early on in [my airline career], and he always said, 'If you get in trouble, you don't worry about the trouble; fly the airplane.' The captain was rated as one of the best. He might have been trying to figure out what was going wrong, when he should have been making sure the airplane was flying properly. There was just no procedure at all for what happened; they also pulled the nose up, and let the airspeed back, following a different emergency procedure, but if they had kept the speed they had already, it might not have gone so quick.[23]

Earl Morrow in the author's classroom, May 2011.
Credit: Robert H. Miller

My time in the service was the smartest move I ever made.

To be frank with you, I was flunking out of college. I got to see the wheels turn; this thing opened

---

[23] *There was just no procedure at all for what happened* - In researching this incident, one of the worst aviation disasters in U.S. history, the author discovered that the lead federal investigator at the Chicago crash site was none other than Elwood P. Driver, a former Tuskegee Airman who flew with Clarence Dart, who is profiled in the sequel to this book. Mr. Dart and Mr. Driver appear together in a wartime photograph there; after the war, Mr. Dart and Mr. Morrow were great friends. *"Tuskegee Airman Heads Chicago Crash Site Probe,"* *Jet Magazine*, June 17, 1979.

up and I didn't figure I would ever make it, but I applied for it, and I made it—out of thirty-something of us who went in, I made it. And I couldn't have had a better job after I got back home. It was just never boring when I was flying. I had a little motto: 'If I don't learn something today, I'm going to quit flying.' And I never had to quit flying, because I was always learning something.

CHAPTER NINE

The Extra Gunner

We first met Richard Alagna in Chapter Six. Here, he brings us up-to-date on his later duties and adventures near the end of the war. He told me that his ball turret gunner days ended when they decided at some point to take the ball turret out of his B-24 completely.

'Did you know the ball turret was adding about a thousand pounds to the weight and drag on the airplane? Manned with a gunner like me, about 1,200 pounds. So they took it out and I became an extra gunner.'

Richard G. Alagna

'Dropped Into An Insane Asylum'

I think this brings us up to when we're going to go overseas and to show you the mentality of my flying officer. We were about to go over by ship and we had an opportunity to go home—we were in New Jersey, I don't know what port it was—and he volunteered his crew for KP duty. Nobody else would have done a thing like that but a first-class rat. We all had a chance to go home, call your mother or your girlfriend, but he volunteered us for KP. We did not become sergeants until we were overseas so therefore we could pull KP.

On the ship going over I wrenched my back very badly and I couldn't bend over at all. I went to the medics and they taped me up; they put tape from here [*points to upper chest*] down to my belly button and tied me up. There was no fresh water on the boat to shower, only salt water. When we were in the Irish Sea, we were on the top deck of this luxury liner and we're all standing there looking at the Irish Sea, and everybody screamed, 'Fighters coming in!' and they all fell to the deck. I couldn't move because I was taped. I wasn't mesmerized—the only way I could fall would be to fall on my ass or flat on my face. Before they skimmed by, I said, 'Three Spitfires,' and they thought that was wonderful, what tremendous aircraft recognition this kid had.

So now we're overseas and I'm all taped up and I'm itchy. We get off and we're in England, and we go to a place where we're going to be assigned to a squadron. I'm desperate because I can't get at this tape. You must also remember that I was issued a .45; a lot of people wondered about that, because in the Pacific I understand crew members were issued shotguns or carbines, but I was issued a .45 sidearm. As soon as we got to base and we dumped our bags, I immediately went to sick call. You have to picture it: I had on a flight jacket and I had a .45 under my armpit.

I go in and I said to the corporal, 'I just got here. I didn't have time to sign the sick book, but I really have to see the doctor. I've got to get rid of this tape; it's driving me crazy.'

He said, 'Don't worry, I'll get you in.'

I heard a voice say, 'Are there any more? No? That's it, nobody else on the sick book.'

'No, sir, we have one more man out there.'

This is what this officer and gentleman says: 'I don't care if he has appendicitis; if he hasn't signed the sick book, I'm not seeing him.'

He stepped out of the office, and I said, 'You son-of-a-bitch, they told me that when I got overseas, you guys were going to lighten up a little bit. I wouldn't let you touch me with a ten-foot pole!' He wasn't being shot at; he was in England. He was taking care of guys who had colds, athlete's foot, et cetera; I don't know what his problem was. Well, my jacket was open and his mouth was agape; I think he saw the .45. I was slightly beyond the edge at that moment.

The corporal was dumbfounded, and I turned around and walked out. Nobody came after me.

I went back to where I was billeted, and I said, 'I think I'm going to be arrested,' because that's what they do to people—you don't yell at officers.

A nice kid from Brooklyn said, 'Don't worry, you stay here in the barracks. I'll bring you food; you'll stay hidden.'

I said, 'But the tape!'

He said, 'Come with me,' and we went into the shower. He grabbed the tape, he took off every hair on my chest, on my back, and then I managed to get some sleep.

*

Now here comes more fun and games, and this is an important one. We end up in the 445th Bomb Group, 700th Squadron. The very first night we get there, I honestly thought I had been dropped into an insane asylum. The crew that had been there had been wiped out, and these fellows were absolutely bonkers, at least that was my impression. One fellow had a bolt from a .50 caliber machine gun, and he slipped a .50 caliber bullet in the facing, and he had a hammer and he's going to hit it. When you do something like that, it's going to explode, the whole thing is going to rupture, and you're going to be in trouble. It didn't explode, but the slug went into the door. I didn't know that he took all the stuff out of the thing; it was a gag.

They also had set up a guy that would come in the door, and just before he'd come in, some guy would throw a knife and it would hit the door. I turned to one of my fellow gunners and said, 'I think they're going to kill me before the Germans do.'

Later they told us that it was sort of like an initiation to their barracks. I had never belonged to Greek societies or anything like that; I vowed that I would get my revenge.

After being there some time and flying quite a number of missions and being slightly insane, I took a belt of .50 caliber machine gun rounds; there must have been about twelve of them in metal links. I pulled all of the cordite out of them, but I kept the caps and I put back the slugs. I had it draped over my bed as a souvenir. I have Romanian and Sicilian blood coursing through my veins, and we all believe in getting revenge.

They were playing poker. It was the afternoon and nobody was flying; it was raining like hell. I went through my act, 'I'm too young to die'—it was a pretty good act. They're playing poker and paying no attention to me.

I said, 'I can't stand it, it's driving me crazy, sooner or later it's going to kill me, I'm dying' of this and that.

Somebody said, 'Shut up!' I took the ammo, walked over to the potbelly stove, said, 'To hell with all of you,' and I dropped it into the stove.

Well, one guy went through the window and into the mud, into the rain. [*Laughs*] Guys hit the doors, they went all over, and I'm standing there screaming, 'What did I do, what did I do?!' All it did was go pop-pop-pop, and fortunately none of the slugs went through the stove. They chased me and threw mud pies at me, but I didn't care because I got my revenge. [*Laughs*]

We used to play poker, and when they played poker, the guys would sit with their cards up close. We would steal—'take home,' let's put it that way— the Very pistol cartridges; we didn't sell them to anybody. It goes in a Very pistol—it's a flare gun, the flares would either be red-red, red-green, whatever colors, and we'd snap off the shotgun shell part and I'd roll it up in newspaper, and we'd feed the fire. When they're playing poker, we'd just drop it in and suddenly the entire barracks room would turn full of red smoke, green smoke. When it cleared, [they would still be sitting there] with their hands on the cards and the money; it was hilarious. One hand was always on the cards, the other was always on the money, because we were all conditioned to this gag. Gags, there were quite a few. When we'd go to the latrine at night, we'd take a Very pistol out, load it, and fire it. The MPs would come, and they'd say, 'Who did that?'

We'd say, 'The guys over there,' and they would roust those guys and give them hell. [*Laughs*]

The 'ground-pounders,' the ground personnel, disliked us immensely. They had a perpetual hate because we made more money than they did. I was a staff sergeant and I made the equivalency in pay of a captain. Overseas pay, flight pay, and we threw our money around like it didn't matter for the simple reason that the next morning you might be eating sauerbraten someplace. There was [one of them] who I hated, a guy who came up after a mission and said, 'Thank God you got back!'

He was an armorer. I never heard anybody say, 'Thank God you came back.' I was really quite thrilled.

I said, 'That's very nice of you.' Now he was going to take out the guns and do the dirty work in the plane.

Then he said, 'Because I left my coffee cup in your plane and I couldn't get a cup of coffee.'

Aborted Missions

Let me tell you the story about the oranges. An aborted mission means they send you back, something happened, somebody changed their mind. We went to the briefing, then we went to breakfast, and they came in and said the mission was aborted. That was very good, marvelous, and all hell broke loose in the mess hall. As we were very privileged, we did get fresh eggs, I think, and good meat and all that nonsense. We got oranges. They started to throw the oranges around. I grew up during the Depression and I didn't think that was funny. They had just gone bonkers. I kept picking up the oranges that weren't spoiled, and I had a gas mask kit that the first thing I did when we got to England was throw the gas mask away and put my underwear and socks in and use for an overnight bag. I stuffed it full of oranges. When you weren't flying, there was nothing to do. The only duty that we had would be at night, to guard your airplane— they would trust us for that—but we had no KP and we didn't pull guard duty other than on the plane. I went back and I got into my Class A uniform and I went to town. I changed trains at

Ipswich and went to Norwich, which was a delight because I liked old things and castles and to go around and see things. I figured I'd spend the day at Norwich, have dinner there, and then come back. I took the oranges and I got off the train, and I'm there on a corner and I called the little kids over. The kids always wanted chewing gum and chocolate and cigarettes, and they wouldn't take the cigarettes that we got for free; they wanted the good cigarettes. The English didn't have oranges or any kind of citrus; we didn't bring in anything for the English. I'm nineteen or twenty, and I'm giving away oranges, and a woman comes out of a house with an umbrella and she starts to beat me with it! My mother always said you never ever hit a woman; you can restrain a woman, but you never hit her. I ran into a pub and I'm out of breath, and guys there are laughing, and I said, 'What did I do wrong?'

An Englishman said to me, 'She thought you were a dirty old man.' I didn't know what a 'dirty old man' was, and when they explained it to me, I was furious, and that time I came close to hitting a woman. I didn't think it was funny that she would accuse me of something like that.

Another time, we were in the air and they aborted that mission. It was a bad one to begin with because planes were running into one another. We didn't see the planes hit; you just saw the big explosion, you saw the big red, you felt the vibration. We took off in fog, and you got up to six thousand fog, ten thousand fog, twelve thousand fog; you're going up there and there's nothing but fog. And then it wasn't fog anymore, it was contrails. We had to form on the flares, the flare color. That's when I discovered all the fun things we did with flares. That's also when we found out that our nose gunner was colorblind. [*Laughs*] He had joined the Air Corps because he figured he would not have to worry about mixing up the color of friendly and enemy uniforms.

So the pilot was pretty smart. He was a good pilot, he was just not a nice person. He decided that we'll fly around, burn up gasoline and do whatever we have to do with the bombs, [and return home]. So we're flying around in the North Sea all by ourselves and the navigator is getting upset, and rightfully so, because the fighters are going to pick up a single aircraft and you're a dead goose. So he sees a bastard squadron—we all had different tail markings, and you could tell from the tail markings that these guys were doing the same thing; they had the smarts to say let's stay together. He tacks on and the navigator was still pretty bright.

He said, 'What if it's a German weather ship?'

Sometimes when B-24s went down, they didn't always break up completely and some of them were actually captured with just the landing gear broken. They would rebuild them, fly them up, and try to infiltrate our squadrons. They would find out where we're going, listen to the conversation. You'd just be stuck because if this was a German leading us around on a merry goose chase, we're in deep trouble. He goes up front, writes down all the data on the guy's tail, all that crap. I think they talked to one another with something or other. He said we're going to pull the pins on the bombs. So we went into the bomb bays—you had to take the cotter pins out of the bombs. Then all hell broke loose. The place turned into a shooting gallery, and we were hit and we dropped our bomb. We didn't know who we hit, what poor stupid bastard on the ground was so upset that he decided to fire. If he didn't fire at us, we wouldn't have dropped the bomb. Our pilot was very upset because he wanted to be, and he did eventually become, a lead pilot. He wanted a promotion so badly.

Anyway, we get back and all the other members of our squadron had gotten back much earlier. We come back, one engine's out, all kinds of holes in the plane, the crew chief is mad as hell because he would rather we'd gone down so that he wouldn't have to repair the plane. It's true, that's the way the guy felt, that's what he said: 'Look what you did to my plane—do you know how many hours I'm going to be working on this?!'

I wanted to kick his butt. Now you have to understand that I'm dead, and I go back to our barracks and everything is gone. The bedding is gone, my footlocker is gone, my shirts, pants, my stuff that's hung up—everything gone. What's going on? It seems that the practice was that when a crew went down, they immediately took the footlocker because they were going to send things home to the families and they would go through it to make sure there wasn't anything in it that would upset a wife—girlie pictures, whatever some idiot might have in his footlocker. Everything was fine; I got everything back except my tunic. There were no tunics to be had on my base. This is old Catch-22 again—you can't get off the base unless you were in a Class A uniform. You can't get a Class A uniform because they don't have any, right? If I could get off the base, I could buy one, because the English had these Army-Navy shops, and I could go in and for 30 to 40 bucks I could get another jacket, but I can't get off the base. I was very upset.

Along comes a guy with my jacket on. I could tell my jacket because I could not sew, couldn't do any of those girl things. I was actually the worst soldier in the world; I would take cotter pins and put the buttons on with cotter pins and hide it so no one would see it. I had a special pair of silver wings that I had bought, a little fancier than what the other guys had because I thought it was kind of cute. Also, the jacket had my name stenciled in the back with my serial number.

I said, 'That's my jacket!'

He said, 'But it fits me.' It was an invitation to a fight; he wanted me to fight him for my jacket.

I just looked at this guy. I put my hand in my jacket, pulled out my .45, pointed it right at him, and I said to him in a very nice, calm voice, 'On the jacket is a marksmanship medal for the .45. I'm going to cock it, I'm going to take the safety off, and I'm going to shoot you, and I'm not going to get any blood on the jacket.' I had it pointed just where the jacket ended. He took the jacket off immediately, threw it down, and away he went.

I've been asked by many guys would I have shot him. I think I would have. I honestly think, at that point, after the aggravation I had that day, that this clown is stealing something that belongs to me right in front of me and he wants me to punch him in the nose, I think I would have shot him.

Somebody said, 'Why didn't you call an MP?'

I said, 'I never called a cop in my life.' When I was a kid, the cops used to hit us with billies, make us move, because we were playing stickball or we were disruptive or we were too noisy or this or that.

*

I became an extra gunner. My pilot did some silly things but he got away with them. They promoted him; he was a good flyer. The tail gunner went, I went, the engineer went, everybody off the crew went, and he got other personnel to train him to be a lead pilot. I'm doing nothing now. I'm without a crew, walking around, having fun. I could do anything I want, but I couldn't go home until I finished my tour. It's driving me slightly crazy. The war was coming to an end and I wasn't going to see it, but I really did love to fly.

An Old Friend

Let me tell you about meeting an old friend. I had a buddy who was in the infantry and he got lucky. Just before going to France, they discovered he had flat feet. Just like the Army, [they all of a sudden] discover you only have one leg or something like that. They had him at a repo depot someplace in England.[24] I wrote to him, he wrote to me, I didn't know where he was, he didn't know where I was, and I'm not supposed to tell him

---

[24] *repo depot*-replacement depot located near the battle fronts, so that individual soldiers could be sent to infantry companies to replace the men who became casualties.

where I am because God forbid the Germans would find out, although the Germans knew exactly where we were every minute of the day. Every night before a mission the Germans would tell us where we were going [before we were even briefed]. That was very nice, I enjoyed that immensely. We'd go into a room with MPs and a screen and they'd lock the door, just like in the movies, and then they'd pull it up and you'd find out what the mission is for the day—except I knew what the mission was for the day because the German with the best jazz program told me where we were going. [*Imitates radio broadcaster*] 'The 445th, you will be our guests,' blah, blah, blah. The cook knew where we were going; the guys in the hallway knew where we were going.

Getting back to my friend, I wanted to find my friend. I went to London, to headquarters, which was a mistake. All I wanted was for them to tell me where my old buddy was. I got into headquarters and when I told them what I wanted, they threw me through the door, they literally kicked me out. They told me I was insane and that the Army doesn't function that way.

So using what knowledge I had, I had an officer un-censor my letter. I go to him and I [had written], 'Sal, I'm at this base, I'm at this telephone number. You can reach me, that's where my squadron is. Kindly tell me where you are.' This officer was nice enough. He said, 'You're absolutely right, it's stupid,' and he signed it and stamped it. It went V-Mail all the way to the States and all the way back again. Sal finally got it. He phoned me, and I got on a train because I had all the time in the world, because by that time I was an extra gunner. I went to see him, and he was in a repo depot, which means all these poor guys who had gotten broken up had to be rehabilitated and reassigned, things like that.

I said, 'Get on your Class A's, let's get out of here and have dinner.'

He said, 'The food here is better than the food in town.' It was hospital food but it was beautiful food.

I saw some guys in black uniforms; I didn't like the black. We were told if you got shot down, you didn't surrender to anybody but a guy in a green uniform, never to a man in a black uniform—they were the SS and they were bad news. So we're sitting at this table having coffee, and I said, 'Who are those people?'

He said, 'They're ex-paratroopers that are broken up, and they're here training everybody to get them in shape, and they wear these black gym suits.'

Then I said in a very loud voice, 'You mean that stupid son-of-a-bitch over there is an ex-paratrooper, the one with the big nose? That god-awful-looking piece of shit?'

My friend Sal is now going crazy, he says, 'He's going to hear you!'

I said, 'I want him to hear me!'

The guy came over. It was a kid I knew from grade school, and we hugged each other and we all had coffee and laughed. He had jumped the day before D-Day, when they put guys on the ground.

Guard Duty

We're in England and we're in the war. I think I told you that you had to pull duty by taking care of the airplanes at night just before they took off; that was the only duty you had to do. One time I was called to do it, and it was cold and wet and I was very tired, and I had been carousing and I couldn't keep my eyes open. I knew that if you fell asleep you could be court-martialed. It wasn't very nice to fall asleep because the Germans were doing very nasty things. They were dropping paratroopers down, espionage kind of guys, and they would drop fountain pens into our airplanes. They looked like fountain pens but they were altimeter bombs, so that when the bombers got up to a certain altitude this thing would explode and the plane would go down. It was a very good method. We had to make sure nobody got near the planes. I broke into an escape kit and I took out the stay-awake pill. When you were shot down you had certain things in this thing. You had morphine, which was never there, and you had other stuff, and you had this pill. I guess it's what the kids use in college to stay awake, but this was a super pill because this was supposed to make you feel like Superman. I did not want to be court-martialed so I took the pill, took some water, and I felt great. I'd never taken drugs in my life, but this was marvelous. They told me they weren't going to come for the plane until 4:00 or 5:00 in the morning, and wouldn't you know it, at 2:00 in the morning they come over and they say, 'You can leave now.' I asked why and they said they had changed the mission to something else. I went back to my barracks and I put my head on the pillow. I closed my eyes and it was like when you snap a window [shade] up, it rolls up. I couldn't keep my eyelids closed; my eyelids would not close. Around 4:00 that afternoon it was like somebody hit me with a baseball bat; I just collapsed. That was a great pill.

Sergeant Grayboy

Going back, we took off on a mission to Berlin. Berlin's a nasty place to go; it had a bad reputation. We were the first wave over wherever the hell we were going, the target area. It's a long, long flight, and when you flew in those planes you got down on the ground, and you always knew who flew that day, because they would be shouting, everybody had to shout. Nobody could hear, your hearing had gone. Those engines—you were eight hours, maybe nine hours, who knew how long you were in the plane.

This guy runs up to me and says, 'You were in the first wave, how many went down?'

I said, 'We were lucky, they caught hell behind us.'

Well, he cursed like a son-of-a-bitch—he had the book on us, he was running a pool. This was Sergeant Grayboy, my buddy, one of my favorite friends. Sergeant Grayboy would book on anything.

Now, Grayboy—he was into black market, he was into everything—he had a beautiful leather jacket. I never got a leather jacket, I'm a deprived person. We had a deal. He wanted my camera, which I wouldn't sell him—oh, the camera story...

When you were flying, when planes got hit, guys would bail out. They would want to know how many guys got bailed out, but everybody had a different count so taking a photograph was rather important. Photography was very strong with me, and I picked up this K-20 camera, like a Speed Graphic, and I took some beautiful pictures. When we came down from the mission, I went to the photographic unit. I knocked on the door, wanted to see my pictures. They said it was classified.

I said, 'What are you talking about, I took the pictures, I want to see how they came out!'

He said, 'Sergeant, if you don't go away, we're calling the MPs.'

I'm banging on the door, I want to see my pictures, I don't see anything wrong with just looking at them—give me one little snapshot for a souvenir. Under the threat of calling the MPs, which I knew would be trouble, they gave me a batch of pictures and they sent me away, but none of the mission I flew!

Anyway, back to Grayboy and the camera. He wanted my camera; I wanted his jacket. We couldn't make a deal so we made an announcement in the barracks that if Grayboy got killed, I got the jacket, and if I went down, he got the camera.

One morning he went up to fly, and he had on the jacket and I told him to take it off.

He said, 'It's cold outside.'

I said, 'I don't give a goddamn, take the jacket off.' I made him take the jacket off and wear a sweater, because we had that deal!

Let me tell you the story about Grayboy and flying the last mission. Everybody wanted to go home, be a hero or whatever you want to call it. One night in bed, Grayboy slept in the bed next to me, and he was doing something I have never seen anybody do. He was putting out his cigarettes with his fingertips, and then he'd throw the cigarette down on the ground and light another one. He had plenty of cigarettes. He's lighting cigarettes and putting them out with his fingers.

I said to him, 'Grayboy, you've got a problem; you want to talk about this?'

He said, 'This is my last mission, this is it.'

I was a poor kid; he had money, he was into the black market, and he could get you anything you wanted. He wanted me to fly his last mission.

We had different deals; I was an extra gunner, [with time on my hands]. You ask how could a guy do that? Well, it was very easy. When somebody was sick and you were flying their mission, your name is Grayboy, mine is Alagna, so they know on the roster that Sergeant Alagna is to fly in Tom Jones' plane. Or you'd show up and you had your helmet on, you had your goggles on the top of your head, the pilot never saw you before; this is wild, dark, and wooly. All he wanted was a body at a machine gun or in a turret. When I come back, he gets the credit and I get the money, so yes, it was done. How many times it was done, I have no idea, but it was done.

I'm sitting there with Grayboy and I said, 'I'm not afraid of flying and I don't think I'm going to get killed. If I thought I was going to get killed, I'd stop flying.' It was a voluntary thing, and if you really wanted to get out of it without going through any nonsense, just walk into headquarters and punch the officer right in the mouth. You want a nice place to eat and sleep where it's nice and safe? They give you a nice little cage. You just walk in and pop him in the nose. And they say, what did you do that for? And you say, 'I don't know, just don't like officers.' The MPs will take you away.

I said to him, 'I don't think I want to fly your last mission because I really don't know if I'm going to have to bail out,' which I didn't look forward to, ever. If I had to bail out and I float down to Germany, they're not going to look lightly upon me. I'm not a woodsy kind of guy; I'm not going to be able to run through the woods and eat the berries.

I would probably end up being in some stalag someplace.

'So now, Grayboy, think of this—I'm in a stalag somewhere, and you are now me. Being me, you have to fly the balance of my missions, you have to answer my mother's mail that's coming in, my girlfriend's mail that's coming in, and when the war is over and they come and get me out of that prison, do you honestly think they're going to give me a hero's welcome? I will be AWOL, as simple as that. I'll go from a German prison to an American prison, for a couple of bucks. I won't do it.'

He got on the plane. I put him on the plane with a bottle of Scotch. He was drunk; he flew his last mission. He was as nutty as a fruitcake.

Patches

Let me tell you about my time on Patches. There was a plane called 'Patches,' and they should have made a memorial to that plane. They renamed it 'Patches' because it had literally over 100 flak holes in it. It flew at a tilt, which was funny. It sounds silly but it seemed like one of the wings went just slightly out of tilt. If you managed to get Patches, if Patches was assigned to you, you knew you were coming home. I flew home in that plane. Nobody's going to take that plane down, that was a good luck plane.

[When it was about time to come] home, before I got onto Patches, the adjutant officer in the squadron said I would fly with him and I would fly in the nose on the B-24. We didn't know where we were going to go—we had no idea whether we were going to go to India or we were going to go home—but they said we're going to have to do some navigational flights. I'm [going to be] flying in the nose, and first we're supposed to go up to the tip of Scotland, turn around, and come back and land. I'm in the nose, there's no more Germans—by the way, all the Nazis died, they disappeared, there wasn't a Nazi left in Germany. [*Joking*] I assure you, the United Nations knows this for a fact: they all went to Sweden. Anyway, something hit my eyes, sunlight. I was resting, I was probably asleep, nothing to do because there's nothing to see. I see sunlight, a rim of sunlight, and we're supposed to not be flying at night but up there it's always very bright. I look forward and I see nothing but water, look to my left, water, look to my right, water. We are no longer over Scotland. This I knew; you don't have to be a bright boy to know that Scotland is not inundated with water. This is the North Sea or the Atlantic Ocean or God-knows-what.

I turn my head around, and the navigator, I have no idea who he was—it wasn't my old navigator— he was sound asleep. True story, not a joke. In the B-24 from that angle, you could see up into where the pilot's and co-pilot's seats were, and both of them were out like this [*closes eyes, stretches legs*]; they were relaxed, they were asleep. Now the rest of the guys in the back, I don't know what the hell they were doing; they were playing cards or they were asleep, who knows what.

I put my hand to my throat mike, and I said in a very low, quiet, controlled voice, 'Hi, is there anybody in this aircraft that's awake? I don't want to upset anybody, but is there anybody in this aircraft...'

Then the fun started. The pilot yelled to the co-pilot, 'You were supposed to be flying, you were supposed to be.' They had it on 'George.' George is the automatic pilot, and we were flying out to God-knows-where. The navigator woke up, and they were yelling at one another, and I'm saying to myself, 'What a bunch of fuck-ups.' This, to me, wasn't practice, practice, practice; this was screw-up, screw-up, screw-up.

Now we get down on the ground, and I don't know how many days went by, but this [new] pilot said to me, 'Richard.' By the way, he was a decent guy, he called me Richard. He said, 'Richard, do you have a wife?'

I said, 'No, sir, I do not.'

'Do you have a real girlfriend that you want to get home to?' I'd only been overseas for a couple of months.

I said, 'No, I don't mind.'

And he said, 'Look, I've got a young pilot that is willing and who wants very much to fly the nose to come home; he's married, he wants to see his wife. I'll get you on somebody else's crew.' Because he was the adjutant, he could do all this paper-work.

I said, 'Okay, but please, no boats. I've had it with the boats, I don't want to go on another boat.'

He said, 'No, I'll get you on another crew.' And that's how I got onto Patches again.

Let's move ahead. I get home, I get fifteen or thirty days [furlough], and I get back to this airfield; the war is still going on in Japan. Some of my buddies came over, and they grabbed me and they said, 'How the hell did you get out?'

I said, 'Out of what?'

'The adjutant went down in the drink [in the other plane].'

I said, 'That's the way it goes, that's the way it goes.' So sometimes you get lucky.

Let me tell you one last thing. When I finally got home—not swimming the Atlantic—I was asked by a nice corporal, 'Sergeant, I have to ask you, would you like to fly against the Japanese?' I couldn't believe anybody would ever ask me that question, ever.

He said, 'Now you have enough combat hours, you don't have to fly against the Japanese.'

I said, 'Thank you very much, you've made my mother very happy. I would like very much to walk around in my Class A uniform with my ribbons, my wings, chase after all the girls that you've been chasing. That's what I want to do.'

Then I tried to get out of the Army, and that was next to impossible. The war was over, I wanted to go home. I did what I was supposed to do, I volunteered, it's over. Just send me home.

Martin Bezon, World War II.

CHAPTER TEN

The Radar Man

In researching this book, I came across Martin 'Hap' Bezon of Port Henry on Lake Champlain, just to the north of 'Hometown, USA,' and about 110 miles north of Albany, New York. Near here is a statue to Samuel De Champlain, who came down the lake from New France (Canada) in 1609. Martin's grandparents emigrated from Poland; little did he know that he would find himself unexpectedly there during the war, trying to convince advancing Red Army soldiers not to shoot him after he bailed out of his B-24 Liberator. This interview was given at his home in 2012 when he was ninety years old.

***

There is one man in particular who is supposed to know all there is to know about this equipment. Sometimes he does, but often he doesn't. And when the radio operator's deficiencies do not become apparent until the crew is in the combat zone, it is then too late. Too often the lives of pilots and crew are lost because the radio operator has accepted his responsibility indifferently.

Radio is a subject that cannot be learned in a day. It cannot be mastered in 6 weeks, but sufficient knowledge can be imparted to the radio man during his period of training in the United States if he is willing to study. It is imperative that you check your radio operator's ability to handle his job before taking him overseas as part of your crew. To do this you may have to check the various departments to find any weakness in the radio operator's training and proficiency and to aid the instructors in overcoming such weaknesses.

Training in the various phases of the heavy bomber program is designed to fit each member of the crew for the handling of his jobs. The radio operator will be required to:

Render position reports every 30 minutes.

Assist the navigator in taking fixes.

Keep the liaison and command sets properly tuned and in good operating order.

Maintain a log.

In addition to being a radio operator, the radio man is also a gunner. During periods of combat he will be required to leave his watch at the radio and take up his guns. The radio operator who cannot perform his job properly may be the weakest member of your crew--and the crew is no stronger than its weakest member.

—Duties and Responsibilities of the Airplane Commander and Crewmen, 1943[25]

***

---

[25] *Radio operator*-Marty Bezon qualified for many positions on the heavy bombers. Many of his duties outlined in this chapter parallel the expectations for the radio man, though much of his crew activity centered on the radar set, duties which were still highly classified.

Martin F. Bezon

'The Black Cloud Arrived'

I was born on November 8, 1921, here in Port Henry. As a matter of fact, the house that used to be at the foot of this hill is where I was born. I attended the Champlain Academy Parochial School kindergarten through eighth grade, and I went to the Port Henry High School and I graduated from there in June of 1941.

I went to work for Republic Steel. I had hopes of stepping out in the world and getting a better job, but this job was available. So, we started working at fifty-five cents an hour, but come December the 7th of the same year—'41—the black cloud [arrived]; the Japs attacked us at Pearl Harbor and it changed my whole life around.

I was walking up to the village and somebody stopped and said the Japanese attacked Pearl Harbor. The full force of that didn't hit me yet, but I got home and got the news and all that, and I realized that it wouldn't be long before we'd get in the war too. As a matter of fact, it was the next day that Roosevelt [asked Congress to] declare war.

So I waited a little bit, then I went to Albany to enlist and I joined the Marine Corps. They said okay, they'll accept us—there were three of us there—but we have to get home and have my folks sign some papers.

I was still seventeen, too young. I came home and found my father sick. My mother was alone and my brother was in the third year of high school here, and the doctor says, 'No way are you going to the service yet, because the responsibility of the entire family is on your shoulders.' I tried to talk to my mother and the doctor, but they said no. So that fell through.

I waited and worked for Republic. Eventually, I just couldn't take no more and told my mother that I got to go in. In December, I went back to Albany and signed up because they dropped the requirements for the Army Air Force Cadet Program to high school graduate. There was no Air Force at the time, so it was the U.S. Army Air Force. This would be in '42. So, they gave me the physical and the complete tests like they did to everybody. I went down to join the Air Force, and they asked me, 'Are you anxious to get back in?'

I said, 'Yeah, I'll come back tomorrow. I just need to go home for a day.'

The sergeant said, 'All right, I'll give you some advice.' He says, 'We'll accept you as an Air Force reservist, and as soon as the cadet class opens up, they'll put a call out and they'll look into the reservists first.' He says, 'If you really want to get in quick, I'd advise you to get in on the next draft that you can and join the Army Service and get in the Army. When the call comes out for cadets, they will take the ones who are on active duty first.'

So I said, 'Oh gee, I'll do that.'

So as we left Albany, we didn't even come straight home. We stopped in Ticonderoga, because [for us] that's where the draft board main office was. We went into Mr. McLaughlin's office, and he looked up and said, 'What can I do for you boys?'

I said, 'We'd like to get into the next draft, sir.'

He said, 'Great, I need three more men.' He stamped three forms and said, 'Be back here tomorrow morning.'

So, the next day, I went back to Albany, and he said to tell them that you were a reservist in the Air

Force and that you wanted to join the Air Force. So, we got examined. They lined us up on the street and raised our right hand to take the oath of allegiance that we'd be in the Army. Then I didn't even have a chance to ask to be assigned to the Air Force. They just announced that anybody who wants to join the Air Force, to take one step forward. I stepped forward with a guy who later became my brother-in-law, but eventually he dropped out. He got a little leery of being up in the air so far.

I went in and went to Camp Upton at Long Island. I was there for about three days and shipped out of there to Camp Croft south of Spartanburg, South Carolina. I went through six weeks of basic and seven weeks of advanced training. They tried to keep me in as a sharpshooter, but I said, 'No, I'm waiting for the Air Force.' I had to wait a couple of weeks and then the call came out. I was happy that we were picked out of, I think, eight of us; before we left, three of the boys didn't pass. So three of us did go from Camp Croft to Nashville, Tennessee. We had one week of written tests and one week of physicals. I was accepted into the cadet program then. There were just two of us left.

'As Long As I Fly'

Even though I qualified for pilot and navigator, I was asked to be a bombardier; they needed bombardiers badly. They were building a huge armada of bombers and they said they were getting ready to just bomb Germany off the face of the map. So I said, 'It makes no difference as long as I fly.' They promised when I put in a tour and came back that they would put me into pilot school.

We wound up training and went to Santa Ana, California, for preflight. They had our curtains closed [on the train] because they said we were too valuable; we were the cream of the crop that they could pick. We weren't allowed to raise the curtains on the train until we got way out around Arizona out in the desert. Then we headed north. Everybody was guessing where we were going. We were headed northeast rather than west; we were going to Chicago or something. Nope. Then we headed south and then headed back east. We crisscrossed the country that way until we got out to Arizona. Then the officer in charge comes through and raised curtains now and said, 'You guys are going to Santa Ana, California, for pre-flight.' I remember that there was quite a 'whoop.' They all liked that idea. So we went to training up there.

I think it was about six weeks. I remember a sergeant coming in the barracks one time and he said, 'How many people have never flown in a plane?' I thought I was going to be embarrassed that I would be the only one standing, but quite a few of them stood up. So, we all got a ride in a plane to get the feel of it.

On weekends, we went to Hollywood, Los Angeles, and Long Beach. Every Friday night there used to be about fifty buses outside the gate to take the cadets wherever they wanted to go.

When we finished preflight, we were sent to Kingman, Arizona, for air-to-air gunnery. That was a seven-week course out in the desert. You had to shoot the .50 caliber machine guns way up in the air. You can imagine how far those projectiles would go.

We had different types of training. We had a huge screen coming over for a machine gun that fired only BBs. There were thousands of BBs falling back, and they would just put them back in. Then you would have planes going across and you would try to hit them. Then we were on the shotgun range every day. We had to fire fifty rounds of 12-gauge shotgun at clay pigeons going through the air—some going one way and some the other. That, I loved too.

The final week, we had to fire from the back side of a pickup truck. The guy shooting was tied down so he wouldn't fall, and you had two men with you. So, as you went around the track at, I believe, 30 miles per hour, they had underground cement places that they made with the front secure so you couldn't get hurt or anything. It had a small slit in it, and you looked through the slit. When you see a truck coming and hit a certain spot, you just lean back and pull the thing there, which throws it out. You had to work that for the other crews that came on. It was hard to hit with you moving, with the target coming at you and going away from you— going to the right and going to the left, going straight up. If you got six or seven hits you were lucky.

But the last day, I don't know what happened. I couldn't miss—just couldn't miss. I know a lot of the boys from the city, they didn't know how to fire a weapon, so they used to keep it loose [to their shoulder]. When that recoiled, it would hit them, so they were black and blue all over the arm and the chest. This one guy, he couldn't fire anymore, his shoulder hurt so bad. You're not supposed to do that. So, I fired mine. I couldn't believe it. I think I got 21 out of 25. We got through with gunnery, passed, and got the certificate as 'air-to-air' gunners, and then we were given a seven-day furlough.

We headed down to Albuquerque, New Mexico. We got our advanced bombardier course. There we learned all about the Norden bombsight.[26] We

---

[26] *Norden bombsight*-The physics involved in dropping a bomb from thousands of feet to hit a target on the ground are astoundingly complicated. Carl Norden, a Swiss-born engineer, developed a 50 lb. analog computer that was so valued by the U.S. military that it invested 1.5 billion in 1940 dollars in it (for comparison, the Manhattan Project came in at around 3 billion). Bombardiers went to school for months to learn how to use it; it was installed in the bombers under armed guard and set to self-destruct upon the crashing of the aircraft. Unfortunately, its accuracy was highly questionable, given all of the combat conditions and high altitudes; the bombardier

learned everything about the ins and outs, and made our practice runs. We flew AT-8s on a bombing run. I had a close call there. We did have one man killed. One of our cadets was killed on training. A couple had to bail out.

After we got through and everything was good, we had time on our hands. The pilots liked to fly up through the canyons. One time we saw one plane coming out while we're going in. We had enough room, but in the planes you don't know. So, as they were ready to pass, they both flipped over and flew by. It turned out good—no problem.

We enjoyed our weekends in Albuquerque. Sunday, we had to come back, because every Sunday they had a huge parade and everybody on that base had to be in that parade, even the KPs, no matter who it was. If you were on toward the tail end of the parade, you had to stand out there for a few hours, just standing [at attention] for your turn to go. It took that long—at least two hours before the last few would get to march. Whoever was picked the best would get an afternoon off to go to town at twelve noon the next Friday instead of five

---

also had to be able to visually sight the target. See www.ted.com/talks/malcolm_gladwell, for an interesting discussion.

o'clock. Finally, we got close one day; we felt we were going to make it. We came out there and everything was good. Then they gave 'eyes right' and we did, but there was a little Italian guy who had a little bit too much to drink the night before. He snapped his head right and his hat flew off and he stooped to pick it up. They gave us a good mark, but it kicked us out of first place! But we graduated—graduated as 2nd lieutenants. This was January of '44.

*

We were sent to a place called Boca Raton, Drew Field in Florida. It was on the east coast of Florida near Tampa. As a matter of fact, we used to live on the spring training grounds for the Cincinnati Reds; we had our tent pitched on second base.

We flew missions. A bunch of bombardiers came in, a bunch of navigators and a bunch of pilots, and they formed crews—our crews that we were going to go into combat with. I ended up with Lt. Tuttle as pilot and Lt. Burkes as co-pilot. We had a good crew. Then there is Zielinski and

Donovan. We were really like a family and blended together good.

'Who's Our Navigator?'

The first [training] mission, we didn't have a navigator, and I looked up on the board and we had a navigational mission that night. We had to take off at midnight. I went back to the pilot and said, 'Bob, I think we got a navigator.'

He said, 'How come?'

I said, 'Because we're going on a navigation mission.'

We went up to the instructor there and said, 'Who's our navigator?'

He said, 'What crew?'

I said, '92.'

'You don't have a navigator,' he said.

I said, 'But we've got a navigation mission.'

He said, 'Who's your bombardier?'

I said, 'I am.'

He said, 'You'd better know what navigation to learn because you're the navigator.'

I said, 'Oh boy.'

So, we had to fly from Tampa over to just below Miami, I'd say 20 miles. You could see it all lit up, and then out in the ocean, out there 50 miles or so, the land disappeared. I had to head north in pitch darkness to a point where we'd turned a little bit north-northeast and we headed down toward the Alabama area—the swamplands down through there in Florida, and then we had to go out into the Gulf of Mexico. From there we turned into our home base.

Where we were stationed, St. Petersburg was not too far away, and they had a long bridge there—I think it was the Gandy Bridge—and way off in the distance as dawn was breaking, you could see that string of lights. So Tuttle says, 'Marty, what's those lights ahead?'

I said, 'If that's not Gandy Bridge, we're lost.'

So we landed right on course and I felt pretty good since it was the first [navigation training] mission, and we did that good on it. But we had some trouble on the bombing runs—it was B-17s that we were flying; we were dropping bombs. No matter what I did, I followed all procedures and did everything we were supposed to do to make the bomb run, but the bombs wouldn't leave. I think it was about three missions we wasted where we never could get the bombs off.

I remember the co-pilot was getting a little grumpy about it. They were short of instructors, and we were one of the few crews that never had an instructor. They take you out of an AT-6 and put you into a B-17, which was quite a difference. They finally gave us this one plane, and we went up night bombing. We had to fly to Orlando, Florida, and the targets were all around Orlando. My job was to call the station as soon as we reached the area. They taught me how to do that, and they would say, 'Bezon, ask permission for bombing the target'—you couldn't go on a target until they gave you permission and told you which one. They would have to tell you what elevation so you wouldn't be on the same elevation as some other plane; the planes going around the target would be pretty close to each other at times. There was one time the pilot happened to go down to see if there was a broken wire or something. I didn't realize that and looked ahead of me a few miles. I saw lights, and when I looked up, I said to myself, 'Holy

Jesus, where the heck am I? What position?' I see the lights below me, and that's a plane coming. He kept coming head-on, and as all pilots know, standard operational procedure they follow—that no matter how distant, even 10 miles away, you need to make a left diving turn, both of you, so you go away from each other. I'm waiting for him to make the turn, and I look and he's getting a lot closer. I'm looking and thought I can't make it now, so I grabbed my parachute and put it on, which was foolish, because if we were going to hit then we're not going to have time to parachute. In the meantime, somebody there woke up, and they did the dive but didn't flare off to the left. So him and I are still coming right together, and it was close. At the last minute the pilot was underneath us and saw our plane, and he revved it right up. I could see that plane. It was closer than that wall [*points to wall in room*]; we went belly-to-belly. So it shook us up, because in just a matter of another few seconds we would have all been killed.

In the meantime, I'm over my bombsight and look up to see the lights down below, over here or over there. So I knew the plane was twisting around, but you don't realize it right away because they are not sharp turns.

So we landed, and the instructor came out and asked, 'What's the trouble?' And we told him.

He said, 'Get in the Jeep. Get another plane. You're getting back up.' He said, 'Don't land for six hours.'

We flew up with another load, and this time the plane worked good. I dropped the bombs quick—twenty of them, twenty runs. So I asked the pilot where we could go to get loaded up for twenty more. Like I said, we were two missions behind already. We landed again, and they loaded up quick, and I dropped 20, 40 bomb loads that day, and from then on, I had no problem.

*

We graduated from there and we're ready to go overseas. We went up to Langley Field, and they took me off the crew. I didn't know why, but they said, 'You'd be notified.' But then I noticed all of my buddies that were bombardiers from several of the crews. So there were about ten of us that knew each other, and we were all taken off, and the rest of our crews left.

We were taken into a church, and they used that for a hall. All of the officers had to be there. They said, 'You're here for a four-week course in radar, and after that, you are going to have two weeks' furlough. I am going to name all of the guys first who are going to start school, and then I'll name the guys who are going to go on furlough for two weeks first.' I wasn't in either group! So after they got through, I walked up to the front of the church and asked the sergeant, 'Sarge, you didn't read my name.'

He said, 'What is your name?'

So, I told him, 'Lt. Bezon.'

He said, 'You're going overseas right away.'

I was happy as heck. He put me with my buddy 'Broadway.' He and I went through everything all the way. They told us, 'They are out on Langley Field waiting for you.'

'The Last I Would See of My Mother'

So, we left. We didn't get in the training program there; we got to Langley Field. We were going to fly a brand-new B-17 over in a few days. We went out that night and partied up pretty good.

We had to take the plane for a thousand-mile hop. They named three places—one west, one down towards the south, the other up here near Burlington, Vermont, going right by the town here. So, I asked the pilot, if nobody has any choice, I'd like to make one. I said, 'How about going to Burlington?' I called up my mother on the phone and told her that I would be flying over Port Henry and we had permission to drop a little bit low. We could get down to ten thousand feet. I said that I would be in a little window in the middle of the plane, the waist, and I'll be waving a white flag. I said, 'I'll drop something from the airplane with a little white chute on it.'

I made a parachute out of some silk I found there and put a little gift for my mother in there and calculated the wind; I knew how to drop it. We were coming up and we flew across the bridge [over Lake Champlain, connecting New York to Vermont] and made a few circles. We dropped down over the village of Port Henry to about two thousand feet with the B-17—I see my mother! She is shading her eyes, looking up, waving, and I'm waving back. Then I threw the thing out and I saw that she got it. That was the last I would see of my mother for quite a while.

Then we flew around the bridge once more and I tried to get the pilot to go underneath the bridge. He said, 'Geez, Marty, we won't fit.' We had second thoughts and decided we better not, so we went to Burlington. Everything was good; everybody checked his position to make sure that nothing was wrong with it. That was the reason for the test flight [to Burlington].

The next day we took off for Bangor, Maine. We still didn't have a navigator; I was doing the navigation with my radar set. We got to Bangor, Maine, and stayed overnight and loaded up our plane with a bomb bay full of mail for the GIs overseas.

We took off the next day to Labrador—Goose Bay, Labrador. We had a near miss up there. They gave us a navigator; he'd never flown with us before. My orders were not to use the radar and to help the navigator. We started and got up to elevation and all of that and headed down across the ocean, to go across the ocean quite a long time before landfall would be seen. I went up and asked the navigator, 'What do you want me to help you do here?'

He said, 'Never mind, you're a bombardier. I don't need no help.'

I said, 'Okay, I'll be down in the radio room.' After I got thinking about it, I thought we'd been flying quite a while. We should have seen land.

I waited there and then I went back up and said, 'Are you sure you don't need help?'

'Nope, I don't need help.'

So, I told the pilot, Bill Tuttle, 'We should be seeing land somewhere. It seems like we've got quite a-ways to go from land yet.'

He said, 'Lower the radar set.'

I had to get the enlisted men to lower my scope. In the bottom of the ship, the scope hangs way down. Inside of it, it's a scope enclosed in this cylinder that they lower down. I warmed up my radar set; it takes five minutes for the first switch to go on. You wait five more minutes before you throw the primary in. [*Points to documents on his desk*]. If you see land, you see all of that light. Water, you see all black. When I send the pulse out, if it's water at 90 degrees, none of that comes back [to me];

that's always black. Over cities and ground and terrain and all of that, a lot of them come back to you. The rest go up. So, you could see well-lit areas. When you hit a city, about 75% or better of them come back at you. So, the city's much brighter. It's a great navigation tool. We never got lost.

He said to lower that down. So, they lowered it down. By the time they got it down there to about 15 minutes later I got it set. You have gradations on your picture and you can make these settings 10 miles, 50 miles, 100, 150, 200 miles.

I put it on 50 miles each and looked out 200 miles. There was nothing in sight but water. I finally went up to 500—nothing—and then 600. All I see is a boat out there 550 miles away from us. We were over 600 miles away from shore and we'd been flying too long!

I went back up to the pilot and said, 'Something's wrong. I can't get landfall.'

He said, 'Go up there and I'll call him on the speaker to let you look at what he's doing.'

So, I went up. In the meantime, the Air Force got a new type of compass. Flying over here [in the North Country], there is so much ore in these mines up here in the hills that the compass is off fifteen, sixteen degrees. If you don't realize it, you get lost flying around here. All over the world, there are these little deviations plus or minus. Up here in the Champlain Valley, it is high. The new compass that we got had a little furl nut on the side and a little window on the inside of the thing and you could preset the variation. Then you read the true heading. If you didn't use that, on our log, the first thing we would note is our observed heading. The next column down is deviation, and it was subtracted or added on to it. That's your true heading. If you don't use that, you could see how far off you're going.

I looked down and saw that he's got the fluxgate compass [an electromagnetic compass]. Good. I said, 'Let me see your log.'

He said, 'What's the matter?'

I said, 'What's the first column?'

He said, 'Heading.' I said, 'What's the second column?'

He said, 'My deviation.'

I said, 'What did you put it in the compass for? You've got it both places. You're going off 16 degrees since we left Goose Bay!'

We were way off course. I said, 'I am going to tell the pilot take it 270, give another heading.' So, I went up and told the pilot to take it 270 degrees, and to start praying.

We made it. The land came in, and we came in right on target. We landed, and the engines all conked out after we stopped—we couldn't even taxi to our revetment. As a matter of fact, we would have all died [if we had not seen land within those few minutes]. They got rid of him pretty quick when we got overseas.

Radar Man

From there we went from Goose Bay to Reykjavik, up in Iceland. We landed there and had something wrong with one of the engines, so we stayed there two or three days. Then we took off and headed down to England and landed there, and they took me off the crew again. I was sent to a one-month English radar school to learn their type of navigation and everything. I remember when we were first taking radar classes, they told us that if we ever say the word 'radar' in town, we would face a court-martial. It was very secretive. You had one classroom where you had to go through an MP. If you want to go from this classroom to the other one, there would be an MP just across the hall. You would have another MP checking you very close. The radar man was known as a 'Mickey operator,' 'H2X operator,' or 'Pathfinder.'

We arrived in England about July of '44. We were all stationed just outside of Norwich—all of the bases of the 2nd Division. I used to meet my buddy there every time I went into town; we went to the same pub. I don't think I ever got into trouble with anybody. I had an argument with one of the guys in the barracks but we settled it all up. That's the way we lived.

The Quonset huts were very cold huts, just a little metal inside and outside covering it. It had one stove in the middle. They would give you a quota of just so much coal. You would burn it up in a day or day and a half and then you were going to be cold for a while unless you could find wood, and where were you going to find wood in England?

So, you had to kind of conserve it. Toward the evening just before you go to bed, you just had to warm it up a bit. It was cold in the barracks. Somebody came up with the idea of taking the discarded oil from the oil changes on the airplane engines. They had barrels and barrels of it available. It took a certain amount of oil and a certain mixture of high-octane gasoline. We stirred it all up and put a can up near the top of the roof and piped it into the stove. Oh, that was good. We rigged one up and we had a red-hot stove all day, twenty-four hours a day. Then somebody put too much octane in one of them and it blew up, so they made us take them down. [*Laughs*]

*

We were assigned to the 466th Bomb Group in the 8th Air Force. I went up to headquarters the next day after I got settled down and asked if I could get on a plane and start flying my missions as quick as possible. I said that I'm a qualified navigator and qualified bombardier. I'm a qualified air-to-air gunner and I said that I would sure like to start 'em up. They said that they can't do it, that there was 'too much money spent on you radar guys'—that there was a lot of expense to train one of us. Then the officer said, 'Are you that anxious to start your missions?'

I said, 'Yes, I am.'

He said, 'The next group to us—the 467th—has a crew that is waiting for a radar man. Do you want to transfer?'

I said, 'Yes, I do.'

That was the first time Broadway and I split. I went over to the 467th and got on with [pilot] Bill Chapman and his crew and flew my missions with Chapman. We flew together until our 18th or 19th mission, when we got shot down.

What they would do is get these planes for radar men, planes that have proven themselves a little superior to the rest of them. They pick them out for lead planes, the first or second planes. They both are equipped identically alike, so if one gets knocked out, the other can take its place. So, they were all lead crews, and all lead crews were in the 791st Squadron of the 467th Bomb Group. And that's how I went into the 467th Bomb Group as a radar man in a lead plane.

I met the crew and all of that and we started our missions. I was not very happy with the navigation. With radar, you couldn't really navigate. You would see little spaces sometimes on the map with a small channel to go between two cities. On the way to a target, you would pass pretty close to the different cities or towns. They've got flak guns around a lot of them. They know the distance that the flak could reach us at the elevation we're flying. You can only be so far; if you get closer to them, they are going to reach you. If you head right between those areas, marked with the red, you were okay. There was one [corridor] that was very narrow, but [my crew] always liked to go through there because I always hit it dead center.

For our targets, the objectives were in different phases. First of all, it might be oil, and then we would only have oil production facilities as our targets. Next would be industrial, and we would bomb only industrial targets. So, I think there were three different phases that we went through. Later on it was some pinpoint bombing, like bombing a bridge going over some waterway.

They kept sending squadrons to a target until they finally blew it up.

The Buzz Bombs

The English wanted us to bomb to kill people, because [their cities had been attacked]. Then the Germans turned around, got the 'buzz bomb,' and started sending them over to England.[27] It was a great big bomb with wings and it had a motor on it. I remember the first day that I got to England, I was standing in line going in the movie house, I heard the 'bzzzz.' Everybody said a buzz bomb was coming. I didn't realize that we were the closest air base to where they launched the buzz bomb. Every buzz bomb went over our base, and if it kept going we didn't worry about it. But if it sputtered and stopped making noise, sometimes they keep going through the air, other times they would turn and come right down. When it stops, you head for the

---

[27] *buzz bomb*- In mid-June 1944, the Germans began launching a new type of weapon—a small, medium-range cruise missile—from bases in northern France, the Netherlands, and western Germany. It was the forerunner to the modern rocket; indeed, some of the German scientists involved in the program later worked on the U.S. space program. The loud noise that the primitive pulsejet engine of the V-1 ('Vengeance Weapon 1') made could be heard approaching from more than ten miles away. See www.museumofflight.org/Exhibits/fieseler-fi-103-v1.

bomb shelter. This one is going and it started sputtering and stopped and everybody ran. Somebody looked up and said we were okay. Then, we just watched it. It got down behind the hill, and all of a sudden [it detonated] and you could see the concussion coming before you felt it.

One night, they were sending a lot of buzz bombs, and it had rained and it was muddy outside. They had the planks to walk on. Somebody said 'buzz bombs,' and we all ran out in our pajamas and jumped into the shelter and went back. We weren't then sleeping another fifty or sixty minutes, and then another buzz bomb came, and another one. By the time of the fourth one, I said 'the heck with it,' and I slept the rest of the night. They kept coming up every night [for a while].

*

Most of the missions you'd get flak—some more intense than others. A couple of times, we had fighters come in. The CO of our group, Colonel Shower, was a stickler on tight formations. The tighter the formation is, the less the fighters bothered you because you have too much concentrated firepower. So, we weren't attacked as bad as the other groups flying with us. Once in a while they'd come over, but didn't bother us too much. But outside that, like Dresden and Nuremberg and places like that, they had a lot of flak.

Dresden, 1945.[28] 'View from the city hall (Rathaus) over the destroyed city.'
Taken between 17 September 1945 and 31 December 1945, by German photographer Richard Peter. Credit: Deutsche Fotothek

---

[28] *Dresden, 1945*-One of the most 'notorious' missions of the war was the February 13/14 raid to Dresden, where at least 35,000 people, mostly civilians, were incinerated. American PoWs were used to remove the bodies, among them Kurt Vonnegut, Jr., where the incident would feature prominently in his novel *Slaughterhouse Five*.

Dresden

Dresden was a bad one, one of the worst missions. It was one of our early ones. Well, what happened there was we got hit bad, and [we got off course]. We were leading three hundred planes. I loved the crew that I was on. They were great—Chapman, Wallace, and our other navigator. We had two navigators on the lead ship—a DR navigator [dead reckoning] and myself, a radar navigator.[29]

We're in the front and all the planes have to go where we go, so we have to [be very accurate]. We're on the flight deck. The pilot was here [*points to table*] and the DR man was sitting right next to him back-to-back, and I was here [*motions again*], just cut in behind the co-pilot.

We had signals [because it was very loud on the plane], and the DR man said, 'Okay, five minutes, take a fix.' I would check my watch quickly and he would get a fix with the radio, and I'd get a fix with the radar and he would compare them and then

---

[29] *DR navigator-*'dead reckoning' is the process of calculating one's position by estimating direction and distance traveled by using a previously determined 'fix' (position) and advancing that position based upon estimated speeds over time and course, rather than by electronic navigation methods.

give me the okay. He never gave me a sign that we were off.

Dresden had heavy, heavy flak, and we got hit with flak the size a little bit bigger than a softball; I would say about a six-inch piece of shrapnel came up through about the middle of the plane. The fuselage was open. Thank God nobody was hurt.

[There was some confusion on the bomb run.] I called out the first course correction on the bomb run, an eight-degree correction when we went from the rally point heading for the target. That eight degrees would have been okay. It's like you turn here and the target's up here [*points to piece of paper*]. I came to eight degrees. I was supposed to be heading there, and the bombardier calls up and says, 'I don't want that. I'm making a visual bomb run.' Okay, so I'm going to kill the course for him. Two minutes later, I gave him a ten-degree [approach] and he still wouldn't take it.

He said, 'No, it's a visual bomb run.' So, I wouldn't navigate the bomb run for him. He's going to make it visually.

I said, 'I can kill the course for you.'

He said, 'Never mind.' So what happened was, we kept going way off course instead of coming up. Instead of doing about a 45-degree course to the target, we got off so far that when the bombardier found out where he was, he had to almost turn it north. Now what happened was all these other planes came up, and they were now underneath us! I looked out the bomb bays to see the bombs drop. I looked down when they were ready to drop and saw a plane right below us! So, I hollered, 'Don't drop the bombs!' It was too late. They went; one bomb went between the wing and the fuselage of that plane and almost killed ten men.

Coming back, we ran into a [weather] front. We were advised to look out for it, but where they told us it was going to be was way off. I checked my radar continuously to take a fix on it. We hit the front, but it was a lot earlier than we had been briefed on. I realized something was wrong and I found that we were being blown way off course. So, I got on to the rally point where we had to meet and head home. I called up the pilot and said we were about 15 miles off course.

I said, 'We got a new heading we should take.'

Now we were flying deputy lead and there was the wing lead. Everybody wants credit for the big lead because you get promotions that way—to Wing, to Division. We had a pilot and co-pilot and a command pilot. The command pilot is there to make sure that everything is running. He is in charge of everything.

Our pilot evidently called up and nothing was said. I never got a response, so I called up again, 'Mickey to pilot.'

He said, 'Go ahead, Marty.'

I said, 'We're twenty-five miles off course. Something better be done.'

I marked the heading that we were going towards, and we're heading right for the Ruhr Valley, and that's an all-industrial place. There must be a thousand anti-aircraft guns around there. It was heavily, heavily, heavily defended. They make their steel and everything else down there.

He didn't say anything, and I called up again, 'Mickey to pilot. Chappy, we've got to get something done. We are thirty-five miles off course, and we're heading to an area that we will be getting flak soon and we are going to lose several planes.'

There was going to be forty or fifty men killed, guaranteed.

He said, 'I checked with everybody, and everybody said we were on course except for one guy who said we're fifteen miles off.' All the other planes said we're on course, and we weren't! We were thirty-five miles off, and I was right!

We got over the Ruhr, and I said, 'We were going to be getting flak soon.' The guys in the waist said, 'It's already popping out ahead of you, waiting for us!'

So, the lead plane finally said, 'Since you know where we are, take over!'

So, we swung up to the lead, and I said, 'Take it up north quick and get the heck out of here!'

The Germans would have shot many of our planes down. I headed north and got on our old track that was on the map to follow home, and we went across the French coast across the Channel. You could see the White Cliffs of Dover coming up, and you know you're home. I finally relaxed a little bit.

'I Cried Like A Baby'

We got in and had a meeting, and they had all of the officers from the base. I said to myself, 'Geez, they are probably going to pat me on the back for doing a good job.'

I got up there and they wanted to crucify me, take my wings, and they said they wouldn't let me fly. They said, 'What's the matter, were you sleeping to get that far off course?'

I had a good crew and I didn't want to lose them. I didn't want to tell [the brass] that I gave the course [correction] several times to the pilot. I didn't want to tell them that when I gave the first course correction on the bomb run [which was not accepted], we first made a big 'boo-boo.' I gave an eight-degree correction when we went from the rally point heading for the target. That eight degrees would have been okay, but now I was blamed for [that mishap, too]. The plane [below us] didn't get hit [with the bomb], but it was close. It was the command pilot's fault, really. He should have told Chapman to go with that angle. By the time the bombardier gets a target in sight, it's got to be about a seventy-degree angle. Hell, if we were forty miles away from there, I could kill that course dead. You don't have to correct it more than one or two degrees with the bombsight after. They didn't do it.

I didn't want to say what I did, but I thought one of them would stand up and speak for me—the pilot, the command pilot, or any member of the crew, the bombardier. They'd heard it all. I suppose they were all scared that I might say something; I didn't want to say something. So, [the brass] said to me, 'One more move like that and you're off your crew.'

I went back to the barracks. I felt bad, real bad, because I could have blown the whistle but I didn't want to get off my crew. I took my shoes off and went to bed with my clothes on; I covered my head and cried like a baby. Then I heard my pilot and Captain Sidney come in. Sidney was in charge of all radar men.

He said, 'Chappy, I don't know what happened up there but I know this man wasn't to blame.' He said, 'He's the only one that comes to this shack after every mission to find out if he could have done better with the radar. If anything's wrong, he wants to find out. He's the only guy to ever come up there! He's very interested in his bombing. He's good. I know it's not his fault. I know it.'

Chappy said, 'No, it wasn't. It was my fault as well as the bombardier.'

I woke up in the morning and everything's okay. I went up to see the commanding officer and asked him if I could have a meeting with our crew. I would like to talk to the crew about my position and what I am there for. He gave me permission.

I went up there and we had the meeting there. I told the guys what I could do. I could navigate when all other systems are down, or blacked out by the Germans; they can in no way block off my signals. I said I've got perfect navigational equipment. I said that I'd never been lost and don't intend to be lost. I went up to [one of the crew] and said, 'If you ever countermand a correction that I give you, I am going to punch you in the head and there'd be another hole in this plane! Don't you ever do that again. It's your fault!'

He said, 'I know.'

Everything was forgotten. We had a great crew, flew some great missions. After that, when I gave corrections to them, they took them.

Berlin

[Our last mission was on March 18, 1945.] It seems like our worst mission was on a Sunday. They gave fresh eggs, so we knew it was going to be a rough one. If it wasn't going to be a rough mission, you usually get powdered eggs for break-fast.

We went outside after the briefing. There was a Catholic priest there. He's there at every briefing— not at the briefing but outside waiting. We would come out, and a lot of us Catholic boys would kneel down and some received communion. He gave us the blessing, then we all jumped in the wagons and went out to our planes. The target was Berlin. By the looks on their faces, a couple of guys kind of almost knew it was going to be a bad one.

Going over was good; navigation was super—we were leading the squadron at that time. We were coming up on the bomb run. We had a little plane that attacked us for a while and then the flak started greeting us; up ahead we could see it. The sky was black with flak. You can't swerve [or take evasive action]. You've got to go right through it.

We got right into it. I had my bomb bay doors open. I was ready to turn it over and get the bombs off. We got an explosion; I thought it was inside the plane, it was so loud. Directly underneath the plane we had taken a direct hit. We had fires in the bomb bays. Up where the pilot was, there was some kind of white-hot metal that landed. The co-pilot stamped on it. It burned right down through the ship, and a hole was left behind.

The pilot and co-pilot had bucket seats made out of heavy steel. The rest of us had safety vests that sometimes stop the flak. There was fire where I was, around my legs. I turned around and grabbed the extinguisher; the plane went into a dive, and of course, it was hard to maneuver. It forced me down on the deck. I finally got the fire extinguisher and stood up and started to put the fire out. I got the fire pretty well out and looked around; my navigator wasn't helping me. I noticed he was lying down and his eyes were very grey. His brains were hanging down the side of his head. All I could think of is that they looked like frog eggs. I went over and picked up the brains with my hands. They were warm yet. I didn't know what to do. Hell, he's dead. So, I spread some sulfa on it and went up to the pilot. [The engineer was supposed to be] in the bomb bay just below me where I could [normally] tap him on the head. I looked down. He was gone. I could see a piece of his clothes and stuff on the side of the plane; he was shot off when it hit. He just dropped out of the plane without a parachute.

The nose was burning pretty good. They got that fire out with the wind that was coming through the nose; it put that fire out. The waist wasn't hurt too much. Nobody got hurt back there. The steel seat the pilot was sitting in was hit so hard that [he had a minor injury on] his backside, but nothing serious at all.

'Thanks, Van'

We were blown into a dive, and to this day, I don't know how we could have managed to pull out of that dive, because the number one and number two engines were shot out altogether. The number three engine was only pulling half power and was running at around twenty; number four was the only good engine, and he was pushing it to the limit, about sixty-two, sixty-three. If we had flown another hour, that engine would have blown up. There must have been terrific pressure. They pulled it out of the dive.

We were also still carrying a full load of bombs in to the target. Because the explosion tangled up the releases and everything so bad, they asked me to go back in the waist into the bomb bays. I took my parachute off. It was only a six-inch walkway; there was nothing underneath me but a six-inch catwalk. I had a big screwdriver and I put all the weight that I dared to put on it to try to open the releases and drop the bombs.

I unhooked the arming wire. The arming wire goes from the nose of the plane up to the little place you hook on, and down to the point where it's going to the arming pin. When the bombs hit with the nose, the arming pin drives it in and makes the explosion. I unhooked that wire so they wouldn't go off when they dropped. I fixed the ignition and all of that so they wouldn't explode, and shut a cotter key in it so there's no way they could slip forward. So if the plane did land, [hopefully] none of the bombs would explode.

We were over the middle of Berlin. I remember when we pulled out of the dive, I put my parachute on. Of course, the navigator [who had been killed], his parachute was okay. Mine had a hole in it; it was just burnt a little bit but I knew I couldn't use it. So, I took his and remember saying, 'Thanks, pal. Thanks, Van.'

I'm up talking to the other navigator and the bombardier. I was kneeling right between them. I tell the pilot that Van [DR navigator] is gone and George Fuller [engineer] is gone. I contacted the waist. The waist was okay. I said, 'The waists are all okay.' So I said that we had two killed in action. I told him where we were, and I gave him a heading to pull and said, 'Take it 90 degrees for the time being.'

The Russian Lines

I went and set up and used my drift meter and all of that, and I gave him a corrected heading more south because that's the closest the Russians were to us, to the German boundary line, or rather the frontlines. As we were heading there, the plane stayed level but she kept losing altitude. So, it was only a matter of time before we would have to bail out, and there was no way we could land it because everything was shot up on the flight deck—the controls and everything. How he kept it level, I don't know.

We got over the lines and we started getting strafed by a German plane; he had one landing gear down, I remember, the other one was up. He made a pass and turned around to get another pass at us. Then, three Russian Yaks came in. The German flew away and they circled us a couple of times, and then they came in and started strafing us to knock us down!

The emblem was American on the plane, but I don't think they could tell [from the angle]. After years went by, I think they must have seen the bomb bay doors open and saw the bombs in it, so probably figured maybe we were on a bombing mission. However, that day we were bombing Berlin, three American ships were knocked down by Russians. So, the Russians did it every once in a while. Of course, a couple of Americans knocked down a couple of theirs, too.

They started strafing us, and Chapman asked me to give the waist gunners the signal to bail because the radio system between the waist and the flight deck was out. So, I had some object there that I heaved at the doors, so they opened up the door going into the waist and I patted my parachute and said, 'Go!' He nodded okay.

We got ready. I went over and touched my dead navigator again and went out and sat down by the bomb bay. I climbed down the bomb bay and sat on the walkway there—that six-inch beam. I sat with my feet dangling out. I never jumped out of a plane before. I waited for the co-pilot to come close to me, that way we'd be close enough that when we landed, we'd find each other quick.

The waist gunner, Twyford, jumped first. I bailed out and put my head between my legs and rolled out and fell far enough to make sure that I wouldn't be around the plane. I pulled the rip cord and nothing happened, and I started clawing at the thing and then finally it popped open—there's an auxiliary parachute in there. It's under spring tension and that popped a little parachute out; that auxiliary chute is fitted into your main chute, and it pops out first and drives the main chute out. All I remember was an awful jar.

As I was going down, I see the three Russian planes come down again. One picked on the pilot. One picked me, one was on the waist gunner. He started strafing me while I was falling, and I waved my hands at him and everything, and he's coming right at me. I saw him and thought, 'Lord, what am I going to do?' What you should do if you are far enough from the ground, you pull the cord on one side and it collapses the chute right away, and you freefall and just let it go and you get away before you hit the ground.

I chose to play dead. I waited until he went around, and he came back around and he's heading square at me. I see the guns going off. I slumped down, put my hands along my side, and hung my head down to my chest. He circled me two or three times then flew off.

Then I heard popping and looked on the ground, and I could see it looked like a hundred people on the ground shooting at us! I heard the bullets, maybe two or three went through the canopy. I [later] cut that piece out to take it home, but somebody on the ship coming home stole it from me. I was not hit.

We were dropping down, and as I looked down there was a sharp-peaked house coming up right in front of me. I moved over a little bit with the shroud line.[30] Down along the side of the house, there's a little cavity in the ground, like some kind of excavation, I would say maybe three feet deep. I landed right in there, and, of course, it cut the wind, so my chute collapsed there and didn't have to be dragged along or anything.

I see the emblem on their hats and uniform that they're Russians, so I started yelling. My mother and father came from Krakow, Poland, back in 1911, so as we were growing up we had to learn Polish, because that's the only way we spoke. I knew enough of Polish to say, 'I beg you, do not shoot, I am an American.' I said, 'I have some papers, easy, easy!' [*Speaks in Polish*]

I reached in. We had these papers. They were small—you fold it, you take them out and open it,

---

[30] *shroud line*-parachute suspension line

it's a big poster. It had a picture of Stalin and a picture of Roosevelt on it, and underneath them it says 'Komrades,' then it had a lot of Russian writing underneath it saying that we're American and all of that.

A couple of Russians started saying, 'Americans, Americans!' Then a big, black 'Cadillac' lookalike limo came along and had three officers in it. I could see that they were high-ranking officers, and they were told we're Americans. One reached down, took my hand, and pulled me up out of there. That was the first time I had a sigh of relief.

They found Wallace almost immediately. I told the Russians that the guys falling out of the sky, they're all Americans. So, they sent word around to make sure that they're all right. They were able to find my navigator. His body was burned up but they found he was all in one piece.

Chapman collapsed his chute, then free-fell and opened it up again. When he hit the ground, they put him in a truck, and some Russian on a horse came up to him with a pistol and put it to his head and pulled the trigger three times, but the gun wouldn't go off. Then the truck pulled away; he could see the guy working on his pistol. He finally fixed it, but the truck was too far away so he didn't chase it.

So, Wallace and me and Twyford, they brought us to this building. They had some interrogators there. They asked me first; I told them I spoke some Polish. They brought a woman over to act as an interpreter, but I couldn't understand her and she couldn't understand me. They then brought in a fella by the name of Walter. He was a big, gangly guy and the type of guy that you see that you like him. We spoke to each other just like talking to my mother or father. He told the Russians that he knows what he is seeing.

They asked through the interpreter what were we bombing. Of course, generally you don't give information to the enemies except the name and serial number. But in this case, the newspapers would be blasting that, I think it was, 2,000 planes would hit Berlin that day in an all-out effort.

I told him we were bombing Berlin. He said, 'Good, good. How many planes?'

Again, I knew the newspapers would give the amount of planes. I said, '2,000.'

They were pleased with that. He said, 'How come you didn't shoot us down when the Russians were strafing you?'

I didn't tell him all our guns were all knocked out and that we couldn't shoot any of the guns. I said, 'We knew you were Russians so we didn't want to shoot back.' I had to lie a little bit.

Then they brought out a bottle of some kind of white liquor. He said, 'Have a drink.'

I said, 'Yeah, I need one.' So, they gave me a little shot. Then some woman there said to put some water in it.

The Russian said, 'No, he can drink it.' I drank it and, boy, was it strong! It went down and I felt better after I warmed up. The waist gunner [drank his] and almost went down to his knees. They put us up, and the next day got the rest of the crew together. There were two more missing but we were going to meet them at the end of the day. They said we were going to bury the navigator. They found him and they found my log. I was hoping that they'd give it to me. It was partially burnt but you could still read it.

They picked us up in two trucks. One of these flat-bottom trucks with green cloth or something over the bottom had a casket on the front. There were two Russians in the front and two in the back with rifles riding with them. The other truck had three seat benches. We sat on that and rode backwards.

We went up to a cemetery in Landsberg and they had a ceremony there. They said something in Russian. They asked me through my interpreter if one of us wanted to say something. I told Chapman they wanted to know if anyone wanted to say the last few words. Chapman said, 'Yeah, I would.' He gave a nice talk about Van Tress being a good navigator. He had been just married for one month; he married an English girl. He was a wonderful man, not only a great navigator.

He ended up having a great big tombstone there. They came to see me and asked me what I wanted on it. I put 'Harold B. Van Tress, born 1923/Killed in action today March 18, 1945/bombing mission Berlin'— they had that all inscribed overnight, they had it on there. That was a big stone that stood up there at least four or five feet. I asked the girl taking the photograph of everything if she would send me or give me a photograph. She said she'd try, but I never got it.

'Crazy Amerikanski'

We stayed there in Landsberg for a couple of days. Then we went to [Posen]. From there, we were taken to Lublin, Poland. That was a pretty good size city. The Russians came in and told us at 9:00 there is a curfew—nobody on the streets. They said, 'If you listen tonight you might hear the Russians holler '[*speaks Russian*],' which means 'halt,' and then you hear a shot. The next day looking out of your window, you will see a funeral going by.' He says, 'We're not fooling.'

We said okay. Chappy and I walked around and found a nice English pub. It was a nice clean place run by a husband and his wife and they had a young daughter about eighteen—a beautiful girl. She's kind of the receptionist. She met everybody at the door. We went in and had a few vodkas. The next night we went down again, but this time we overstayed. It was 10:00 before we came out. I said, 'Oh boy, Chappy, this is going to be a lulu.'

We were walking up the street; he was a little bit pie-eyed. We kind of leaned on each other and then heard a son-of-a-gun Russian holler, 'HALT!'

Chappy hollered, 'Halt your butt,' but he didn't use 'butt,' he used the other word. I was just waiting to feel the bullet go through my chest; I was just wondering how it was going to feel. Two Russians came up and said, 'Crazy Amerikanski,' and they helped us up to the hotel. So, every night they'd meet us down there—they knew we were coming out—and escort us back.

*

I went to church on Palm Sunday. Over in Poland they have what they call a continuous mass. It starts from twelve midnight Sunday morning to twelve midnight Sunday night. There were no Saturday masses then. Anytime you walk into the church, whatever part of the mass was going on, when that part came up again, you walk out.

There were people going in and out all the time. It was full. I went in. I don't remember if any of the other crew were Catholic or not. I took, I think, 20,000 of those zlotys [that I got on the black market for my watch], and a bearded priest came in; he had a nice big beard on him. He was slowly passing down and you could see people giving a bill or some coins to him. He comes to me and I chuck 20,000 of them in there. He bowed three times to me and took off. I never saw him again.

I stepped out of the church that day and two guys came up to me. One talked English pretty well—very well. I said, 'Where did you learn English?' He said that he was a professor at the Lublin University, and he said, 'I'd like to talk to you sometime.' He invited me to come down to his house the next day for dinner. It wasn't too far from the hotel we were living in.

They sent a guy to take care of us, and I asked him for some food because I was having dinner with this Polish family. I said I would sure like to get some food I could give them, because food is scarce to them and I didn't want to go down there and eat their supplies. He gave me a lot of K-rations and a chicken that was still frozen, cans of different vegetables. So, I went down and gave it all to them. You would think I gave him a million dollars!

We had a nice visit and he asked me if I would take a letter for him and smuggle it back to the country; the Russians wouldn't let him mail it out. As a matter of fact, while I was walking the streets of Lublin, I must have got about eight letters from people who begged me to send them to their relatives in the States. So, I took them all.

A couple of incidents happened while we were there in that hotel. The hotel was just a bombed-out half-building, and we had a nice woman come in every day to straighten our beds, which were just two planks with hay on them. She would straighten up the hay and fold the parachute on them [that we were still using as a bedroll]. Eventually, I cut off a little piece of the shroud lines and I pulled all these threads out of it—very fine threads just like you sew clothes with, and I said, 'You can't break it. It would be good for sewing. You take this parachute too.' She brought me something to cover myself that night, and she took and hid everything I gave her so the Russians didn't see her taking it from there. I hope she finally got it out of there.

Another time we were in the room and in come three Russians. You could see they were a little bit looped; I guess they wanted to fight. One came up to me and said, 'Me, boxer.' I said, 'Me, football player.' He went to the next guy. Then he went over to Chapman. I looked at Chapman. He was a little Southern boy, and I could see he's not going to take it. So, I told Yarcusko [the bombardier] to get ready.

This Russian hits Chapman on the chest, and Chapman hauled off and belted him one. I belted one and somebody else grabbed the other one. So, there we were fighting, and somebody fired a pistol. Some big shots came in—big officers, high-ranking. We all stopped when the shot went off. My interpreter came in and asked me what happened. I told him that we were resting and relaxing here and these guys busted in and they wanted to fight. Well, they threw them out of the place. I don't mean pushed them. They threw them out! One gave me a Russian pistol, and he said, 'The next time somebody comes in to bother you, don't talk to them, don't answer them, don't ask them questions—just shoot them. Don't drag them out in the hallway, throw them out the window and we'll pick them up.' So they left and I took the bullets out of the gun and said, 'Don't fool around, boys.' The next day they came and took the pistol away from me.

*

We weren't prisoners. Though we were kept in confinement by the Russians, we had quite a bit of liberty. Whenever we pick up a Russian girl to take her to her house to talk with her, they would pick up the girl the next day. The KGB, they would question her and tell her we were spies. But none of them believed it.

One time, they came in and said, 'We can't ask you officers to do manual labor.' I guessed by the rules of the Geneva Convention, the enlisted men were going to work today.

I said, 'Doing what?'

He said, 'Shoveling some fill onto the truck.'

I said, 'I'll go with them.' [The Russian] said, 'No, you're an officer.'

I said, 'I want to go with my men.'

He said, 'Okay.'

So I went with them, and I took a shovel and helped them fill up a big truck; there were two trucks to load up. So, they're going down to [deliver] the first load, and I said, 'Can I go with you?'

He said, 'Sure.' It was into a prison. They dumped the load there. I went in where all the prisoners were; I had never seen anything so sad in my life. I see one guy there with nothing but bones sticking out of his face. You could count his ribs so easy and his face was nothing but bones sticking out. His eyes looked at me, and here I am fat as a hog and smoking a cigarette. I see he is looking at me. I took a cigarette and walked over to him. The guards said, 'No, no,' but I said, 'The hell with you, you're not going to shoot me.'

I see some of the others looking around. I had about twelve cigarettes left. I broke them in two into twenty-four and gave everybody a half cigarette. There was no filter so they could smoke either end.

'We're Going To Crash!'

It was a lot of fun. I wanted to go to Krakow but they had no way of transporting me there. I knew that I had relatives all over the area.

They finally flew us from there to Poltava up in the Ukraine over Russia. We were trying to take off. We were on a grass field—just a meadow. They had a Jeep loaded on there already and all of us went on. I sat in the seat just behind the steering wheel. They started going on the grass and all of a sudden hit a hole. They pulled it out and tried again; it hit [another crater]. I said, 'Holy cow!' Finally, they took us off and sent us down a few miles away, where they had a cement runway—a hardtop runway. They had heavy screens over the thing. When we got there, they loaded us on the plane and flew us to Poltava.

We finally found a plane there over in Poltava that was in good shape except the landing gear was pretty badly mangled. What had happened [at Poltava] a year or so before was that there were these 'shuttle missions'—they take off in England and bomb Germany, then Poland, and over to Russia. The next day they take off loaded with bombs again, hit the southern part of Germany, and land in Italy. The third day, they fly from Italy, bomb Germany again, and then land back at the base. They called it a shuttle run—three runs. You'd get three missions in three days.[31] They had had seventy-five of these planes come in. They lined them up in two rows. The Germans came in and demolished all of the planes. Never took off again; that's where we got our landing gear and stuff. We found landing gear on one of the other planes there that was in pretty good shape, and, with Russian help, we jacked the plane up, got the thing off, and put the other one on. We worked on the engines—whatever we knew about it. We never had any experience with them.

Each plane had a small generator on it because you don't have any electricity in the plane until at least one engine is going. So, we start them up to give us power while checking the position that we

---

[31] *shuttle missions*- Operation Frantic was a series of World War II shuttle bombing operations conducted by American aircraft primarily based in Southern Italy, which then landed at Soviet airfields in Poltava, in the Soviet Union (Ukraine). The operation began in June 1944 and ended in September. The Germans contributed to the discontinuation of the program with a German air attack on the Ukrainian bases; deteriorating relations with the USSR also hastened the demise. See www.history.com/this-day-in-history/united-states-begins-shuttle-bombing-in-operation-frantic

were flying. When we got that all done, the Russians took all seventy-five auxiliary engines—they called it—and put them all in the bomb bay—all seventy-five of them! Then they said, 'We've got sixteen more men we want you to haul out of here.' There's eight of us left, so there would be twenty-four men.

We went up to test-op [our rebuilt plane]. Chapman, Wallace—the two pilots and myself acting as the engineer. I knelt between the pilot and co-pilot. It was one of these steel mat runways—you could hear that rippling noise as you go over them. Usually, you should get over 100 miles, 115 miles, 110 miles an hour before you like to take the plane off. I watched the speedometer. I leaned. Both of their heads are close by me. I hollered, 'You're doing 60, 65,' but when I got around 80, it didn't climb very high. 'Eighty-four, eighty-five!' Oh boy, I looked up and we were at the point of no return, and gone too far.

When I got up around 88, 89, Chappy pulled back on the plane and said, 'We're going to crash!' The plane took off and he quickly folded his landing gear. That worked, thank God. We started going down again, and just before we hit the ground she picked up enough speed and kept going—success!

We landed right away. The Russians gave us heck. They thought we just taxied down the runway to turn off, but here we are going full speed. So, we told them, 'We've got to do some more work on those engines.' We have to take all those auxiliary engines out of the bomb bay, and the other men—we can't take off with 16 more of them—they've got to wait for somebody else to come in. So, they fixed the plane up, and they said, 'Okay, take off this time, and don't come back.'

All the guys assembled there. Something told me this time when we got on that plane, we're going to be searched. As soon as I got to my navigation position up there on the flight deck, I opened a big huge fuse box about that wide and about that high [*makes gesture with hands*] with all the fuses in there. I opened it up. It had two screws on top and one on the bottom. I took the bottom one off and loosened up the others, and removed it and put the letters in it and put the screw back in quickly. I went to my position, and then they came on and said, 'Everyone out.'

We all had to go out of the plane. They took about four men and they went in and searched that plane from one end to the other. So, I kind of held my breath.

Then they said, 'All right, get on, close that door, and don't come back.' They said, 'You're going to Bari, Italy.'

He gave us the elevation of the flight at ten thousand feet and gave us the wind. I forgot how many knots it was and the direction the wind was coming in. Like anybody flying an airplane, you've got a heading, and if the wind is coming [a certain direction] and you want to go there, you better go this way so the wind would blow you on the right track.

So, I told the Russians, 'One minute, when I go up in the air at ten thousand feet, I am going to take three different headings. I'll only be a minute—a minute or so on each one.'

He said, 'What do you want to do that for?'

I said, 'I want to get my own wind and the knots.'

He said, 'We gave you winds.'

I said, 'That's all right, I want to get my own.'

He said, 'All right.'

So, I took a heading so-and-so and I told Chapman to take another thirty, forty feet the other way and then the third way. Each time, I marked our heading and how much drift we were making. I put all this on the E6B computer. We carried a small computer. I set them all on there. I could turn the dials and show you exactly what degree the wind was coming from, the exact knots up to half a knot; I think it was five knots an hour. Anyway, I put the wind on the E6B after I erased it and put my heading on there and applied the wind. I put the course on there, the exact course I wanted to make. I put the heading on and it showed me how much correction to make into the wind. I put that all down and we took off. They told us if we get one mile off course, we've got to shoot you down.

We went down across Yugoslavia over the mountains. We came over the top of a mountain and looked down and saw the bluest body of water that you've ever seen. You couldn't see the other side, and I remember the co-pilot saying, 'Marty, what's that blue water?'

So I told him, 'If that's not the Mediterranean Sea, I don't know what country we're in.' We flew across it, and once we got over the Mediterranean, we still couldn't see land yet.

He said, 'What's our ETA and course?'

I said, 'The course looks pretty good, but I have been taking a drift of the top of the white caps on the Mediterranean,' and I could see we were drifting a little bit more than we did before. I gave a one-degree correction and checked my ETA and gave the time we should be there. We came into Bari right over the runway, and our time was off by half a minute. It was a perfect hit.

We landed, and they gave us hell for coming in with that plane. We had no parachutes, nobody had a parachute. They told us to get out of the plane and gave somebody orders to tow that out to the junkyard and junk that plane. Everything was beat up on it but we made it.

*

[The war wasn't over yet.] They took us up to Naples and they deloused us. They put us naked into a shower with a strong stream of water and they deloused all of us—head, ears, everything, any crevice in the body, to make sure. There was a lot of lice; we were loused up from Russia. They put some kind of powder on us and put it under our armpits and stuff like that.[32] Before we went into the shower, we had to take all our clothes off and shoes and stockings and put them in this rubberized bag, and then they sealed it off so no air could come outside of it or anything. Inside of it you could feel a little tube, a hard metal cylinder. They said, 'Put it on the ground and put your heel on it.' That was before we went in the shower. We had our shoes on yet and stomped on it. [The cylinder] opened up and put whatever [is inside of it all over inside of the rubberized bag], to delouse our clothes. Everything was clean. We then went in the shower and put our clothes back on. It did a good job.

In Naples they gave us a couple of days there and we went into town—Chappy and I. We got a little bit looped. We were so happy to be back in American hands.

---

[32] *put some kind of powder on us*- DDT, an insecticide used late in WWII to control malaria and typhus among civilians and troops. A white powder was generally sprayed on the subject; it was banned for agricultural use in the USA in 1972 as a threat to wildlife.

'We Were All Killed'

[We flew to England and] we went back to the base. It was about eight weeks that had gone by; [we got there] at supper time. Of course, we weren't dressed in Class A uniforms. We went up into the hallway, and they lined up to go into the mess hall outside, and the line goes into the door. You pick up your metal plate. We were walking up and everyone turned around looking at us. They were all young kids; Christ, they looked like they must have just gotten out of school or something! I didn't see any of the old-timers. They were all gone. When we got shot down, word came back that we were all killed. As we turned to go in the mess hall, I could see inside. There was a long table in the front. It had the CO, Colonel Shower, and all the brass from the base, all on that long table. They were waited on while the rest of us had to go through the line.

The minute I walked in, I noticed this Captain Novak looking up. He said something to Colonel Shower, and Colonel Shower jumped up and came running over to us. They had been notified that we were dead. He took us back to the table and we were waited on that night. Captain Novak asked who spoke Polish. I said, 'I did.' He said he was Polish, too. I asked where our clothes and all our belongings were.

He said, 'I think they are up in the post office. I hope they haven't sent them out yet.'

I got out of there as quick as I could, and Chappy said, 'Where are you going, Marty?'

I said, 'I am going to see if I can get up to that post office.'

So, I took a bicycle; I don't know who it belonged to. I rode off because the post office was on the outskirts of the base. I knocked on the door. It had a screen wire mesh glass on the front of the door, and way in the back, I could see one guy working. He points to his watch and says 'No.' I kept banging and banging and banging. He finally comes up to the door and says, 'Sir, we're closed.'

I said, 'No, no, I just want to ask you a question. Do you have any boxes of clothes that are going to be shipped out here yet?' I gave him the names.

He said, 'Yeah, we've got ten boxes out there.'

I said, 'What's the names on them?'

He went back and said, 'There's a Chapman, there's a Twyford.' And he named three or four.

I said, 'Geez, don't ship them. Please don't ship those clothes out. Ship Van Tress and Fuller. George Fuller and Harold Van Tress. Ship them home, but the rest of them, we're all back on the base.'

He said, 'I'm glad you came here because in the morning, they were going out.'

I still have the board where the address was marked 'Killed in Action' that they were going to mail to my mother. I hadn't been able to get in contact with her. I did send her some letters from Italy and England. She finally got two of them. The rest of the letters, I gave to the guy that used to audit all of the mail going out. They checked the Polish letters and said that they were all right. So, we mailed them out.

I went to town that night. I knew my old buddy would still be worrying the hell about me. He was over in the corner of the bar crying his head off...he jumped up [when he saw me], and boy, did he cry! We saw each other then, but it was the last time that I saw him. We were supposed to head out. They weren't going to form any more crews here. The front lines were moving so fast, they did very little bombing after that.

After the war [in Europe] was over, everybody went celebrating, but they restricted us to the base and wouldn't let us go out. But we all had .45 revolvers and we went around shooting the smoke stacks on the buildings. Then they thought they'd better let us go into town or we'd kill ourselves.

*

Coming Home

I asked to go back by boat. I flew over, and I'll never be able to cross the ocean on any kind of ship again. I got on this ship, I think it was the *USS Frederickson*. We did see a whale. I was seasick for about three days. I lay on my cot and never moved. We slept eight above on little cots. I think it was eight above each other—one on top of the other. I was on the very bottom and only had about that much room [*makes gesture with hands*]. So I came back on that, and put all of the clothes down in the hold. Somebody, during the trip, took whatever they wanted, and that's how I lost a lot of the stuff.

I came home and landed in Boston. They had to give us furlough papers to go home for a month. I went home and then back to Langley Field. There was a sergeant interviewing all of us, getting information from us. He said, 'Where do you want to go? You can be based any place you want.'

I said, 'No, I got a little more [fight] left in me, I would like to go to the South Pacific.'

He said, 'You don't have to go down there.'

I said, 'I want to go down there.'

He said, 'Wait a minute, you were missing for over six weeks.'

I said, 'Yeah. Missing in action. Eight weeks.'

He said, 'You can't go. You have to go home for two months—one month at home and one month in the recuperation center. You can go to Long Beach, Atlantic City'—of course, there were no casinos there then—'or Lake Placid, New York, for a week. Do anything you want. Say anything you want. Dress the way you want. You just have to have one month of recuperation. Then you come back and get reassigned.'

I said, 'No, skip that. I want to go to the South Pacific.'

He said, 'You're crazy!'

So, they assigned me to a group in Boca Raton—B-29s. I was going to be trained there for combat in the South Pacific.

I was going down. I was a couple of days ahead of schedule, so I stopped in Atlanta, Georgia. The guy that sat next to me in preflight—he was a kid that was killed; Devine, I think his name was. Him and I used to talk many a time lying in the bunks at night. I thought I would find his folks and go over and visit with them and tell them about their son, and maybe I'll get a supper out of it.

I bought a quart of whiskey first— $2.49. I put it up in my room and I went downstairs and was going down to have dinner, and thought I would make the phone calls first. I went into the phone book and I thought that there would be two or three, but there were a couple of pages of Devines, so I said forget it. My God, there must have been fifty of them.

I went down to order a steak dinner, and I put the fork in and I noticed going in that there is a package store across the street—a liquor store. I was just ready to cut the steak when Harry Truman came on the air and announced that the war in Japan was officially over. We are now at war with no one.

So, I didn't even cut the steak. I went across the road and bought eight more quarts of whiskey and took them up to my room. Ten minutes after it became known—maybe fifteen minutes—liquor went up to $20 per quart. I got them for $2.49!

I went outside and saw a Marine and said to come on with me. We hugged each other and said that we did it!

I said, 'Listen, this hotel room's going to be open and I got all the liquor in the world. You come here and take a drink any time you want.'

He took me in the poolroom and there were quite a few rows of tables. He said, 'Third table. Third table up, look on the upper left leg, reach down there, you'll see a bottle of booze at the leg. You come in here and take a drink any time you want.'

Then I met some sailors and I took them up. I wasn't doing that much drinking, but they were. The next day, they were really celebrating there. I got tangled up with five other people celebrating and dancing and eating and all of that, so I was a day late coming down to my base in Boca Raton. The little sergeant says, 'Sir, you're a day late. I've got to mark you AWOL.'

I said, 'Oh, come on. The war's over. I did my duty.'

I pleaded with him, then I made up a story. 'My car broke down up in Ft. Lauderdale and my wife's there with two kids, and you're going to give me AWOL.'

He said, 'I'm sorry, sir, that's what the rules say.'

The master sergeant came walking in. I look across his chest; he's got his name—Polish, a 'ski.'

He said, 'What's going on here?'

I said, in Polish, 'I got drunk as hell and I'm a day late coming down for my arrival. He wants to mark me AWOL.'

He said, 'Write in here that he came in two days ago.'

He signed me in two days early. I hung around for a while and asked for a discharge, and I came home.

*

'They're All Gone'

[Near the end of World War II], I was put in for a captain rating. It had to get approval of headquarters. I don't know if Doolittle had anything to do with it or not. Then we got shot down and word came back that we were killed. So, they put all that off. When we got back to England, all promotions were frozen. I got like a belated captain rating, which considered [the possibility] that I would have made captain, to appease me a little bit. I never got it. I was a first lieutenant [at the end].

I came back at the end of '46 and went back to Republic Steel. In between strikes and all of that, I worked construction here and everything and never drew unemployment. I had 31 years credit with Republic Steel. It wasn't the actual time I spent there, because our service time was counted as years worked and they called me back during the Korean War. I had to go back again to serve. So, I trained on the B-29s. Then I became an instructor. I became the staff officer of the radar men. I know they grumbled at me, but I put them through the paces every week. I said, 'By God, I want to get home, and I know most of you want to get home, too.'

*

Van Tress had a son born. He was married for a month. Chapman and I tried to talk him out of it, to wait until the war was over. He married this girl he was wild about. Then he died.

After we got shot down and then came back to base, there were a couple of guys who came over from some other base and wanted to talk to me about Van. His mother asked them to go see me because Van slept right next to me. I gave them a whole bunch of pictures of Van and his new wife and all of that. So, they took them with them. The last time I talked to Twyford, he said he heard from Mrs. Van Tress. Her son's wife and his son are coming over. So, he would be her grandchild.

I could never find the co-pilot, Wallace. He sent me a letter in 1947. He was taking engineering up in college. He let me know that he and his wife Betty are good and he hoped that I go to college too. I wrote him a letter back and then we kind of let time slip by a little bit. One time heading out to Las Vegas I landed in St. Louis, where I last knew he lived. We had about a three-hour layover and I called up his home. The people who were living there then never remembered him. My son found around ten Wallaces around the area. I called three but none of them were there. The next night I called three more, so I gave it up. I even put an inquiry in *American Legion Magazine* and the *VFW Magazine* to see if anybody knew his whereabouts; called the 2nd Air Division Association, which I belonged to, and they tried to find him and they couldn't.

All the rest of the men are gone. Chapman was the last one. I used to call Chapman several times. We talked to each other quite a bit. I know the first time I sent him a Christmas card, he sent one back. He wrote, 'Please, if you ever come down and see me, don't ever talk to my wife about what we did in the service.' [*Laughs*] He lived in Alabama. He became quite wealthy. He had a crew of men out— carpentry work, anything. He worked the whole of Alabama and even part of Florida doing construction or anything he'd want or excavating or whatever. He owned a local Howard Johnson franchise and he owned a big share of the local bank. He had a loan company and a motel. He said, 'If you ever come down, I don't want you paying for any meals or rooms. You come here; I've got a place, and I am looking forward to seeing you.' We tried a couple of times, but something happened. He wasn't feeling good or I wasn't feeling good or something.

I called him up. Every Christmas Day I'd call him up after twelve noon; I'd just call him up and have a talk. The last time I called just a few years ago—it can't be over five years ago—his wife answered. Of course, down there they don't use your first name. They just go by your last name.

She said, 'Who is this?'

I said, 'That Polish Yankee from upstate New York.'

She said, 'Oh, Bezon! Just a minute. I'll see if Bill can get on the phone.' I said to myself, 'Oh, sounds like he is not good.'

He got on and he said, 'Martin, you don't know what this means to me when you call.' I think it bothered him what happened the time that I was [reprimanded] and got chewed out, and I think it might have bothered him quite a bit later in life.

I said, 'What's the matter with you, Bill?'

He said, 'I just had open-heart surgery and I'm recuperating.' And then he had something wrong with his leg.

I said, 'Geez, Bill, we've got to get together at least once.'

He said, 'Boy, we've got to!'

I got worried about him. A few days later I called up again.

I said, 'I just want to know how Bill's doing.'

His wife said, 'I am sorry to tell you, he died last night.'

So then Twyford died, and that was the last of them.

Anderson was on the police force and died from a heart attack. Yarcusko was out in California laying rugs and he died. So they're all gone, and I stay here.

*

Marty Bezon passed away at the age of 90 in April 2012, only three weeks after this interview took place.

Seymour 'Sonny' Segan, World War II.

CHAPTER ELEVEN

The Bombardier

I got to know Seymour Segan during a visit to his house in the fall of 2002. A former student worked at the local copy center, and Mr. Segan had brought in some World War II era photographs to be reproduced. 'He asked me if I'd be interested in talking to you. Even the manner that he asked me was with the right courtesy, you know? Not imposing—he thought it was very important. I think you had an influence on him; he was on the ball.'

He invited me to his home on a chilly November evening in 2002, about a week before a planned symposium on the air war at my school, which I had invited him to be a part of. We sat down in his living room; his wife Shirley joined us.

On December 7, 1941, Mr. Segan was nineteen and leading a troupe of Boy Scouts in New Jersey on a camping trip. A forest ranger told him about the attack, and he decided to enlist. He went into the Aviation Cadet program. 'I'll bet you that three-quarters of the guys in my crew, if not all, volunteered. Definitely the pilot, the co-pilot, the navigator, and myself. Because you weren't drafted to get into the Aviation Cadet Program. When I went into the Aviation Cadet Program, you had to have two years of college or an equivalency test to do it. Originally, it was four years of college, in order to become an aviation cadet. Ford Motor Company's Willow Run plant was knocking out B-24s like crazy. They needed you fast, so they made it two years of college or an equivalency test, which I was able to pass. I didn't have any school or college at the time.'

Segan wound up in the 485ᵗʰ Bombardment Group flying missions on the B-24 Liberator out of southern Italy with the 829ᵗʰ Squadron. He opened up about the trauma of World War II, and the miracles that saved him.

'I ended up in I think 22 or 23 different hospitals. Service-related, but mostly for my leg. Post-traumatic war syndrome was the worst. A combination of that with alcoholism—I found AA. That was a deciding factor in my [post-war] recovery.'

***

Duties of the Bombardier

Accurate and effective bombing is the ultimate purpose of your entire airplane and crew. Every other function is preparatory to hitting and destroying the target.

That's your bombardier's job. The success or failure of the mission depends upon what he accomplishes in that short interval of the bombing run.

When the bombardier takes over the airplane for the run on the target, he is in absolute command. He will tell you what he wants done, and until he tells you "Bombs away," his word is law.

A great deal, therefore, depends on the understanding between bombardier and pilot. You expect your bombardier to know his job when he takes over. He expects you to understand the problems involved in his job, and to give him full cooperation. Teamwork between pilot and bombardier is essential.

There are many things with which a bombardier must be thoroughly familiar in order to release his bombs at the right point to hit this predetermined target.

He must know and understand his bombsight, what it does, and how it does it.

He must thoroughly understand the operation and upkeep of his bombing instruments and equipment.

He must know how to set it up, make any adjustments and minor repairs while in flight.

He must know how to operate all gun positions in the airplane.

He must be able to load and fuse his own bombs.

He must understand the destructive power of bombs and must know the vulnerable spots on various types of targets.

He must understand the bombing problem, bombing probabilities, bombing errors, etc.

The bombardier should be familiar with the duties of all members of the crew and should be able to assist the navigator in case the navigator becomes incapacitated.

After releasing the bombs, the pilot or bombardier may continue evasive action--usually the pilot, so that the bombardier may man his guns.

—Duties and Responsibilities of the Airplane Commander and Crewmen, 1943

***

Seymour 'Sonny' Segan

'In Maxwell, Nebraska, there's a separate cemetery just for group burial—lots of men are buried there. There were ten of us on that plane. Three of us survived. One got out before the plane went into the dive—it was in a straight dive from about 13,000 feet—one was blown out of the plane when half of the plane blew up on the way down—and I got out just before it hit the ground, maybe a second or two; I think I was pushed out. I have a 1947 [area search investigation] report that says, 'Were fingerprints taken?' 'No.' 'Why not?' 'No hands.' You know, that type of thing where they bury thirty-five pounds of a guy that weighed 200 pounds.'

*

I was one of the original 485th Bomb Group. We trained in the United States, in Nebraska. We went overseas; we flew from Nebraska to Florida, then we flew down to Trinidad, and then we flew to Brazil. And from Brazil, we flew across to Dakar. Then we came up to Marrakesh, where we lost a crew in the Atlas Mountains—they flew right into them.

When we flew the group over, the ground crew came by ship. One squadron lost their ground crew because the ship was one of the largest [troop carriers]; the Germans got them in the Mediterranean and sunk the delivery ship. We were in Tunis for about four or five weeks, and then flew across to Venosa, Italy, where we started our missions.

The first mission to Yugoslavia was a 'milk run.' A milk run is an easy mission where you don't run into fighters and have little to no flak. It was probably planned that way, because at the time the group was a whole bunch of neophytes. Later on, when you have a mixture of [more seasoned crews] and replacements, that's where it gets tougher. When I was in North Africa [before the missions in Italy], we'd go into Tunis, and you'd run into some guys who had already finished their fifty missions. You got a hold of them right away and you would try to pick their brains the most you can. And the usual question we always asked was, 'How many guys made it all the way through?' It was usually two, three, and occasionally four crews or so. Out of eighteen planes in a squadron. There were four squadrons in a group. We were the 828th, 829th, 830th, and 831st. The group commander was Colonel [Walter] Arnold, a very famous leader at that time. His uncle was Hap Arnold, the head of the United States Army Air Corps in those days. He got shot down, too; he was shot down after I was.

We were there for about four or five weeks. You hear of two, three, four crews coming through. And I got cocky. Because you go on a mission, and you lose one, you lose two, sometimes three or four planes. You start to look out when you're flying and...

By the way, we flew to Africa in the planes that were [painted] 'ODs.' You know what OD is? Olive drab. Our planes were all painted that dark green, but later on they found out that the paint was hundreds of pounds of weight, and also the friction against the rough paint was reducing the air speed. So they would start to leave them straight shiny aluminum. But it really didn't change things; the Germans found you either way. [*Laughs*] Olive drab was not camouflage, not while you're up there.

We'd be in the air and I would look out and I would see all these silver planes around me. I'd say, 'Hey, I'm one of the ones that's going to make it'; there's always a few that make it all the way through. You look around at all the replacements and you're one of the originals! You know some of the originals are going to make it, it's a good chance it'll be me. After 25 missions, we were down to that. That was the mission before my last mission. It was a false sense of security I had.

'Controlled Fear'

Still, it might sound funny, but you always accepted the fact that you might not make it; you were stupid if you didn't. You flew with what I would call 'controlled fear.' You were scared stiff, but it was controlled. My ball turret gunner—he couldn't take it anymore. As a matter of fact, he tried to shoot his leg, but he didn't hit his foot; he just took a piece of skin off it. He didn't want to fly anymore, but they wouldn't ground him. I guess he was right. He's dead now. But he had lost control of the fear. Ball turret is a tough place to be, too. He never got out of that ball turret; he died in that ball turret. You have to depend upon somebody else getting you out. You got to crank it up [*makes hand motions*]. It goes down below the plane and you can't land with the turret down, otherwise you'll be scraping along the runway. Somebody has to crank him up and then you turn yourself around to be able to come out the hatch.

But I really thought I would complete the fifty missions. You'd get to go home. [But] the fifty missions is a fallacy. The reason they called it 'fifty missions' was because anyone who had 25 missions in the Eighth Air Force was okay. The reason we had fifty is because on some missions we got credit for two, depending on the severity of the mission. Ploesti was two. Wiener Neustadt, Austria, was two. Neunkirchen, Austria, was two.

Munich was two. But when you hit, like, Bologna in Italy…

[*To wife*] Should I tell him the story about Bologna?

[*To interviewer*] You know the [local Italian-American restaurateur family]? She had her Italian restaurant; one night we went in with another couple, and on the wall was a pictorial map of Bologna, Italy.

I looked at it, and I said, 'Oh! Bologna! I bombed that in World War II!'

And she said, 'My father was killed in that raid.'

She wasn't upset or anything; there were quite a few raids on Bologna, it was hit quite a few times. Anyway, that was a shorter run, and would be credited as one mission.

The worst targets were in Ploesti and Budapest, where the oil refineries were. Those were the worst, in the same category as Wiener Neustadt in Austria, which was where aircraft factories were. Those were rough. There was heavy, very heavy anti-aircraft flak and fighter planes.

On D-Day, we were sent to Ploesti early in the morning. We were like a diversion to pull fighters to the east instead of to Normandy and that area, on June 6. Your Tuskegee Airman, is he coming [to the air war symposium]?[33] They were great; they were great. I want to compare notes with him about missions we were on. Any time we saw our American fighters coming in, it was one of the greatest sights.

The problem was, on our long missions, most of the time our fighter planes couldn't go all the way [to the target with us]. A fighter plane usually had a belly tank [with extra fuel]. But they couldn't fight in combat with the German fighters with their belly tanks on—it would decrease their maneuverability. So the minute they would come in contact with any fighters, they had to drop their tanks. [They were with us] in Italy, depending on what the mission was. We even went to Munich [together], which was a long mission. And we went to Czechoslovakia, you know, those types of places.

---

[33] *air war symposium*-In November 2002 the author organized a panel discussion at our high school on the air war featuring Mr. Segan, pilot Earl Morrow, and Tuskegee Airman Clarence Dart. Mr. Morrow is also featured in this book, and both Morrow and Dart are featured in the sequel to this book.

These were long missions, in those days. Today it's not. Our airspeed wasn't that high, maybe 150, 160, sometimes 170 mph, you know. The fighters can go much faster. But they couldn't use their belly tanks; they'd have to jettison them for combat.

'Maximum Effort'

The missions to Ploesti, Romania, had begun in earnest in midsummer 1943, when in the first disastrous low-level raid flying out of Libya, 54 bombers were destroyed by German fighters and flak; over 660 men were killed or shot down and taken prisoner. As strategy was refined, sustained attacks on 'Hitler's gas station' over the next fourteen months crippled the flow of oil from what had once supplied at least a third of the Reich's supply.[13]

On the day we were shot down, we were not even in our own plane. Our plane had been badly damaged in the mission before this one, badly banged up from flak and needed a lot of repair. They wanted the maximum effort on this mission so they sent us up in an old plane from the 831st Squadron. I was the 829th. That plane should not have been flying. We had trouble with one of the plane engines; it started to go out, that number three engine. Later, when I was brought out of Romania back to the hospital in Bari, Italy, one of the crew members of that ship said, 'We would not fly in it. I don't know why they sent you up in it, that plane was not in a condition to fly.' That's why we got shot down.

The day we were shot down, the target was the oil refinery in Bucharest. Normally it would have been about a seven to eight hour mission; you lose a lot of time getting off, and then you have to circle until you get into formation. Don't forget we were taking a lot of ships up; you have to get into the other groups' formations. The whole concept of that type of combat we flew in was to have as many planes as possible all bunched together.

'A B-24 flying over a burning oil refinery
at Ploesti, Romania, 1 August 1943.'
United States Army Center of Military History, public domain.

You have an upper box, a middle, and a lower box of planes together. When you have the firepower of all those .50 caliber machine guns concentrated, an Me-109 or Fw-190 will not come in on you. Each ship has a nose turret gun, which is two .50 caliber machine guns; a top turret, two more; a ball turret gunner, two more; two waist gunners, one each—they would hold them out the waist window; you also had the tail gunner. So you have got 2, 4, 6, 8...10. Ten .50 caliber guns, but when you're flying in a formation of 18 planes, and close by that is another formation of 18 planes, that is multiplied. There are 180 machine guns from that one box, and you have those three boxes, one right there with the other one. We flew formations so close that you could see the faces of the guys in the plane off-setting you. It took flying skill, it took coordination over the radio and everything like that, and that was the best protection you had from enemy fighters.

From flak you had no protection. The only way we had protection from flak was we would throw out tinsel to try and screw up the radar that they had, so the air would be full of metal. But still, you know, [in daylight] they more or less could figure us out. Flak was a deadly, deadly thing.

Once you go up to your 'IP,' the initial point to begin the bombing run, the plane cannot veer or take evasive action from the flak. As a matter of fact, the pilot is not even flying the plane at that point; it was my job as the bombardier, taking over. When we made that turn to the target, we have to stay in that course until I dropped the bombs. Then we had to [turn, in formation] as fast as we could to get out of the flak.

Now their fighters would be ready. They did not want to go into their own flak, most of these German fighters. So, one good thing was, when you were over the target with all of that flak, you were not being hit by fighter planes. Although on some missions they did come in to attack us through their own flak, the majority of times they did not. When we began the group turn, after we dropped our bombs and started to turn to go home, that's when we lost our group. That is when fighter pilots attacked us. They will always go after the stragglers.

We could not keep up with the group; we had that one engine out, and another one was not in good shape. We had also lost our radio communication as we were being attacked by the Me-109s. We had lost altitude from about 22,000 feet to 13,000 feet when they hit us. Some reports say nine, some reports say seven; I remember that there were a lot of them coming in. I was dry in the mouth. I was in my bombardier compartment, there was a nose gunner in front of me, and then there was a bubble over the top of it that I could put my head up in to call out the fighters: 'At twelve o'clock,' 'three o'clock,' 'two coming in at three,' 'two coming in at two,' you know, that type of thing.

The ironic part about it was that I was the best gunner in my crew. I had gone to gunnery school and I was an excellent machine gunner prior to going to my advance training as bombardier. That's a frustrating feeling, not having a gun.

I had to give testimony when we got back. [*Reads from an official 'Reports of Death' identification memorandum dated June 10, 1949*]:

> Date: June 28, 1944
> Time: 10:30 AM
> The location was approximately 35 miles southwest of Bucharest, Romania. The plane was in a dive when I bailed out. It went into a dive at 13,000 feet, stayed in it all the way down.
> I was hanging out the escape hatch when it went into the dive and managed to bail out just before it hit the ground. I bailed out approximately 300 feet from the ground. To my knowledge, none of the crew were killed or wounded before she crashed.
> The plane was on fire when it went into the dive. The fire was in the bomb bay

command deck and waist. All engines were shot out. In the dive, the tail blew off. While on the ground, I saw part of the stabilizer floating down. This was confirmed by radio operator, Tech Sergeant Scott, who was blown clear when she blew. Lieutenant M. J. Hirsch, Navigator, Tech Sargent Scott, and myself bailed out and our chutes opened. The plane exploded and smeared all over the ground when it hit.

After reaching the ground I saw Tech Sergeant Scott, whose parachute came down after me. He came over to me and tried helping me with my leg, which was injured upon hitting the ground. Near the fire of the plane was a parachute, and Romanians who picked Scott and I up told us that this man was dead. I did not see who it was but I have reason to believe it was Sergeant Peterson, who had been the only one reported killed.

While in the prison camp I heard from Lieutenant M.J. Hirsch, whom I later saw being freed. As for the rest of the men I heard nothing. I did not examine the wreckage, and all I could see was fire along the ground. We did not land in water.

I believe my other crew men are dead as the ship was in a straight dive down, making it nearly impossible to bail out. I (barely) got out as I was hanging out the escape hatch when we went into the dive, having only inches to go, and it still took

me 13,000 feet to get out. Sergeant Scott was
holding on the waist gun and was blown out
the waist window. Lieutenant Hirsch got
out before she went into the dive. Another
reason I believe they are dead is because
no one ever saw their parachutes and they
never showed up at the prison camp after
we were freed.

*

Last year I got a really interesting phone call
from Milwaukee, Wisconsin. The nose turret
gunner came from Milwaukee, he was married, he
had just had a little baby girl; she was about six
months old when he died. He got killed in the
crash; he might have pushed me off and out of the
plane. You have to understand, it's like centrifugal
force. It was like a stone wall that you are up
against. You got to get out—I can't get out, I die. I
don't want to die, I got to get out! I can't get out,
that type of thing, and then all of a sudden, bam, I
am out! He was a big, powerful guy. I don't know.
I was hanging out the escape hatch of the nose
wheel.

His grandson called. The nose gunner was killed
on June 28, and a few months later his wife died
from tuberculosis; this little girl was left alone. Her

family brought her up. She had five sons. One of her sons called me, his grandson.

I said to him, 'I am almost 90% positive that your grandfather saved my life.' To be honest with you, I do not know. The pressure when the plane went into the dive was so great, it was like pushing us back. This man who called me never knew his grandparents; his mother never knew her own mother and father. I didn't even know about that until he called.

*

I don't remember pulling the ripcord, but when I hit the ground, I smashed my left leg. I was about 50 or 100 feet away from the burning plane. I took off the Star of David from around my neck and tossed it as far as I could; Romania was also very anti-Semitic and working with the Nazis. My radio operator, Scotty, came over and then the Germans arrived. They took us to an airfield. Because my leg was so bad, they took me to a civilian hospital in a small town, Budesti; Bucharest was in flames at the time from bombardment.

The first day I was there they brought in this big guy; he looked like he was cast for a beer wagon driver in the 1890s with the big handlebar mustache, the big cheeks, you know. [*Chuckles*] They were telling me that my bombs injured him! I was a little scared, a twenty-one-year-old kid. Then he starts yelling at me, 'For Vayne! For Vayne!'

I did not know what he was saying but I figured it was the F-word. [*Laughs*] One of the nurses spoke a little French and I spoke a little French, my high school French. It turns out he had a brother in Fort Wayne, Indiana; he wanted to know if I knew his brother! [*Laughs*] He gave me a big smile. He wasn't angry with me.

They had girl Russian prisoners, paratroopers, working in the kitchen there. The Romanians shaved off all of their hair so they could not escape, so they would be able to find them, you know, looking for a bald girl. [*Chuckles*] They heard that there was an American prisoner there, and they came to my bed with some food that they took from the kitchen, some fruit, and gave it to me. I liked it there but they did not keep me there long; they sent me to a Russian prison camp. I was there about four or five days until some [Romanian] officer came in one day. The men in the camp, the

Russians, were enlisted men. Most of the Romanian officers were all members of the nobility. They were second and third and fourth sons of the nobles, so being an officer in the military in Romania was a very high echelon thing. Civilians in the street, as they passed, would have to salute them. So, it would be against their whole belief system to put an officer, even an enemy officer, in with prisoners who were enlisted men. So they put me in a hospital with another Romanian officer, who treated me very nicely, gave me extra food and things like that. The only thing that was bad there was the doctor. There was a three-inch gap between my tibia and fibula and he told me to walk on it. I didn't know; I was a twenty-one-year-old kid. A young Romanian intern, who couldn't speak a word of English, made me understand not to. He did it secretively, afraid of getting caught. Then, a nun brought in a picture of Jesus Christ and hung it on the wall. And I found out that the Romanian officer was anti-Semitic. I am Jewish. Finally, I told him I was Jewish. He never spoke to me for the next couple of days, and they moved me out into Bucharest.

We had a French doctor, who was interned, who took care of us in Bucharest. He took X-rays of my leg. He saw what had happened to my leg. He put me on a table and he got some guys from the camp downstairs. Real strong ones, you know, six-footers and 200-pounders. Three on each side, they held me down, and he re-broke the leg so it could have a chance to heal properly. It worked, although much later, I had to have a bone graft. I had a bone taken out of this leg [*touches right leg*] and put into that leg [*touches left leg*]. She healed beautifully. She healed so well that—you can feel it right here [*pulls down sock to show the area where the bone was grafted*]—that even in November 30, 1947, when I turned a car over five times, my car landed on top of the leg. If it had landed on [the rest of] me it would have killed me. I was thrown out as the car was turning over. It didn't break here [*points to the graft area*]; it broke here [*points to higher on leg*].

As the Red Army poured into Romania, the pro-fascist government was overthrown in a coup d'état near the end of August and Romania joined the Allies. The PoWs' situation was precarious; as the Red Army *approached the capital, the Germans carried out a series of reprisal terror bombing raids.*

The bombings started by the Germans. As a matter of fact, the guys were looking up in the sky thinking maybe it was our boys, and it turned out to be Dorniers, which are German bombers. When the bombings started as the Russians were coming in, all of a sudden there were Romanian tanks around the hospital ward we [Americans] were in, to protect us, because we were their greatest asset at that time.

We were terror-bombed for three days and three nights. Before that, we were bombed by the Americans and the British. The first night we were in the basement of the hospital. This was a very, very, very old building. The rats were all over. We decided to go out, and I was starting to fall on my crutches when a couple of guys grabbed me. My radio operator had come out of a building that most of the GIs ended up in. It was the tallest building in Bucharest; it was a sixteen-story building, steel and concrete, owned by the Franco-American Oil Company. [*Laughs*] They also had two 40mm anti-aircraft guns, on the roof. Our guys had taken it over [with the Romanians' blessing].

He had come to look for me, and I thought that he should have gotten a medal for that. They grabbed me. They had no stretcher, so they used a door that had been blown off, and they carried me to the safety of this building, which was a few blocks away. We were on the eighth floor, we took over the whole eighth floor. Our officers went to the Bank of Romania and they borrowed $75,000. We got equipment and rifles, things like that. We had our guards around the perimeter. We set up our own kitchen there. It was the safest place to be because you were in the middle of a building. You had the anti-aircraft guns on the roof. Not only did we go there, but as many of the Romanian people who could get into the building got in to there. The only difference was we had food.

'Like Ants Scurrying Back and Forth'

One of the saddest things I ever saw, after the third day of bombing by the Germans, these people had not had food at all. Bread trucks came to the courtyard of the building; this building had a courtyard in the middle of the building. The bread trucks came in and the Romanians started to cue up the civilians. All of a sudden, the sirens went off again and we could hear the German planes in the air. I watched from the eighth floor... [*hesitates; gets choked up*] I'm sorry. It was like ants scurrying back and forth... [*pauses, composes himself*] I'm sorry.

They were... [*pauses*] they wanted the safety of the building. But they needed bread, they were hungry. You could see them [*motions his hands back and forth*], they were torn—do we go to the building for safety, or for the bread? [*Takes a deep breath and regroups himself*] When you fly, you don't see that. You are up at 20,000, 25,000 feet. All you can see is the landmarks and soccer stadiums, the oil refinery you are going to hit or the marshalling yards, the railroad yards that you are going to hit. When I saw that I just broke down, and at that time I swore I would never drop another bomb. But I came to terms with that; if I had to do it again, I would. But actually seeing it was a very, very traumatic experience for me, still is.

*

I was a prisoner for two months. In early September, the first and largest evacuation of American PoWs during the war occurred; they flew us back to Italy.

Over a thousand American PoWs were flown out of Romania on converted B-17s. On September 4, 1944, the commanding officer of the 15th Air Force, Major Gen. N.F. Twining, wrote to the evacuees:

> You are going home. You are the returning heroes of the Battle of Ploesti. Your safe return to my command marked the culmination of an outstanding campaign in the annals of American military history. The German war machine's disintegration on all fronts is being caused, to a large extent, by their lack of oil-oil that you took from them. I only have one regret on this jubilant occasion. I wish it had been possible to bring out of Romania every officer and man who went down in that battle.

Of the 3,781 men shot down trying to destroy Ploesti, only 1,185 came home.

'Missing in Action'

When I came out of Romania, I was in the hospital in Italy. A neighbor's kid from home came up to see me. He had heard that they had brought us guys back. His family had been writing to him to see if they could find out about me, where I was, how I could be reached.

I asked him right away, 'How are my mother and father?'

He said, 'Well your mother is dead, don't you know it?'

I just broke down. I was in bad shape; I weighed about 100 pounds at the time. I had just gotten out of Romania. So I sent a telegram. It said, 'Know about mother, don't worry.' [*Begins to cry softly*]

I'm sorry, sometimes I get a little emotional, I can't help that. The chaplain was supposed to tell me, but he never did. [*Hands the interviewer some World War II era telegrams*]

'Missing in action.' If you look at some of these telegrams, none of them have my home address; they were addressed to my father's place of business. I purposely didn't want the telegram to go home because I knew my mother had very, very high blood pressure. My father and I had a deal where I'd have it sent to my father's place of business so he would make arrangements to have a doctor come out and be handy, if need be. I got shot down June 28. It came to my father during the July 4th weekend, and they couldn't deliver it because the place of business was closed. So they went through the trouble to find out the home address, Strauss Street, which was delivered on July the fifth. My father was already in Manhattan working that day and my mother was home. The telegram came, that I'm missing in action. According to the way I heard it, she started to walk up the stairs and she keeled over. They called the doctor from down the block. She died of a cerebral hemorrhage.

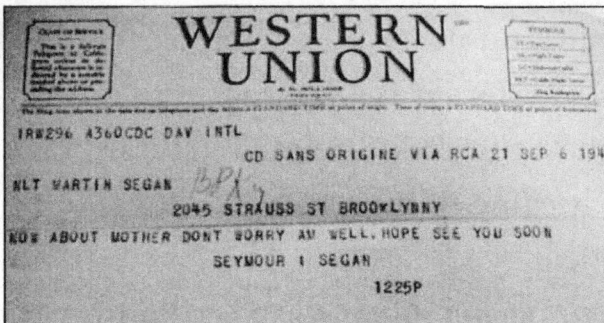

I spent a lot of time in hospitals. I had a lot of trouble reconciling how my mother died from the telegram. How do you think you feel when you find out you killed your mother?

Wife: He was 'Sonny.' He was the youngest and he was the only boy.

Seymour Segan: I used to blame myself that I didn't explain to her the fact that 'missing in action' is not necessarily 'killed in action.' You know? I didn't even think about that. One of the reasons I didn't want to be in a foxhole or be a foot soldier was because, at least in the air, it's often quick and over with, the ship blows up or crashes. Maybe that's what she was thinking. In my case, seven out of ten died and three of us lived.

Did I give you the letter where I'm dead? It was a letter from the Veterans Administration. Let's see if I can find it, it's here someplace. [*Shuffles papers around*] Here it is. 'We regret to inform you of the death of the above-named veteran.' [*Laughs*]

Wife: It came to his parents, but his mother was already dead.

Seymour Segan: That was cleared up very fast. I had a brother-in-law at that time who was very much involved with the military, and he was able to go outside of the channels and find out what was going on.

*

[I experienced a lot of troubles], but I've found, in a way, that everything sometimes turns out for the best. [After the 1947 car accident], they put me in Brooklyn Jewish Hospital and then transported me to the Veterans Hospital. When I had recovered enough, the doctor said, 'Go home for ten weeks, then come back and we will take X-rays and see how it healed.' I said, 'I can't go home; I live in a furnished room. I have no way of making food; I will have to walk in the winter on crutches for seven, eight blocks to find a restaurant for breakfast, lunch, and dinner.' So, they sent me up here, near the Adirondacks, to a veterans hospital at Mt. McGregor. [34] It was originally built in 1903 by

---

[34] *Mt. McGregor*-Mt. McGregor has an interesting history. It is located in Wilton, New York, about 10 miles south of Glens Falls. Originally settled by Native American survivors escaping King Philip's War, it boasts spectacular views. Duncan McGregor built a hotel called the Mountain House in 1876; in 1885, the new owner, Joseph Drexel, loaned the use of his personal cottage on the mountain to his friend, then seriously ill former president Ulysses S. Grant, where Grant finished writing his war memoirs in just six weeks before he died there that July. Today, the Grant Cottage State Historic Site is preserved exactly as it was at the time of his death. In 1945, New York State

Metropolitan Life for tuberculosis patients. It's on top of the mountain there—fresh air, cold fresh air, porches all the way around. They could take the patients and put them out in the cold air so they could breathe. They thought maybe that would help with their tuberculosis, and they did the same thing in Denver, and in Saranac Lake [Adirondacks]. So they also sent me up there.

It was January of 1948, the beginning of January. I fell in love with Glens Falls, just to the north. To me, the whole town was welcoming me from Brooklyn, New York. In 1961, December the 18th, we moved up here. It was a wonderful move for us. We were very happy. The children were brought up here. We have had a wonderful life up here; I am going to be buried up here. I hope it's not for a couple more years. [*Laughs*] Sometimes bad things can lead to good things.

*

To tell you the whole story is almost impossible. Because sometimes things come back to you that you haven't thought of in years. All of a sudden you think of it, and what makes you think of it, you

---

used it for convalescing WWII veterans like Mr. Segan, and from 1976-2014 it was used as a minimum security state prison.

don't even know. I'm one of the lucky ones. It took me a long time, but I was able to put it behind me and go on with my life. Not right away. For quite a while, I was at every veterans hospital in New York City. [*Lists various hospitals*] I was doing life. I was on the installment plan. [*Laughs*]

Wife: He was in and out of every veterans hospital in New York...

Seymour Segan: I ended up in I think 22 or 23 different hospitals. For my leg, for my finger that I lost—and that happened in on-the-job training, so it was covered by the government. One of the machines took it off. Post-traumatic war syndrome was the worst, a combination of that with alcoholism. I found AA. That was a deciding factor. I carry one of these around with me all the time, and maybe I'll be able to cope with everything. [*Takes a card out of his pocket*] The important thing is right here. '*God grant me the serenity to accept the things I cannot change, courage to change the things I can, and the wisdom to know the difference.*' And once I was able to accept a lot of those things, I was able to reach my potential.

Wife: You can't blame any of these fellows who nearly self-destructed. The main thing [to remember] is that they have the wisdom to know the difference.

***

Mr. Segan lost his wife of 59 years, Shirley, in 2007, about five years after this conversation. I visited again with Mr. Segan from time to time at the retirement community he settled into. He passed away a month after his 91st birthday on January 12, 2014.

The author at Clarence McGuire's gravesite at St. Mary's Cemetery,
Fort Edward, NY. 2010. Credit: Kris Dressen.

Resurrection

The phone rang on a beautiful summer evening. It was the cap to another long day at the keyboard and perhaps the answer to a long-shot query letter I had mailed a week earlier, to parts hitherto unknown.

Just a day before mailing the letter, I had had a shock. I wondered what the odds were of finding the exact same photograph that had haunted me all of my life—but now labeled with names!—on the internet. And the webpage it appeared on at the

American Air Museum in Britain looked like it was a tribute to the crew. I looked closely at the caption:

A bomber crew of the 351st Bomb Group with their B-17 Flying Fortress. Handwritten caption: 'Technical Sergeant James E Ellis, Staff Sergeant Maurice J Franzblau, Sergeant Clarence B McGuire, Sergeant Fenton D Strohmeyer, Sergeant Guido Signoretti, Sergeant John Swarts, Second Lieutenant John M Morton, Second Lieutenant Donald Fish, Second Lieutenant William J Fuerth and Lieutenant

McCaleb D Taylor of the 351th Bomb
Group, 511 Squadron.'

I looked for the sponsor.

IN MEMORIAM

B-17 #4238146-Killed in Action (KIA)
Shot down by flak and crashed near
Beendorf, Germany.
Remembered by John S Swarts, Summer-
field, FL

Here was another shock. The tribute appeared
to be sponsored by the man who is labeled as the
tail gunner on Clarence's plane. He's in the photo
with Clarence that has been with me all of my
life—but weren't they all killed? The webpage also
says:

'2nd Lt. Warren J Bragdon filled in
as Co-Pilot for Lt. Donald Fish as he
was flying lead ship on 570 Bomb Group
in Polebrook, England.'

So there were two survivors of the crew photo,
who had not gotten on the plane that day. On the
internet again, I tracked the tail gunner to an address in Florida, and sent off the letter to what I

hoped was the right address. I included the grave-side photograph; I suppose if I had my man, it might come as a bit of a surprise to him.

I picked up the phone to answer the call. Some feedback interference hummed momentarily on the other end of the line, but even before he began to speak, I just knew that my hunch had played out. I found him, an actual survivor of the B-17 bomber crew in the photograph. Or should I say, he had found me.

John Swarts, World War II.
Source: John Swarts

'This is John Swarts,' said the voice with the dis-tinctive Southern twang. 'Me and Clarence were pretty good friends.' A pause. 'You got it right, address and everything. I knew him well; I went with him to his home up there in New York. Me and him even rode horses together; I got some pictures I can send you. His mother used to write me letters afterwards. I'll look for that, too.'

John was the tail gunner in that crew photo. He hailed from Missouri, and later settled in St. Louis.

'Things worked out all right for me. Was married twice, got a boy and a girl. Spent 33 years on the railroad, and then had my own business. I'll be 93 on February 11. I don't get around good like I used to; fell three years ago and broke my pelvis and hip. But it was just me and the co-pilot who survived that day.'

'I was burned in the eyelid by flak a couple days before. I was in the hospital and didn't go on the last mission.' Because of a snafu, his mother got a telegram stating that he was missing in action— 'The Army didn't know I was in the hospital. It took three months to clear up; she thought I was missing for two weeks before I was able to get word to the family that I was not on the plane.'

The plane went down on July 29, 1944. This weekend in the summer of 2017, the 73rd anniversary is upon us as we speak on the phone. 'The name of the plane was *Pugnacious Ball*. Flak got it. Blew it up. But I think they recovered a body bag to send home to his mother.'

'I watched for the planes coming back; you always do when they are out on a mission. You count them. We waited and waited. They didn't come back.'

'It was the worst day of my life. Still is.'

John sent me some material back in the mail— some photographs, scrapbook pages, even a letter from Clarence's mother.[35] 'We were a very close

---

[35] *a letter from Clarence's mother-*

May 1, 1946

Dear Corporal [sic-Sergeant] Swarts:

I am the mother of Sergeant Clarence B. McGuire who was a member of the crew to which you were attached, and who was killed in action on his 6th mission over Germany (Merseberg) on July 29th, 1944. Only Providence knows the mystery which surrounds the entire crew. I had never received any further particulars from the Government, but Clarence's only brother, Jack, was the E.T.O. at the same time, and he worked hard to get any information to be had.

When Jack reached Versailles, France, he went directly to the Graves Information Department there, and found that Clarence had been buried in an isolated grave in Benndorf, Germany, from July 29, 1944 to June 18, 1945 – at which time he was reburied in the U.S. at Margraten, Holland. Jack went to his grave in July 1945. You may be sure that what he was able to accomplish was the source of much comfort to me. I hadn't heard a word from the Government, but in checking with them in December last, they confirmed the information I already had. Clarence's brother and I have erected a very lovely memorial to Clarence's memory, in our own family cemetery, and I crew. This is a photo of us horseback riding in Denver, Colorado, in cadet school training. We enjoyed our time together. We then went to gunnery school in Kingman, Arizona.' Clarence's nickname was 'Barney.' He was the biggest one on the crew. We all got along good. Oh, we had a lot of fun, going to Piccadilly Square and all...'

---

have requested that Clarence's remains be sent to me, just as soon as this procedure is possible.

I am particularly anxious to get in touch with Captain James P. Tounley who was the Commanding Officer of your crew at the time of Clarence's last mission. Captain Tounley wrote my son Jack immediately after, and it was such a kind, fine letter. I wrote to Washington to get Captain Tounley's address, but one of their form cards said the department for such information was closed, and they could not be of assistance. However, it may just be that you know of his whereabouts, and would let me have his address if you know it – I would be appreciative of your kindness in forwarding it to me.

I am addressing you under your military title, though I earnestly hope you are now out of service and have returned to civilian life – in which I wish you much more happiness. If ever you come to New York, do make it a point to come and see me. I should like so much to have you do so; Clarence spoke so highly of all of the men attached to the crew; said they were all such a fine lot.

Thank you again and again for the above address if you can get it for me, or already have it, and with my best wishes to you,

Most sincerely,
(Mrs.) Helen Y. McGuire.

*Riding horses in Colorado. John is on the right with the child;
Clarence is on the left. Source: John Swarts.*

Over in England, they called themselves the 'Ball Boys' after their commander, Col. Ball. Clark Gable, the movie actor, was also in the 351st Bomb Group at the time, enlisting and flying operational missions over Germany.

'He flew with us six times; I got to be with him a few times. He was a nice man.'

John also met the eighteen-year-old Princess Elizabeth and her parents.

'She was pretty quiet. I had a year on her. That's General Doolittle and the King and Queen, too. We talked for a couple minutes; I was just coming off a mission, and they were there to greet us.

Somebody took a picture; it says on the back, *NOT FOR RELEASE*, but I suppose it's okay now.'

From left: John Swarts, General Jimmy Doolittle,
The Queen Consort Elizabeth Bowes-Lyon, King George VI,
and Princess Elizabeth, 1944.
Source: John Swarts.

'I flew six missions with the crew Clarence was on, and seventeen altogether. We flew a support mission on D-Day, knocking out a German ammo dump. I saw a lot of guys getting killed on the beach, getting shot on the ground on that day. It was awful.'

John also sent me newspaper clippings. *'Vet Feels Guilty Because Buddies Died,'* declares one. 'I feel so guilty. They were buried in Germany the same day they were shot down.'

'When they shipped me home, I was training on the B-29 in California when the war ended. I was lucky a lot. Somebody was with me.'

'Everybody was answering their call to duty. I wanted to go; you do it and that's it. I made a lot of friends; I lost a lot of friends.'

'I don't know what to make of the world today. Wars are different. Today you drop a bomb from 8,000 miles away. All the countries think different; always somebody wants to be a dictator. People are trying to divide us—there should be more unity in America.'

I asked John what his nickname was.

'Mickey. I don't know why. I was the youngest, like Mickey Mouse I guess,' he chuckled.

I asked him if he knew who took his place on that fatal mission.

'I don't know. I wondered for a long time...nobody knows, and I'm not sure I'd want to know, now. It could have been anybody—lots of times a mechanic or somebody from the ground crew would jump in, if they were short somebody last minute. Oh yes, that happened quite a bit. They wanted to go, they wanted to fly. Kids are crazy, you know that… anyway, it'd break my heart to find out now.'

John Swarts at the World War II Memorial, Washington, DC.

Our time grew short. We said our goodbyes.

'I get a little emotional. I'm almost 93; I hope to see them all again in heaven.'

'My Best 4 Friends of our crew, all killed in action but me.'
L-R- Clarence B McGuire, Maurice J Franzblau, Fenton D
Strohmeyer, Guido Signoretti, John Swarts. Source: John Swarts.

*

I copy the letter Clarence's mother sent to John after the war. I fold it up and return to the grave of my youth, and leave it under a memorial pebble inscribed by my students:

'We Will Never Forget'

I turn and leave this cemetery to go back out into the world, having gone again to see a hometown boy whose future ended on July 29, 1944. And I take another memorial pebble the kids inscribed not so long ago for such an occasion, and drop it into a padded envelope.

'We Remember'

I taught my students to stop and remember, and I think they remain genuinely grateful for that. John S. Swarts, SN 37619276, tail gunner on the B-17 #4238146, has another surprise coming in the mail soon, from the young people of this 'Hometown, USA,' from the grave of his friend. Time marches on, but the ripples go forth.[35]

***

---

[35] John called me a few days later to tell me that he had managed to get in touch with the co-pilot mentioned in this chapter, that he was still alive, over 100 years old, in Minnesota. He gave me the number, but as of this writing, I have been unable to reach him.

The Airmen featured in this book

Andy Doty: After the war, Andy Doty married his high school sweetheart, Eleanor Baker, the daughter of the local druggist, and raised three girls, settling in Palo Alto, California, and retiring as Director of Community Affairs for Stanford University. You can read more about his World War II experiences in Vol. I or by searching for his out-of-print 1995 memoir with the information provided in the 'Source Notes' in the back of this book.[14]

Richard 'Dick' Varney, Sr.: After the war, Dick Varney was employed at Imperial Color, later known as Ciba-Geigy. When he retired in 1976, he had worked himself up to the plant supervisor. He was active in his church and a local VFW post and also was an avid New York Yankees baseball fan. He also enjoyed talking politics. Dick passed away on April 24, 2008, at the age of 96.[15]

Richard G. Alagna: After the war, Richard completed law school and was admitted to the New York Bar Association in 1951. Active in community organizations, Richard also enjoys painting, photography, and etching. He has won many awards and his works are in numerous private collections and galleries across the United States.[16]

Kenneth R. Carlson: Ken Carlson enjoyed a successful career in advertising and became a youth advocate after the war. He spoke about his World

War II experiences to inspire young people and was a strong supporter of his alma mater, the Collegiate School in New York City, the oldest school in the country. He passed peacefully on July 20, 2022, in New York City, at the age of 101. [17]

Earl M. Morrow: Earl Morrow was a career airline pilot for American Airlines. He retired to the family farm in Hartford, New York, after his career, and was a sought-after speaker in local schools and community events. He passed in December 2018 at the age of 97.[18]

Martin F. Bezon: After the war, Martin worked for the U.S. Geological Survey in Alaska. After being called up for service in the Korean War, he resumed his former job at Republic Steel until the mines closed in 1971. He later worked for the Amerada Hess Corporation. Martin was very active in his local VFW, American Legion, and his church. He enjoyed spending time on Lake Champlain, hunting, and fishing in the Adirondacks and Vermont. He passed away at the age of 90 on April 16, 2012.[19]

Seymour 'Sonny' Segan: Sonny worked in New York's menswear industry and opened a number of successful retail stores, first locally and then throughout the Northeast. In 1989, Sonny was named president of the Menswear Retailers of America. He was active in his temple and community organizations throughout 'Hometown, USA.' He was also instrumental in helping many people in their recoveries through AA. He died on January 12, 2014, at the age of 91.[20]

IF YOU LIKED THIS BOOK, you'll love hearing more from the World War II generation in my other books. On the following pages you can see some samples, and I can let you know as soon as the new books are out and offer you exclusive discounts on some material. Just sign up at matthewrozellbooks.com.

THE THINGS OUR FATHERS SAW ® SERIES:

VOICES OF THE PACIFIC THEATER

WAR IN THE AIR: GREAT DEPRESSION TO COMBAT

WAR IN THE AIR: COMBAT, CAPTIVITY, REUNION

UP THE BLOODY BOOT-THE WAR IN ITALY

D-DAY AND BEYOND

THE BULGE AND BEYOND
ACROSS THE RHINE
ON TO TOKYO
HOMEFRONT/WOMEN AT WAR
CHINA, BURMA, INDIA

Some of my readers may like to know that all of my books are **directly available from the author, with collector's sets which can be autographed** in paperback and hardcover. They are popular gifts for that 'hard-to-buy-for' guy or gal on your list.

Visit my shop at matthewrozellbooks.com for details.

Thank you for reading!

I hope you found this book interesting and informative; I sure learned a lot researching and writing it. What follows are some descriptions of my other books.

Find them all at matthewrozellbooks.com.

The World War II Generation from Hometown, USA-Voices of the Pacific Theater

Volume 1 of The Things Our Fathers Saw® series started with my first book on the oral history of the men and women who served in the Pacific Theater of the war. *"The telephone rings on the hospital floor, and they tell you it is your mother, the phone call you have been dreading. You've lost part of your face to a Japanese sniper on Okinawa, and after many surgeries, the doctor has finally told you that at 19, you will never see again. The pain and shock is one thing. But now you have to tell her, from 5000 miles away."*

— *"So I had a hard two months, I guess. I kept mostly to myself. I wouldn't talk to people. I tried to figure out what the hell I was going to do when I got home. How was I going to tell my mother this? You know what I mean?"* — **WWII Marine veteran**

But you don't have to start with this book—I constructed them so that you can pick up any of the series books and start anywhere—but it's up to you.

The Things Our Fathers Saw—The Untold Stories of the World War II Generation-Volume III: War in the Air—Combat, Captivity, and Reunion

Volume 3 is about the Air War again, and this time I have some of my friends who were fighter pilots, including a Tuskegee Airman who had to deal with racism back home, on top of defeating fascism in Europe. There is also the story of my B-17 crew friends, sitting around a table and telling about the day they were all shot down over Germany, and how they survived the prisoner-of-war experience in the last year of the war. An audio version is also available.

—*"After the first mission Colonel Davis told us, 'From now on you are going to go with the bombers all the way through the mission to the target.' It didn't always work, but that was our mission—we kept the Germans off the bombers. At first they didn't want us, but toward the end, they started asking for us as an escort, because we protected them to and from the missions."* —**Tuskegee Airman, WWII**

— *"[Someone in the PoW camp] said, 'Look down there at the main gate!', and the American flag was flying! We went berserk, we just went berserk! We were looking at the goon tower and there's no goons there, there are Americans up there! And we saw the American flag, I mean—to this day I start to well up when I see the flag."*

—**Former prisoner of war, WWII**

— *"I got back into my turret. Fellas, the turret wasn't there anymore. That German fighter who had been eyeing me came in and he hit his 20mm gun, took the top of that Plexiglas and tore it right off!*

Now we're defenseless. The planes ahead of us have been shot down, we're lumbering along at 180 miles an hour, and these fighters were just [warming up] for target practice." —**B-17 Turret Gunner**

<u>The Things Our Fathers Saw—The Untold
Stories of the World War II Generation-Volume IV: 'Up the Bloody Boot'—The War in It-
aly</u>

Volume 4 in this series will take you from the

deserts of North Africa to the mountains of Italy with the men and women veterans of the
Italian campaign who open up about a war that
was so brutal, news of it was downplayed at
home. The war in the Mediterranean, and particularly the Italian Campaign, is one that for
many Americans is shrouded in mystery and
murkiness. Yet it was here that the United
States launched its first offensive in the west on
enemy soil, and it was here that Allied forces
would be slogging it out with a tenacious enemy fighting for its life in the longest single
American Campaign of World War II.

—"*There was an old French fort there, and we could
look down on it during the day. We gauged the way
we would hit that place so that the moon would set
right between two mountain peaks; we timed it so*

when we got there, that moon would silhouette them, but not us... We carried out the first and only bayonet charge [of the war] by our Rangers; we didn't fire; very few people knew that we carried out an overnight bayonet attack. I'll tell you, that's something. You see that, it'll shake you up real good." —
U.S. Army Ranger, WWII

— *"We attacked another hill, and I shot a German soldier. And then the Germans counterattacked on the hill, and I could not escape, so I decided to just lay down on top of that soldier and make believe I'm dead. They passed me by, I got up and [this German I shot] starts talking to me in English, he says he's from Coney Island, in Brooklyn; he went to visit his mother in Germany and they put him in the army. And he was dying, and he says to me, 'You can take my cigarettes; you can take my schnapps.' Then he died right underneath me. And I imagine he knew I had shot him...."*

—U.S. Army scout, WWII

— *"So there was a terrific fight going on in a place called Santa Ma-ria, south of Rome. While we were going through, in transit, we stopped at a big Italian barn; they had a kitchen set up, and we had our own mess kits. As we were going through the line, we saw this huge rack of shelves with American*

Army duffel bags packed on there. And Hendrickson said to me, 'Hey, Tony, you know what? My brother must be in the area someplace. There's his duffel bag.' The name was stenciled on. So I said, 'That's nice.' [But] I was thinking, why is his duffel bag there? Well, there was a military policeman guarding these bags. I went back to the MP. I said to him, 'What are these bags doing here?' And I told him about Hendrickson. 'Well,' he said, 'I don't know if you want to tell him, but these guys are all dead. They were all killed at Santa Maria.'" —U.S. Army map maker, WWII

The Things Our Fathers Saw—The Untold Stories of the World War II Generation-Volume V: 'D-Day and Beyond'—The War in France

Volume 5 in this series will take you from the bloody beach at Omaha through the hedgerow country of Normandy and beyond, American veterans of World War II--Army engineers and infantrymen, Coast Guardsmen and Navy sailors, tank gunners and glider pilots--sit down with you across the kitchen table and talk about what they saw and experienced, tales they may have never told anyone before.

— *"I had a vision, if you want to call it that. At my home, the mailman would walk up towards the front porch, and I saw it just as clear as if he's standing beside me—I see his blue jacket and the blue cap and the leather mailbag. Here he goes up to the house, but he doesn't turn. He goes right up the front steps.*

This happened so fast, probably a matter of seconds, but the first thing that came to mind, that's the way my folks would find out what happened to me.

The next thing I know, I kind of come to, and I'm in the push-up mode. I'm half up out of the underwater depression, and I'm trying to figure out what the hell happened to those prone figures on the beach, and all of a sudden, I realized I'm in amongst those bodies!" —Army demolition engineer, Omaha Beach, D-Day

— "My last mission was the Bastogne mission. We were being towed, we're approaching Bastogne, and I see a cloud of flak, anti-aircraft fire. I said to myself, 'I'm not going to make it.' There were a couple of groups ahead of us, so now the anti-aircraft batteries are zeroing in. Every time a new group came over, they kept zeroing in. My outfit had, I think, 95% casualties." —Glider pilot, D-Day and Beyond

— "I was fighting in the hedgerows for five days; it was murder. But psychologically, we were the best troops in the world. There was nobody like us; I had all the training that they could give us, but nothing prepares you for some things.

You know, in my platoon, the assistant platoon leader got shot right through the head, right through

the helmet, dead, right there in front of me. That affects you, doesn't it?" —Paratrooper, D-Day and Beyond

ALSO FROM MATTHEW ROZELL

~SOON TO BE A DOCUMENTARY MINI-SERIES~

"What healing this has given to the survivors and military men!"-Reviewer

FROM THE ABC WORLD NEWS 'PERSON OF THE WEEK'

A TRAIN NEAR MAGDEBURG

THE HOLOCAUST, AND THE REUNITING OF THE SURVIVORS AND SOLDIERS, 70 YEARS ON

–Featuring testimony from 15 American liberators and over 30 Holocaust survivors
–500 pages-extensive notes and bibliographical references

BOOK ONE—THE HOLOCAUST
BOOK TWO—THE AMERICANS

BOOK THREE—LIBERATION
BOOK FOUR—REUNION

THE HOLOCAUST was a watershed event in history. In this book, Matthew Rozell reconstructs a lost chapter—the liberation of a 'death train' deep in the heart of Nazi Germany in the closing days of World War II. Drawing on never-before published eye-witness accounts, survivor testimony, and wartime reports and letters, Rozell brings to life the incredible true stories behind the iconic 1945 liberation photographs taken by the soldiers who were there. He weaves together a chronology of the Holocaust as it unfolds across Europe, and goes back to literally retrace the steps of the survivors and the American soldiers who freed them. Rozell's work results in joyful reunions on three continents, seven decades later. He offers his unique perspective on the lessons of the Holocaust for future generations, and the impact that one person can make.

A selection of comments left by reviewers:

"**Extraordinary research** into an event which needed to be told. I have read many books about the Holocaust and visited various museums but had not heard reference to this train previously. The fact that people involved were able to connect, support and help heal each other emotionally was amazing."

"**The story of the end of the Holocaust and the Nazi regime** told from a very different and precise angle. First-hand accounts from Jewish survivors and the US soldiers that secured their freedom. Gripping."

"Mr. Rozell travels 'back to the future' of people who were not promised a tomorrow; neither the prisoners nor the troops knew what horrors the next moment would bring. He captures the parallel experience of soldiers fighting ruthless Nazism and the ruthless treatment of Jewish prisoners."

"If you have any trepidation about reading a book on the Holocaust, this review is for you. [Matthew Rozell] masterfully conveys the individual stories of those featured in the book in a manner that does not leave the reader with a sense of despair, but rather a sense of purpose."

"Could not put this book down--I just finished reading *A Train Near Magdeburg*. Tears fell as I read pages and I smiled through others. I wish I could articulate the emotions that accompanied me through the stories of these beautiful people."

"Everyone should read this book, detailing the amazing bond that formed between Holocaust survivors likely on their way to death in one last concentration camp as WWII was about to end, and a small number of American soldiers that happened upon the stopped train and liberated the victims. The lifelong friendships that resulted between the survivors and their liberators is a testament to compassion and goodness. It is amazing that the author is not Jewish but a "reluctant" history teacher who ultimately becomes a Holocaust scholar. This is a great book."

ABOUT THE AUTHOR

Photo Credit: Joan K. Lentini; May 2017.

Matthew Rozell is an award-winning history teacher, author, speaker, and blogger on the topic of the most cataclysmic events in the history of mankind—World War II and the Holocaust. Rozell has been featured as the 'ABC World News Person of the Week' and has had his work as a teacher filmed for the CBS Evening News, NBC Learn, the Israeli Broadcast Authority, the United States Holocaust Memorial Museum, and the New York State United Teachers. He writes on the power of teaching and the importance of the study of history at TeachingHistoryMatters.com, and you can 'Like' his Facebook author page at MatthewRozellBooks for updates.

Mr. Rozell is a sought-after speaker on World War II, the Holocaust, and history education, motivating and inspiring his audiences with the lessons of the past. Visit MatthewRozell.com for availability/details.

About this Book/ Acknowledgements

*

A note on historiographical style and convention: to enhance accuracy, consistency, and readability, I corrected punctuation and spelling and sometimes even place names, but only after extensive research. I did take the liberty of occasionally condensing the speaker's voice, eliminating side tangents or incidental information not relevant to the matter at hand. Sometimes two or more interviews with the same person were combined for readability and narrative flow. All of the words of the subjects, however, are essentially their own.

Additionally, I chose to utilize footnotes and endnotes where I deemed them appropriate, directing readers who wish to learn more to my sources, notes, and side commentary. I hope that they do not detract from the flow of the narrative.

First, I wish to acknowledge the hundreds of students who passed through my classes and who forged the bonds with the World War II generation. I promised you this book someday, and now that many of you are yourselves parents, you can tell your children this book is for them. Who says young people are indifferent to the past? Here is evidence to the contrary.

The Hudson Falls Central School District and my former colleagues have my deep appreciation for supporting this endeavor and recognizing its significance throughout the years.

For helpful feedback and suggestions on the original manuscript I am indebted to my good friend and trusted critic, Alan Bush. Alan always offers solid advice, diving into the narrative as soon as it arrives in his inbox, saving me perhaps a good deal of anguish with his timely and trusted comments. Cara Quinlan's sharp eyes and ears caught errors that were missed in an earlier edition. Sunny Buchman was one of my early champions and worked to arrange interviews with the folks at her retirement community, The Glen at Hiland Meadows. My wife Laura re-typed some of the seventy-five-year-old letters and reports. My friend Rob Miller traveled to my hometown to take some very special portraits of our veterans and participate in some of our events recognizing them. The Folklife Center at Crandall Public Library in Glens Falls helped with background information on the *LOOK Magazine* series that profiled the Glens Falls–North Country region as 'Hometown, USA' during the war. To my good friend and classmate Paul Dietrich, thanks for finally getting me on board to experience firsthand a deafening, lumbering B-17 flight up Lake George and back.

Naturally this work would not have been possible had it not been for the willingness of the veterans to share their stories for posterity. Andy Doty graciously allowed me to use excerpts from his well-written war autobiography. All of the veterans who were interviewed for this book had the foresight to complete release forms granting access to their stories, and for us to share the information with the New York State Military Museum's Veterans Oral History Project, where copies of most of the interviews reside. Wayne Clarke and Mike Russert of the NYSMMVOP were instrumental in cultivating this relationship with my classes over the years, and are responsible for some of the interviews in this book as well. Please see the 'Source Notes.'

I would be remiss if I did not recall the profound influence of my late mother and father, Mary and Tony Rozell, both cutting-edge educators and proud early supporters of my career. To my younger siblings Mary, Ned, Nora, and Drew, all accomplished writers and authors, thank you for your encouragement as well. Final and deepest appreciations go to my wife Laura and our children, Emma, Ned, and Mary. Thank you for indulging the old man as he attempted to bring to life the stories he collected as a young one.

NOTES

[1] Bailey, Ronald H. *The Air War in Europe*. Alexandria, Virginia: Time-Life Books, 1979. 28.

[2] Bailey, Ronald H. *The Air War in Europe*. Alexandria, Virginia: Time-Life Books, 1979. 29.

[3] Bailey, Ronald H. *The Air War in Europe*. Alexandria, Virginia: Time-Life Books, 1979. 30.

[4] Miller, Donald L. *The Story of World War II*. New York: Simon & Schuster, 2001. 38

[5] Bailey, Ronald H. *The Air War in Europe*. Alexandria, Virginia: Time-Life Books, 1979. 28.

[6] Tooze, Adam. *The Wages of Destruction: The Making and Breaking of the Nazi Economy*. London: Allen Lane, 2007. Location 7803

[7] Miller, Donald L. *The Story of World War II*. New York: Simon & Schuster, 2001. 257.

[8] *45,000 people were killed and 400,000 left homeless* -Miller, Donald L. *The Story of World War II*. New York: Simon & Schuster, 2001. 259.

[9] 'B-17 Flying Fortress', Boeing http://www.boeing.com/history/products/b-17-flying-fortress.page

[10] Ambrose, Steven. *The Wild Blue: The Men and the Boys Who Flew the B-24s over Germany*. New York: Simon & Schuster, 2001. 23

[11] Miller, Donald L., *The Story of World War II*. New York: Simon & Schuster, 2001. 483.

[12] Source Notes: **Duties and Responsibilities of the Airplane Commander and Crewmen** B-17 Pilot Training Manual -1943. United States Government (declassified, public domain). The responsibilities for those in the heavy bombers of the U.S. Army Air

Forces are outlined at the start of many chapters. See 'B-17 Crew Requirements and Standard Operating Procedures', www.303rdbg.com/crew-duties.html. Also, 'Air Crewman's Gunnery Manual, 1944; Aviation Training Division, Office of the Chief of Naval Operations, U.S. Navy in collaboration with U.S. Army Air Forces,' www.ibiblio.org/hyperwar/USN/ref/AirGunnery

[13] Joiner, Steven. *Mission to Ploesti: B-24 Liberators*. Air and Space Magazine, Feb. 11, 2015.

[14] Source Notes: **Andy Doty**. Doty, Andrew. *Backwards Into Battle: A Tail Gunner's Journey in World War II*. Palo Alto: Tall Tree Press, 1995. Used with author permission.

[15] Source Notes: **Richard Varney.** Interviewed by Emily Thomson, December 16, 2003. Hudson Falls, NY. Deposited at NYS Military Museum.

[16] Source Notes: **Richard G. Alagna.** Interviewed by Michael Russert and Wayne Clarke, September 18, 2002. Rockville Center, NY. Deposited at NYS Military Museum.

[17] Source Notes: **Kenneth R. Carlson.** Interviewed by Michael Russert and Wayne Clarke, March 18, 2003, NYC. Deposited at NYS Military Museum.

[18] Source Notes: **Earl M. Morrow.** Interviewed by Wayne Clarke, September 4, 2009. Hartford, NY. Deposited at NYS Military Museum.

[19] Source Notes: **Martin F. Bezon.** Interviewed by Wayne Clarke, March 27, 2012. Port Henry NY. Deposited at NYS Military Museum.

[20] Source Notes: **Seymour 'Sonny' Segan.** Interviewed by Matthew Rozell, November 3, 2002. Glens Falls, NY.

Made in the USA
Las Vegas, NV
24 July 2025

25364513R00282